Computer Dictionary FOR KIDS

...and Their Parents

Jami Lynne Borman

Illustrated by
Yvette Santiago Banek

Dedication

This book is dedicated to Ruth Allen
and teachers everywhere who have touched the hearts
and helped shape the minds of young people.

All inquiries should be addressed to:
Barron's Educational Series, Inc.
250 Wireless Boulevard
Hauppauge, New York 11788-3917

ISBN 0-8120-9079-9

Library of Congress Catalog Card No. 95-16002
Library of Congress Cataloging-in-Publication Data

Borman, Jami Lynne.
Computer dictionary for kids...and their parents / by Jami Lynne Borman.
p. cm.
Summary: Defines over 600 computer terms, explains how to deal with an error message, offers advice on purchasing computer equipment, and suggests ways to best utilize and enjoy the computer.
ISBN 0-8120-9079-9
1. Computers—Dictionaries—Juvenile literature.
[1. Computers—Dictionaries.] I. Title.
QA76.15.B678 1995
004'.03—dc20 95-16002
CIP
AC

Printed in United States of America
678 6550 98765432

Acknowledgments

It takes the efforts of many people to make a book a success. I would like to acknowledge and thank some of the people who helped me write and edit this book. In addition to all the talented people at Barron's who helped put this book together, I had the help of two highly skilled adults: **Scott Borman-Allen** and **Thomas M. Schach**.

From the beginning of the project, **Scott Borman-Allen** assisted me in writing and editing the manuscript. Scott also drew the original sketches for many of the illustrations in the book. **Thomas M. Schach** came onto the project later, and has been invaluable for his Macintosh expertise. Tom wrote the background text for all the Macintosh terms and provided guidance and advice on how Mac technology and the Mac experience differs from the PC.

In addition to adults, seven very talented kids also worked on this book. I wanted the book to appeal and be useful to young people, so I brought several kids onto the project as student editors. These special editors gave me a kid's perspective on things, asked very perceptive questions, and even designed several of the games and puzzles that you see throughout this book. I took their comments and opinions very seriously, and hundreds of changes were made to the manuscript as a direct result of their input. So, many, many thanks to my seventh- and eighth-grade student editors who helped make this book easier to read, more fun to use, and just plain cool. They are: **Suzanne Bentley, Meredith Coticchio, Orin Davis, Amanda Frey, Joe Hyer, Danielle Lejnieks,** and **Greg Lockard.**

Also, special thanks go to **Jonathan Allen** (age 15) for assisting me with research, designing some of the games, and proofreading the manuscript; and to **Ed Hahn** and **Kathleen Keiderling** for their help in promoting the book.

PC Keyboard Layout

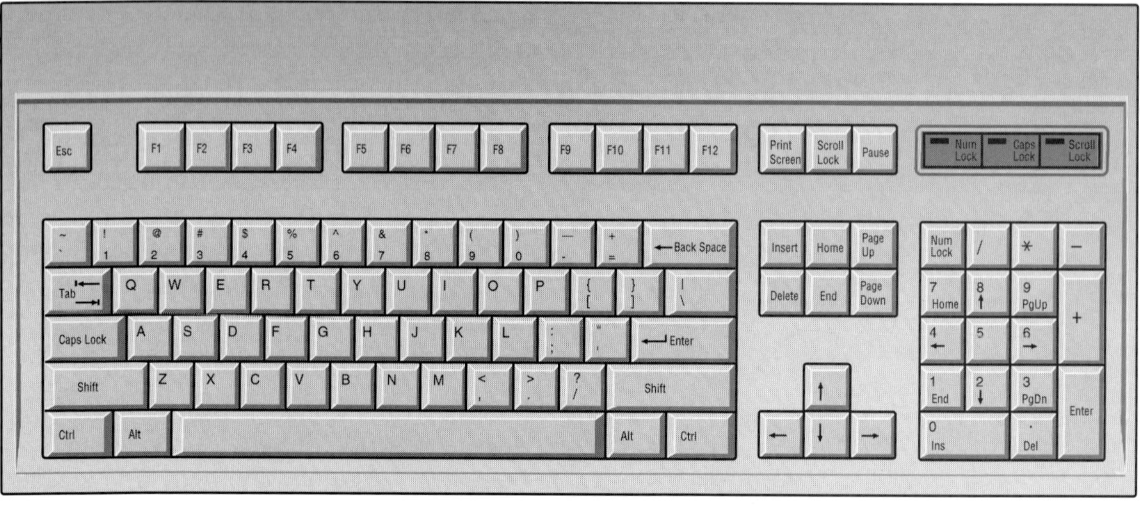

Macintosh Keyboard Layout

TABLE OF CONTENTS

Where is a kid like you supposed to get answers to questions about computers? You can get answers at the arcade, from your friends, or by reading one of those thick books collecting dust near the family computer. But are these good sources? Besides, most of the adult computer books contain a lot of techno-babble that even the grown ups have trouble understanding!

Some computer terms are easy to understand. **No problem.** But some computer terms can be a little tricky to understand. That is because you need to know the meaning of other computer terms before a word you are trying to understand will make sense. For example, suppose you were trying to explain how good a peanut butter and jelly sandwich is to a kid from Jupiter who had never heard of peanut butter or jelly. You would need to explain both **peanut butter** and **jelly** at the same time so you could describe how to put them together to make a great sandwich.

Just like the peanut butter and jelly example, some computer terms make more sense when they are explained together. In this book, you are sometimes asked to look up another computer term that will help you understand the term you are reading about.

Use this dictionary to look up words you hear on TV, at school, at the dinner table, from your friends, or that you are just plain curious about. Computers are **cool**, and understanding them makes everything you do on the computer more fun. By the way, if you discover that *Computer Dictionary for Kids...and Their Parents* is missing a term or explanation that you think we should include in the future, just send me an e-mail message at CD4KIDS@AOL.COM or write to me at the address shown below.

Jami Lynne Borman (author)
Computer Dictionary for Kids...and Their Parents
Barron's Educational Series, Inc.
250 Wireless Boulevard
Hauppauge, New York 11788

Introduction for Parents

Worried that your kids may be passing you by when it comes to understanding computers? Well, it is time to catch up. *Computer Dictionary for Kids...and Their Parents* will help you understand those cryptic computer terms you see in computer manuals, come across at the office, and hear from your kids and their friends.

Written for kids in fifth through eighth grade, this book is a mini course in computers for you and your family. Try working with a few words each evening at the dinner table or at bedtime. Learn the meanings of *cyberspace, desktop publishing, Internet, information superhighway, multimedia, screen saver, snail mail, sneaker net,* and much, much more. You'll be amazed at how quickly you begin to understand conversations that used to sound like a foreign language.

Going beyond simple definitions, *Computer Dictionary for Kids...and Their Parents* explains:

- **What to do when you get an error message.**
- **What to do when you accidentally erase a file.**
- **What to look for when purchasing computer accessories (such as a CD-ROM drive).**
- **Ways to get more use and enjoyment out of the equipment you already have.**

The colorful illustrations, games, puzzles, and examples help explain complex ideas. I also clearly point out what computing tasks the kids can try on their own and when they should first get your permission.

In this book, I was careful to use examples that break stereotypical roles for boys, girls, and adults. My examples show families purchasing and installing computer equipment in stages (on a budget). Some kids in the examples have computer accessories (like a sound card) and some do not. The examples show families making sensible purchasing decisions—not just purchasing the most expensive options available.

Knowledge is about sharing. There are not many opportunities today where you and your children can explore a new area from the same point of understanding. It is a wonderful opportunity. I encourage you to take advantage of it.

How to Use This Book

omputer Dictionary for Kids...and their Parents contains nearly 700 computer words, terms, concepts, phrases, and messages. All the words are listed in alphabetical order.

Numbers and spaces are in alphabetical order.

When a computer term begins with a symbol (such as *) or a number (as in **486 computer**), the term is listed before the A's in the section called *Symbols & Numbers.*

data

↓

data_center

↓

database

When a computer term has two or more words, it contains a space between the words (as in **data center**). When putting a term in alphabetical order, the space comes before the letter A. For example, the word **data center** comes before the word **database** because the space in the word **data_center** comes before the *b* in data*b*ase.

Look up other words to learn more.

When you see the words "look up" and the 👁, you can explore other terms for more information on the topic you are reading about. Just look up the terms that follow the 👁 .

Computer terms can have more than one meaning.

Just like other words you know, some computer terms have more than one meaning. When a term has more than one definition, the first definition begins with **(1)**. The second definition begins with **(2)**. Each definition is separate, and lets you know that the term can be used in more than one way.

Some definitions are for PCs, some are for Macs.

Most computer terms apply to all computers. But there are some computer terms that only apply to PCs or only apply to Macs:

When you see a term in the color blue, it means that the term only applies to IBM and IBM-compatible computers.

When you see a term in the color red, it means that the term only applies to Macintosh computers.

Drawings of PC and Mac keyboards are shown on page 2. You can look at these drawings whenever you see a key mentioned in a definition.

Terminology can be fun.

Technical terms that were once found only in science fiction movies are now used in homes everyday. Ten years ago, if you *zapped* someone, you shot them with your ray gun. Today, *zap* means to heat up your lunch in the microwave. Technology and terminology can be a lot of fun. Check out **bells and whistles**, **garbage-in**, **garbage-out**, **morph**, and **sneaker net**, and see how you can use these terms around your house.

Early computing machines used thousands of switches (called electromechanical relays) to hold numbers. One of these computers, called the Mark I, was made in 1944 by Harvard University and IBM. The Mark I was less powerful than some of today's calculators.

The first bug. One day, while trying to find out what was causing a problem with the Mark I, some programmers found a moth caught in one of the switches. From then on a problem with a computer was called a *bug*.

The computer gets a vacuum. During World War II, the British designed a computer called the Colossus that used vacuum tubes (instead of switches) to process information. The Colossus had one job: breaking the secret codes that were used by Hitler and his army.

Vacuum tubes, which look like old-fashioned light bulbs, processed information much faster than switches, so they were also used in the ENIAC computer at the University of Pennsylvania in 1946.

The ENIAC is called the first modern computer since it was the first electronic computer to be used for more than one purpose. The ENIAC had over 17,000 vacuum tubes, more than 500 miles of wiring, and weighed 30 tons. It was so big that it was stored in a room the size of a small warehouse. The ENIAC could perform about 100,000 calculations per second. That may seem like a lot, but the computer in your home today can perform about *5,000,000* calculations per second.

Like the Mark I, the ENIAC had its problems. First, it used lots of power. Every time the University turned on the computer, the lights dimmed all over the campus. Second, the vacuum tubes got so hot that they kept burning out. When the computer was on, some of the students had full-time jobs just running back and forth replacing burned out vacuum tubes.

Computers get faster. In 1948, the transistor was invented. Transistors were much smaller and cooler than vacuum tubes. As transistors were used in more and more computers, computers became smaller, used less electricity, and ran much faster than the computers that used vacuum tubes. By 1953, around 100 computers had been built in the entire world.

Integrated circuits make computers even faster. Traditional circuits (like vacuum tubes and transistors) have parts that are connected with wire. Integrated circuits contain many electronic components on a single chip. The chip is *very* thin. It is made up of several paper-thin layers of semiconductor material (such as silicon). By the 1970s, thousands of components could be placed on a single chip. Today, millions of components can be placed on a single chip. Placing more circuits on a chip has been very important in the development of computers. As circuits get smaller they can be placed closer together—so electricity passes through them more quickly and computers process information faster.

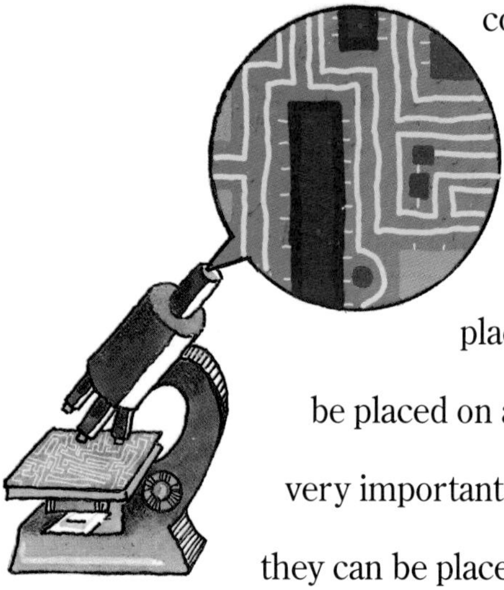

The Apple II becomes the most popular microcomputer. By the mid-1970s, Intel had invented the microprocessor and many companies began making microcomputers. In 1977, Apple Computer introduced the Apple II, which quickly became the most popular microcomputer of the time. Other companies that made microcomputers included Tandy-Radio Shack, Atari, and Commodore—but each company used its own operating system. So if you owned an Atari computer, you could not share a word-processing file with a friend who owned an Apple, a Tandy-Radio Shack, or a Commodore computer.

IBM begins selling microcomputers. IBM introduced its first microcomputer, the IBM PC, in 1981. It was a huge success. The IBM PC used an operating system called DOS, which was written by Microsoft. Many software companies went into business to write software programs for the IBM PC.

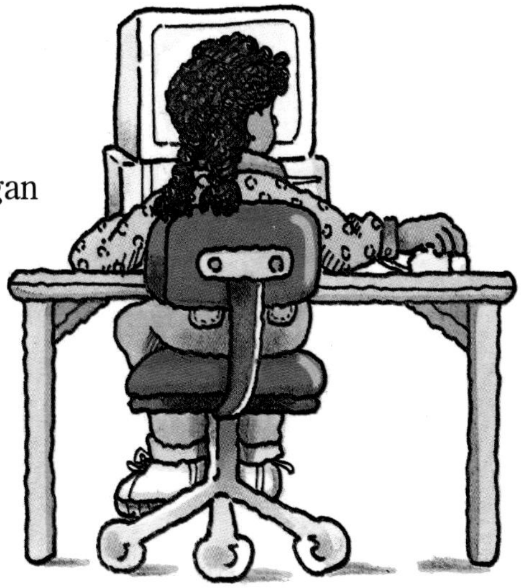

In 1984, IBM introduced the PC/AT. IBM's microcomputers were so popular that many other companies began making personal computers that were copies of the IBM machines. These copies were nicknamed *clones*, and sold for hundreds of dollars less than the IBM machines.

Apple introduces the Macintosh. In 1984, Apple introduced a computer called the Macintosh (or Mac). The Mac was the first widely used personal computer to have a graphical user interface (GUI). The Mac used a microprocessor made by Motorola called the 68000.

IBM and IBM-compatible computers outsell Apple's computers. IBM is a company that has been around for many years. Apple Computer was started in 1976. IBM is well known as a company that makes some of the best large (mainframe) computers and office equipment (such as typewriters). It was natural for the IBM computer standard to be chosen most often by businesses since it was a name they knew and trusted. And since people were familiar with IBM computers at work, they bought IBM computers for their homes.

IBM also made their designs available to other companies that wanted to make IBM-type computers. So IBM-compatible computers were produced by the thousands. Apple did not make their designs available until very recently.

In 1987, Microsoft introduced its first version of Windows, a graphical user interface (GUI) for IBM and compatible computers. Windows is the second-best selling software program ever made. (DOS is the best seller.) Windows's popularity has helped keep IBM and IBM-compatible computers selling better than Apple computers.

The future is fast and powerful. Companies such as Intel and Motorola continue to develop new and faster microprocessor technologies. Computers are getting smaller, faster, less expensive, and more powerful.

In the future, features that are provided by sound cards, video cards, modems, and other accessories may be built right into the microprocessor. Desktop computers are already replacing minicomputers and may someday replace even the largest mainframe computers.

Symbols & Numbers

? A *question mark (?)* can be used to replace a single letter in a filename or the filename extension. You can use a question mark as a placeholder for each letter in the filename or extension that you cannot remember. When you use a question mark to replace a letter, the question mark is called a wildcard. Look up *extension*, *filename*, and *wildcard*.

---

* An *asterisk (*)* can be used to replace some or all of the letters in a filename or the filename extension. You can use a maximum of one asterisk in the filename and one asterisk in the extension. When you use an asterisk to replace one or more characters, the asterisk is called a wildcard. Look up *extension, filename,* and *wildcard.*

¦ The *pipe* (¦) is used to separate two DOS commands. You can usually locate the pipe symbol on your keyboard by looking above the backslash (\) character. The pipe character can be difficult to find because it looks different when printed (and displayed on your screen) than it looks on the keyboard. On your screen and when printed, the pipe looks like a straight line (|). But on your keyboard, the pipe looks like a dashed line (¦). Look up *MORE command* and *TREE command.*

 The apple with a bite out of it on the far left-hand side of your screen can be selected to reveal the Apple menu. The Apple menu is a special menu where you (or the owner of the computer) can select what items go on the menu. Look up *Apple menu.*

---

020 machine A *020 machine* is a Macintosh computer with a Motorola 68020 microprocessor for its brain. Look up *68020* and *microprocessor.*

---

030 machine A *030 machine* is a Macintosh computer with a Motorola 68030 microprocessor for its brain. Look up *68030* and *microprocessor.*

---

040 machine A *040 machine* is a Macintosh computer with a Motorola 68040 microprocessor for its brain. Look up *68040* and *microprocessor.*

---

286 computer A *286 computer* is an IBM-compatible computer that has an 80286 microprocessor for its brain. The 286 computer is considered outdated for most business uses and is close to being outdated even as a home computer since it cannot run the most popular software programs. The 286 computer is also called an AT-compatible computer, since it has the same microprocessor used in a computer made by IBM called the PC/AT. Look up *compatible* and *microprocessor.*

3½-inch diskette A diskette (also called a disk or floppy disk) is used to hold software programs and computer files. A *3½-inch diskette* can be used by either a Mac or a PC. However, since Macs and PCs put information onto a diskette in different ways, the same 3½-inch diskette cannot usually be used by both a Mac and a PC.

The 3½-inch diskette comes in two densities: double-density and high-density. The density indicates how close together information is placed on the diskette. High-density diskettes let you store more information than double-density diskettes.

A 3½-inch, double-density diskette looks almost identical to a 3½-inch, high-density diskette. The exceptions are the letters HD (for high density) in the upper right-hand corner of the high-density diskette and a hole in the bottom right-hand corner of the diskette. Look up *density, diskette, diskette drive,* and *SuperDrive.*

386 computer A *386 computer* is an IBM-compatible computer that has an 80386 microprocessor for its brain. Look up *microprocessor.*

486 computer A *486 computer* is an IBM-compatible computer that has an 80486 microprocessor for its brain. Look up *microprocessor.*

5¼-inch diskette A diskette (also called a disk or floppy disk) is used to hold software programs and computer files. The 5¼-inch diskette comes in two densities: double-density and high-density. The density indicates how close together information is placed on the diskette. High-density diskettes let you store more information than double-density diskettes.

A 5¼-inch, double-density diskette looks identical to a 5¼-inch, high-density diskette. Sometimes the company that makes the diskette will label the diskette to let you know whether it is a double- or high-density diskette. But unless there is a label on the diskette, you cannot tell them apart. Look up *density, diskette, diskette drive,* and *disk jacket.*

68000 The Motorola *68000* microprocessor was used in the first Macintosh computers. Almost every monochrome Mac that is still in use has the 68000 for its brain. The 68000 processes information very slowly (it has a slow clock speed) and is now considered outdated. It was very popular in Macs that were made during 1984–1990. Look up *clock speed* and *microprocessor.*

68020 The Motorola *68020* microprocessor was used as the brain in the first color Macintosh computers. Even though the 68020 is about four times faster than the 68000 microprocessor, it was quickly replaced by the 68030 microprocessor. A Mac with a 68020 microprocessor is often called a 020 machine. Not many Macs were made using the 68020 microprocessor, although it was used in some of Apple's laser printers. Look up *microprocessor.*

68030 The Motorola *68030* microprocessor has been used as the brain in more Macintosh computers than any other microprocessor. Although more powerful microprocessors are available, Macs with a 68030 can still be purchased today. A Mac with a 68030 microprocessor is often called a 030 machine. Look up *microprocessor.*

68040 The Motorola *68040* microprocessor was first used as the brain in a Macintosh in 1991. A Mac with a 68040 microprocessor is often called a 040 machine. Look up *microprocessor.*

8088 computer An *8088 computer* is an IBM-compatible computer that has an 8088 microprocessor for its brain. The 8088 computer processes information very slowly (it has a slow clock speed) and is now considered outdated. The 8088 computer is called an XT-compatible computer since it has the same microprocessor that was used in a computer made by IBM called the PC/XT. Look up *clock speed, compatible,* and *microprocessor.*

80286 computer An *80286 computer* is an IBM-compatible computer that has an 80286 microprocessor for its brain. The 80286 computer is commonly called a 286 computer. The 286 computer is considered outdated for most business uses and is close to being outdated even as a home computer since it is not fast enough to run the most popular software programs. The 286 computer is also called an AT-compatible computer, since it has the same microprocessor that was used in a computer made by IBM called the PC/AT. Look up *compatible* and *microprocessor.*

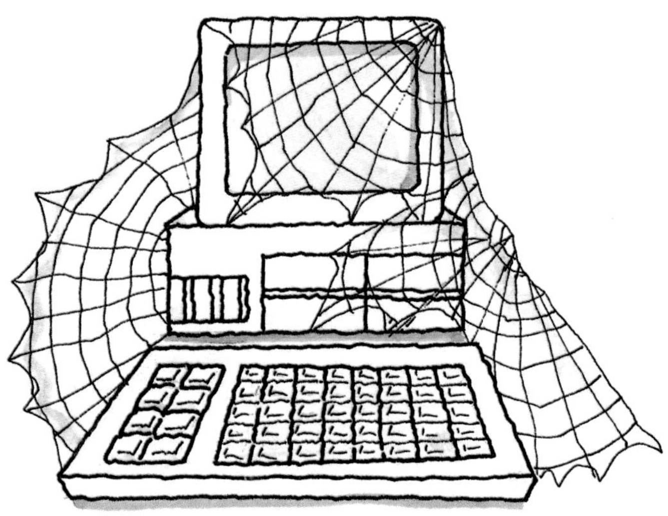

80386 computer An *80386 computer* is an IBM-compatible computer that has an 80386 microprocessor for its brain. The 80386 computer is commonly called a 386 computer. Look up *microprocessor.*

80486 computer An *80486 computer* is an IBM-compatible computer that has an 80486 microprocessor for its brain. The 80486 computer is commonly called a 486 computer. Look up *microprocessor.*

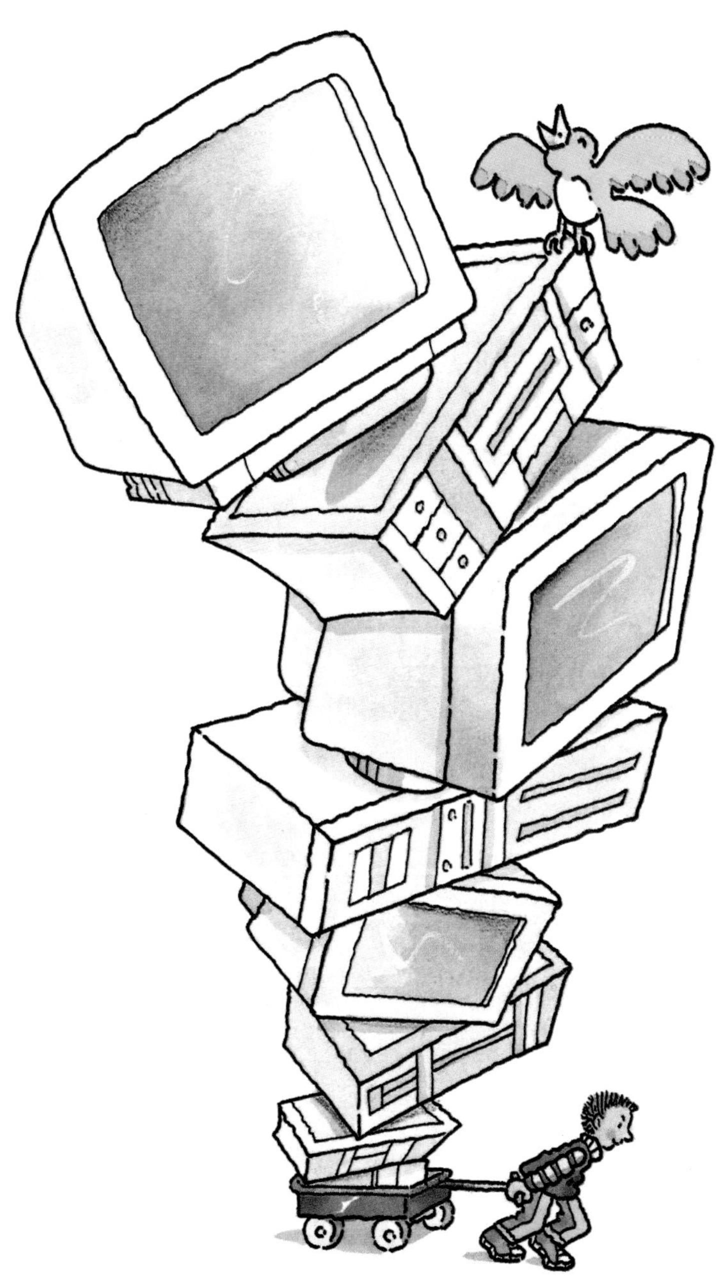

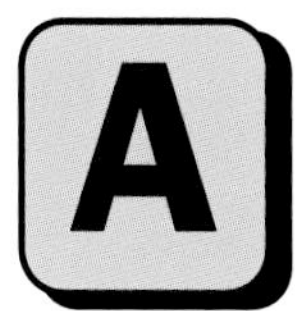

abort To *abort* a computer program is to stop the program after it has started but before it has ended.

> *Sarah was attempting to solve a case in Where in the World is Carmen San Diego? when her mother called her for dinner. Sarah* **aborted** *the game when she stopped the program after she had begun the case, but before she had solved it.*

access **(1)** One meaning of *access* is to go and get something. Did you ever play a computer game where the action, picture, or sound stopped for a second or two? If so, your computer probably went to get more information (like a picture, animation, or sound) from the game software on your computer's hard disk or the CD in your CD-ROM drive. A computer can only remember part of the pictures, sounds, and rules of the game at a time. Depending on your selections or actions in the game, the computer needs to access more information from the game software to keep up with your choices.

> *Orin was helping his mom explore the deserted islands in Myst when his sister Michelle came over to watch.*
>
> *"Why does the sound stop when you move from one room to another?" Michelle asked.*
>
> *"Do you think maybe ghosts were left on the islands?" asked their mother.*
>
> *"No," laughed Orin, "it's just the CD-ROM drive* **accessing** *the next sound effect."*

(2) Another meaning of *access* is to get into a secret area that is protected with a combination lock, or to use a software program that is protected with a password. The combination or password that gives you access to the secret area or software program is called the access code. Look up *access code* and *password*.

access code An *access code* is the combination or password that gets you into a secret, secured, or private area. Computer rooms and other secret areas often have combination locks on their doors. Your parents may have a password on some of their software programs so that you cannot see certain information that they store on the computer. When you need a password, the computer or software program is password protected.

> *Andrea uses the computer lab in school to write stories for her English class. Andrea's English teacher gave her the* **access code** *for the lock so Andrea could get into the computer lab. Once in the lab, Andrea turns on a computer and types her password so she can use Ami Pro, the software program that she uses to write her stories.*

access speed The amount of time it takes your computer to find information on its hard disk or a CD-ROM.

Access speed is measured in milliseconds (which is abbreviated ms). One ms is one one-thousandth ($^1/_{1000}$) of a second. Hard disks usually have access speeds from 9 ms to 30 ms, while CD-ROM drives have access speeds from 140 ms to 800 ms.

Think of access speed as how long it takes your computer to find information. The slower your computer accesses information, the longer the access time. Look up *access*, *CD-ROM*, *CD-ROM drive*, *data transfer rate*, and *millisecond*.

Pretend that you are a CD-ROM drive and your best friend is a hard disk. (Be prepared to lose this race!) To demonstrate the **access speed** *of a CD-ROM drive compared to a hard disk, ask your friend to race you to a piece of candy that you place on the kitchen table.*

As a hard disk, your friend is allowed to walk directly to the candy very fast. As a CD-ROM drive, you have to spin around before taking each step. Starting from the same point in the house, race to access the candy on the kitchen table. Your friend, who plays the hard disk, should be able to get to the kitchen more quickly than you.

access time The amount of time it takes your computer to find information on its hard disk or a CD-ROM. *Access time* is the same as access speed. Look up *access speed.*

accessory In computers, as in clothes, there are essentials and there are frills. An essential is something you must have to survive—not something you want to have to be cool. The essentials of getting dressed for school may include jeans, a T-shirt, sneakers, socks, and underwear (though you probably don't put them on in that order). The essentials of a computer setup are a monitor (the TV portion), the keyboard, and the CPU (the box the other stuff is plugged into).

A frill is an extra, and is called an *accessory.* Your clothing accessories may include a belt, jewelry, vest, jacket, bow, or any other item that makes what you are wearing more comfortable, attractive, or fun. Your computer accessories may include dust covers, a joystick, sound card, CD-ROM drive, modem, printer, or other items that make your computer better, easier to use, or more fun.

acronym An *acronym* is a special type of abbreviation that is pronounced like a word. An example of an acronym is RAM (which is pronounced the same way you pronounce the name of the animal with curly horns). RAM is an acronym for random access memory.

Look at the abbreviation for the United States of America. The first letter of each main word is capitalized and a period is placed after each of those letters.

United States of America → U.S.A.
United → U.
States → S.
America → A.

Unlike normal abbreviations, acronyms do not use periods. But to make matters even more confusing, most computer abbreviations also do not use periods.

If an abbreviation does not always have periods, how can I tell an acronym from an abbreviation? The best way to tell whether a word is an acronym or an abbreviation is to pronounce it. When you pronounce an abbreviation, such as U.S.A., you say each letter separately: U—S—A. When you pronounce an acronym, like RAM, you read it as a single word. You would not say R—A—M, as you do with U—S—A.

Can you match these computer acronyms to their meanings?
Answers appear in the Answer Section in the back of the book.

Acronyms	Meanings
1. ASAP	A. random access memory
2. BASIC	B. special interest group
3. GUI	C. what you see is what you get
4. LAN	D. as soon as possible
5. MIPS	E. wide area network
6. RAM	F. local area network
7. ROM	G. beginner's all-purpose symbolic instruction code
8. SIG	H. millions of instructions per second
9. WAN	I. graphical user interface
10. WYSIWYG	J. read-only memory

active When a menu item in a software program is *active,* it is available for you to use. When a menu item is inactive, you cannot select it. An active window is the area of your screen that you are currently using. The title bar shows you the name of the window.

PC You can tell which window is active because the title bar of the active window is in a different color than the other title bars.

Mac You can tell which window is active because the title bar of the active window has lines running through it. Look up *inactive*, *menu*, *menu item*, and *window*.

ADB *ADB* is an abbreviation for Apple desktop bus. ADB is a special kind of connection that hooks your mouse, keyboard, and/or joystick to your Macintosh. The neat thing about ADB connections is that the mouse, keyboard, and joystick can be hooked to each other (rather than the computer) and they all work—only one of them has to be hooked to your Macintosh.

For example, you can hook the keyboard to your Mac. Then you can hook the mouse and the joystick to the keyboard. Since they all have ADB connections, and one of them (the keyboard) is hooked to the Mac, they all work—even though only the keyboard is directly connected to your computer. Hooking ADB connections to each other is called daisy-chaining. Look up *daisy-chain.*

AI *AI* is an abbreviation for artificial intelligence. Look up *artificial intelligence.*

algorithm An *algorithm* (pronounced al-gore-rhythm) is a set of instructions that gives you an answer or a finished product. Did you ever follow a recipe? A recipe is an algorithm. When you follow the instructions in a recipe you get a finished product—for example, brownies.

Computer programs are made up of many **algorithms**; each performs a specific job. Many logic and math games are algorithms. Try the **algorithm** below. No matter what number you start with, you always get 10 for an answer.

1. **Think of a number from 1–10.**
2. **Add 6** to the number.
3. **Subtract 4** from the number.
4. **Subtract your original number.**
5. **Add 3** to the number.
6. **Multiply** the number **by 2.**

alias Some people (like movie stars and members of rock bands) have more than one name. They have the name that their parents gave them as children, and they have a stage name that they use when they perform. The stage name is called an *alias*. An alias is another name used by the same person.

Each and every file has an icon. An alias is a second icon for the same file. An alias is not a copy of the file. An alias for a person means that one person has two names. An alias for your file means that one file has two icons. Clicking on either one of the icons starts the same file.

Why use an alias? Sometimes you want to be able to find your file in more than one folder. An alias lets you do that.

How can I tell that a file is an alias? There are two ways you can tell the difference between the original file and the alias.

- The filename for the alias is in italics.
- The filename for the alias always has the same name as the original file plus the word "alias." For example, suppose you wrote a scary story called "The Haunted House." The alias would have the filename *The Haunted House alias.*

How can I create an alias? To create an alias, just follow the instructions below.

1. Click on the icon that you want to create an alias for.
2. From the File menu choose the Make Alias command.

Your Mac makes an alias and places it next to the original file. You can then move the alias anywhere you want.

alpha test Before a software company sells a software program to stores (and then eventually to you), it must test the software program to make sure it is working correctly. Software companies usually put their software through two sets of tests: an A test and a B test. But instead of calling the tests A and B, the software companies use the Greek words for A and B: alpha and beta.

A test → alpha test
B test → beta test

The *alpha test* is the first set of tests that are done on a software program. As problems—or "bugs"—in the software are discovered and then corrected, the software is alpha tested again. The process

test → fix bugs → test

is repeated until the software company is satisfied with the software. Unfortunately, the software company is usually satisfied with the software long before it is bug-free.

After the software "passes" the alpha test, it is put through a second set of tests—the beta test. The alpha test is usually made by programmers who work for the software company. The beta test is often done by some of the people who are going to use the software. (The beta test is not typically done by employees of the software company.) The beta testers use the software program and try to find any problems with it. The beta testers then tell the software company about any problems they find.

If big problems are found by the beta testers, the software company usually makes some changes to the software program. Sometimes, after making big changes to a software program, the software company will have the software program alpha tested and beta tested again.

One of the reasons you sometimes have to wait a long time for a new software program to be available in stores is because the new program needs to be fixed after the alpha and beta tests are done.

Some software companies ask some of their customers to beta test a new software program. The customers get to use the new software program for free, in exchange for telling the software company about any problems with the software program. Even kids can be beta testers for games and other software programs made for kids! (If you want to be a beta tester, write a letter to your favorite software company telling them why you would be a good tester.)

Many people like to beta test games and other software programs because they get to try out new software before it is sold in stores. The bad side to being a beta tester is that a new software program usually has a few problems.

alphanumeric The first part of this word, alpha, has to do with letters (as in alphabet). The second part of the word, numeric, has to do with numbers. *Alphanumeric* means having to do with letters and numbers.

ABCDE+12345

Your street address is alphanumeric because it contains both letters and numbers. For example,

237 East Prospect Place
Apartment 2C
Washington, D.C. 20045

When a message on your computer screen says that your answer may be alphanumeric, your answer may be all letters, all numbers, or a combination of letters, numbers, spaces, and (sometimes) symbols such as ?, !, @, #, $, %, and *.

ALT key The *ALT key* is the key on your keyboard with the letters A-L-T. As a matter of fact, most computers have two Alt keys, one on either side of the spacebar. The Alt key is used in many programs to give an Alternate (or different) meaning to another key (usually a function key). Do you know how to use the Shift key? You hold down Shift while you press another key. The ALT key is used the same way. You hold down Alt while you press another key.

What does the ALT key do? It depends on the program you are using. Just as each software program has a different use for each function key, different programs also have a different use for each ALT key combination. The user manual that comes with your software program will tell you whether or not the ALT key is used, and if so, what it is used for.

Does a Macintosh have an ALT key? No, Macs do not have an ALT key. But Macs do have a key called "command" that does the same job. Look up *command key* and *function key.*

"After Dark. What's that?" asked Joseph as he looked at a box sitting on Mrs. Little's desk.

"It shows animations on the screen when I walk away from the computer," replied Mrs. Little. "When I do not touch the mouse or keyboard for a couple of minutes, my computer screen displays a fish tank. When I move the mouse or touch a key, my screen goes back to normal."

"Awesome!"

"I can also make it display the fish tank by pressing Alt *and a special key," continued Mrs. Little.*

"Will pressing Alt *and a key on my keyboard make my screen turn into a fish tank?" asked Joseph.*

"Only when you are using the After Dark program. When you are using another program, Alt *and a keypress may have a very different result."*

ambient temperature Ambient means surrounding. The *ambient temperature* is the temperature of the air that surrounds you and your computer. Basically, it is a fancy way of talking about the room temperature.

Many computer manufacturers recommend that their computers be used in rooms that are not too hot and not too cold. The manufacturer will say that the computer should have an ambient temperature that is no colder than one temperature and no hotter than another temperature, for example 10°C–32°C or 50°F–90°F. Those two temperatures are called the ambient temperature range because the temperature surrounding your computer should not go hotter or colder than that range of temperatures.

android An *android* is a robot that looks human. Today, androids are still science fiction. Our technical knowledge is not advanced enough to create a humanlike robot. Maybe someday we will be able to create androids like the character Data from the television series *Star Trek: The Next Generation*.

animation Do you like to watch cartoons? Cartoons are one type of *animation*. Animation is a way of giving lifelike movement to pictures or objects.

In the case of a cartoon, several drawings are made, recorded, and then played back. To make an animation of a butterfly opening and closing its wings you might include the following drawings:

(1) A butterfly with wings that are closed.
(2) A butterfly with wings that are open just a little.
(3) A butterfly with wings that are open most of the way.
(4) A butterfly with wings that are open.

Each drawing is recorded for less than a second. Then the recordings are played back very quickly, one right after the other. If you were to record the drawings in the following order (1), (2), (3), (4), (3), (2), (1), what do you think you would see when you played back the recording? A butterfly opening and then closing its wings.

anti-virus program An *anti-virus program* is a special type of software program that can look for a computer virus on your computer and get rid of the virus if it finds one. You can also use an anti-virus program to check whether a diskette or file has a virus.

Before you copy any files to your computer from a computer at friends, your parent's office, a bulletin board, or a computer service, it is best to use an anti-virus program to make sure that the files do not contain a virus. Look up *Trojan horse* and *virus.*

antistatic mat An *antistatic mat* prevents you from zapping your computer with static electricity and possibly damaging one of the parts inside your computer. Did you ever walk across a carpet, touch the light switch, and then ZAP!...get a shock? If so, then you have experienced static electricity.

When two objects are rubbed together, an electrical charge is built up. For example, if you walk across a carpet, electricity is built up inside your body. When you touch something that contains metal—like a light switch or your computer, the electricity built up inside you is removed in the form of a little spark—which you feel as a shock.

The same little shock that gives you a tingle can damage sensitive parts inside your computer equipment. By touching an antistatic mat before you touch your computer, any static electricity that your body is carrying is removed from your body into the antistatic mat—rather than into the computer where it can cause a serious problem.

Apple Computer, Inc. *Apple Computer, Inc.* is the company that makes the Apple, Quadra, LC, Powerbook, and PowerPC lines of computers. The Quadra, LC, Powerbook, and PowerPC computers are all Macintosh computers.

Apple Computer was started in 1976 by Steve Wozniak and Steve Jobs. In 1977, Apple began selling the Apple II. In 1984, Apple introduced a computer called the Macintosh (or Mac, for short). The Mac was the first widely used personal computer to have a graphical user interface (GUI).

For a few years, Apple computers were the most popular computers made. But when IBM began selling its personal computers in 1981, the sale of Apple computers fell behind the sale of IBM computers. (See *A Brief History of Computers* in the front of this book.) Apple computers continue to sell well, but not nearly as well as the IBM and IBM-compatible computers. Look up *GUI, IBM, IBM-compatible, Macintosh,* and *PowerPC.*

Apple desktop bus The *Apple desktop bus* is a special kind of connection that hooks your mouse, keyboard, and/or joystick to your Macintosh. Apple desktop bus is abbreviated ADB. Look up *ADB.*

Apple menu 🍎 If you look at the menu bar at the top of your screen, there is an apple on the far left-hand side—an apple with a bite out of it. You can click and hold on the apple to reveal the *Apple menu.*

The Apple menu is different than other menus because whoever owns the computer gets to choose what goes on it. Every Mac comes with some items already on the Apple menu (like the Chooser and the control panels folder). But don't be surprised if the Mac at school has different items on the Apple menu than your Mac at home.

How do I select the Apple menu? To select the Apple menu, click on the apple and hold down the mouse button. You can drag your mouse to pick an item on the menu. When you let go of the mouse button, the Apple menu closes.

How do I add something to the Apple menu? Inside the system folder is a folder called Apple Menu Items. Anything (even an alias) that is added to the Apple Menu Items folder appears on the Apple menu.

- Never change the Apple menu on your school computer.
- Never change the Apple menu on a computer owned by someone else.
- Never change the Apple menu on your family computer without first getting your parents' permission.

Look up *alias, click, drag, folder, menu bar,* and *system folder.*

AppleTalk *AppleTalk* lets you connect two or more Macs to form a LAN (local area network). AppleTalk is built in to every Macintosh computer. Before you can use AppleTalk, each Mac on the LAN must have a special connector called LocalTalk.

Look up *local area network.*

application program An *application program* is a software program that was created to do a job or produce a result. It is software that is used by people. An application program is different than a systems program, which is software that is only used by your computer.

A computer game is an application program. When you play a board game, you set up the game, roll the dice, move the markers, keep score, pay the bank, and play with another person. In a computer game, the computer does all those things for you. Computer games even play with you when you can't get together with your friends.

application programmer A person who writes the computer instructions for an application program is called an *application programmer.* Look up *application program.*

Brad's mom is writing the instructions for a new software program. Brad's mom is an **application programmer**.

application programming The action of writing computer instructions for an application program is called *application programming.* Look up *application program* and *application programmer.*

When Brad's mom writes the instructions for a new software program, she is doing **application programming**.

arrow keys *Arrow keys* are the keys on your keyboard that are used to move your cursor up, down, left, and right. You might think that locating the arrow keys on your keyboard is easy. You might be thinking "...all I have to do is find the keys on my keyboard that have an arrow on them. How difficult can that be?" Unfortunately, locating keys with arrows is not always the same as locating the arrow keys. Although each of the four arrow keys does have an arrow on it, some keyboards also put an arrow on the backspace [←Backspace], tab [Tab ⇆], shift [⇧Shift], and enter [↵Enter] keys.

How do you know which keys are the arrow keys? On most keyboards, the four arrow keys are grouped together to the right of the keys with letters. On some older PC keyboards, the arrow keys are located on the numeric keypad on the right-hand side of your keyboard. On some Mac keyboards, the arrow keys are located to the right of the spacebar. Look up *numeric keypad.*

Wow, what a traffic jam! Can you **follow the arrows** to figure a way out? The red arrows show you how to follow one path that exits at "D." Can you find your way out when you enter at C, H, K, L, N, P, W, X, and Z? *Answers appear in the Answers Section in the back of the book.*

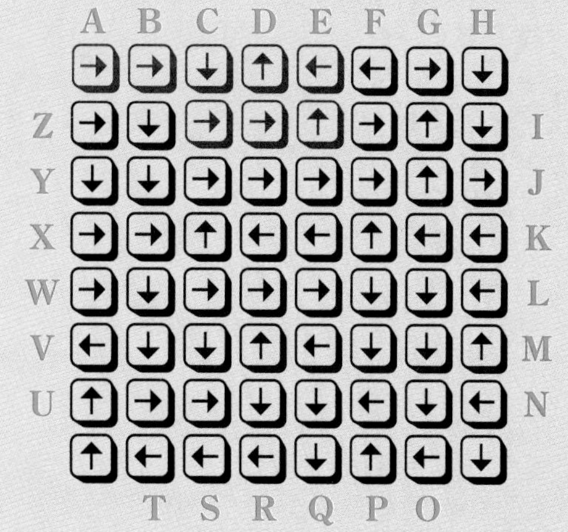

artificial intelligence *Artificial intelligence* is the idea that someday, a computer can be built that will think the way that people think. Some science fiction movies show computers making their own decisions and disobeying—even attacking—the humans who built them! But science fiction movies are imaginary. Real computers can only follow the instructions that are programmed into them.

It's true that a computer can do some things faster than a person. For example, you may have used a program that can check the spelling of all the words in a report in just a few seconds. But this doesn't mean that a computer is intelligent.

When we talk about intelligence, we are talking about a lot of different traits of the human mind. Some of these traits include

- Being creative.
- Figuring things out.
- Drawing conclusions.
- Learning.
- Making choices based on experience.

Computers are not intelligent like people are intelligent. Today, there are computers called expert systems that can select the best choice from a list of choices. But even an expert system only makes decisions that it has been told to make—from the instructions that have been programmed into it. The expert system cannot think for itself and is *not* intelligent. Artificial intelligence is abbreviated AI.

Look up *expert system.*

artificial language An *artificial language* is a language that is made up for a special purpose. Computer languages are artificial languages because they are made up by scientists so that programmers can talk to computers more easily.

There are many artificial languages. Some of the following artificial languages you may have heard of and some may seem foreign to you: Assembly, ADA, BASIC, C, COBOL, FORTRAN, LOGO, and Pascal.

Look up *computer language* and *natural language.*

ASAP *ASAP* is an acronym for as soon as possible. Sometimes ASAP is pronounced AY-sap and sometimes the letters are pronounced individually, as in A—S—A—P.

> *Ted's dad told him that he could invite two friends on their weekend camping trip.*
>
> *"You better ask those kids* **ASAP,***" said Ted's dad, "or they won't have time to get permission from their parents."*

ascender An *ascender* is a lower case letter that is as tall (or almost as tall) as an upper case letter. Look at the illustration below. Notice how the letters "b" and "l" are as tall as the letter "B." Look up *descender*.

Bubbles

Which letters are ascenders? Can you figure out which lower case letters of the alphabet are **ascenders**? *Answers appear in the Answer Section in the back of the book.*

ascending order *Ascending order* is very similar to alphabetical order. Ascending means "going up." Ascending order means going from the lowest to the highest.

When your teacher gives you a list of words to put in alphabetical order, you know that all the words on the list are going to be made up of letters. When a computer puts a list of words in ascending order, sometimes the words are made up of all letters—other times the words include numbers or symbols.

What are the sorting rules for words that have letters and numbers? When a word has both letters and numbers, the words that begin with a number come before the words that begin with a letter. For example, the word "123a" comes before the word "artist." If you look in the beginning of this book you will see that the terms that begin with numbers (like 020 machine) come before terms that begin with the letter "a."

What are the sorting rules for words that begin with a capital letter? In most (but not all) computer programs, a word that begins with a capital letter comes before a word that begins with the same letter in lower case. For example, the word "Arm" comes before "all" even though "all" comes before "Arm" in the dictionary.

What are the sorting rules for phrases that have a space? When a computer is placing words in alphabetical order, the space counts as a letter. The space comes before the letter "a." Look at the three words below.

data

data center

database

The words above are in alphabetical order. Why doesn't "database" come before "data center"—since *b* in base comes before *c* in center? The answer is that the fifth "letter" in data center is a space while the fifth letter in database is a "b." Since the space comes before the letter "a" in the alphabet, data[*space*]center comes before database. Look up *chronological order, descending order, numerical order,* and *sort.*

Do you know your states? Cynthia had to type a list of all fifty states and their capitals for homework. Cynthia used the word-processing program Word to type her list. When she was done, Cynthia asked Word to sort the list in **ascending order** so that all of the states were listed alphabetically. **Can you list** all fifty states in **ascending order**? **Do you know** each state's capital? *Cynthia's list appears in the Answer Section in the back of the book.*

asterisk (*) The *asterisk* can be used as a wildcard to take the place of some or all of the letters in a filename or extension. When the asterisk is used as a wildcard it is called a star. Look up *extension, filename,* and *wildcard.*

audible When a sound is *audible*, it is loud enough to be heard. When a sound cannot be heard, it is inaudible.

> *"Amanda, you are speaking so softly I can't hear your answers," said Mr. Grant.*
>
> *"Sorry, Mr. Grant," replied Amanda in a loud voice, "I will try to be more* **audible.***"*

audio How many different types of sounds can you think of? There are voices, music, animal sounds, nature sounds, sounds that an object makes when it's moved (like a door being slammed shut), beeps, buzzes, gurgles, and hundreds of other sounds. What do all these sounds have in common? When these sounds are recorded, they are called *audio*.

Many software programs—particularly games—have music, voices, and sound effects. In order to hear the audio portion of some programs, your computer must either have a sound card, or have the built-in ability (like Macs) to play audio.

AUTOEXEC.BAT The *AUTOEXEC.BAT* file is read by your computer each time you turn on your computer or reboot your computer. The AUTOEXEC.BAT file contains information that you want your computer to know and use (the PATH for example) each time you turn on your computer. The AUTOEXEC.BAT file can also be used to run any programs you want to run as soon as your computer is turned on. For example, if you use Microsoft Windows, there may be a command inside the AUTOEXEC.BAT file that automatically starts Windows each time you turn on your computer.

How do I change the AUTOEXEC.BAT file? If you are using DOS version 5.0 or later, you can change the AUTOEXEC.BAT file by using the DOS command called EDIT. If you are using a version of DOS that is older than 5.0, you need to use a software program that can edit text. Before editing an AUTOEXEC.BAT, please read the following warnings.

- DO NOT change the AUTOEXEC.BAT file on someone else's computer (such as the one in your class or library at school).
- DO NOT change the AUTOEXEC.BAT file on your computer at home unless you have your parent's permission.
- DO NOT change the AUTOEXEC.BAT file on any computer unless you are absolutely sure that you know what you're doing!
- Save a copy of the AUTOEXEC.BAT file before you change it (just in case your change creates a problem). Use a different name for the copy (such as AUTOEXEC.OLD).
- Print a copy of the AUTOEXEC.BAT file before you change it. That way you will know what was in the file before you changed it. You will need this information in case your computer does not boot after you make your changes.

1. Change to the root directory of your hard disk. From the DOS prompt, type

```
C: [Enter]
CD\ [Enter]
```

2. Type the EDIT command followed by the name of the file you want to edit—in this case, the AUTOEXEC.BAT file. If no AUTOEXEC.BAT file exists on your computer, the EDIT command creates one for you.

```
EDIT AUTOEXEC.BAT [Enter]
```

3. Make any changes you want to make. Then save your file by selecting the File menu and the Save command.
4. Reboot your computer. You must reboot your computer after making a change to the AUTOEXEC.BAT file or the change you made will not be used by your computer.

Look up *DOS prompt, EDIT command, Microsoft Windows, reboot, root directory,* and *word processing.*

availability The *availability* of a product is the date that you can get it. Does your family ever rent movies from the video store? You have probably seen the signs for movies that are coming to the video store but aren't at the store yet. These are movies that are unavailable (not yet available). The availability of the video is the date that it will come into the video store for you to rent. The availability of a software program is the date it will come into a computer store for you to buy.

b The letter "*b*" has two different meanings, depending on how it is used in a sentence.

(1) The letter *b* is an abbreviation for baud, the speed at which your modem can send and receive data. Look up *baud* and *modem.*

(2) The letter *b* is an abbreviation for byte, the amount of space that it takes to store one character on your diskette or hard disk. Look up *byte* and *character.*

back door A *back door* is a secret entrance to a software program.

Many software programs ask you to enter your name and password before you may use the program. The software program might even check your name against a list of names to make sure that you are allowed to use the program.

Programmers sometimes make a secret entrance to a software program. The secret entrance is hidden from most users. Sometimes the secret entrance is a special password and sometimes it is a special way of starting the program.

The secret entrance is called a back door because it lets the programmer use the software program without going through the name-checking procedures at the front door—the beginning of the program.

backslash (\ ) A *backslash* is a symbol on your keyboard. The backslash points back to the beginning of the sentence. The backslash is often confused with the forward slash (/).

\	Backslash
/	Forward slash

Backslashes are used in file names such as C:\GAMES. Look up *forward slash.*

backspace *Backspace* is a key on your keyboard that moves your cursor back one space to the left. When the cursor backs up, it erases the letter that it backed over. The backspace key is always located above the Enter key.

PC The backspace key is sometimes marked "backspace" or an abbreviation for "backspace" (such as BkSp). Other times, the backspace key is just marked with an arrow pointing left ⇦ (the direction your cursor moves when it backs up).

Mac The backspace key on a Mac is marked "delete." You can press Delete to erase the letter to the left of the cursor. You can also press Delete to remove any text that is highlighted on your screen.

---

backup copy It is a good idea to keep an extra copy of an important file or software program. This extra copy is called a *backup copy.* You will be able to use the backup copy if your original diskettes get lost or damaged, or someone accidentally erases an important file on your hard disk. Look up *copy* and *COPY command.*

"Oh no," cried Shara, "I just erased the social studies report I need for school tomorrow."

"How did that happen?" asked Mom.

"I was beginning my report for my science project and I saved the science report with the same name as the social studies report."

"Did you make a **backup copy** *of your social studies report on diskette?"*

"Yes."

"Well, copy the **backup copy** *to the hard disk and give it a different name this time. Then you will have both reports on the computer."*

"Whew, that was a close one."

"Just remember that you cannot have two files with the same name," reminded Mom.

"I won't forget that again," said Shara.

---

bad sector A *bad sector* is a damaged area of your diskette or hard disk. Sometimes there are bad sectors on the disk when it comes from the manufacturer. Other times, sectors go bad because your diskette has not been handled carefully. A sector can even go bad for no obvious reason. If there are bad sectors on your diskette, copy any information that you can still use onto another diskette. Then throw away the bad diskette so you do not accidentally use it again.

Balloon Help Do you read the comics in your local paper? When the characters in a comic strip talk to each other, their words are shown in balloons above their heads. *Balloon Help* looks like the balloons in the comics.

You can use Balloon Help when you need a short explanation about a feature, icon, or part of your screen. To use Balloon Help, just point to an item with your mouse. The help pops up on your screen all by itself. On a Mac, you can turn Balloon Help on and off by clicking on the Balloon Help menu.

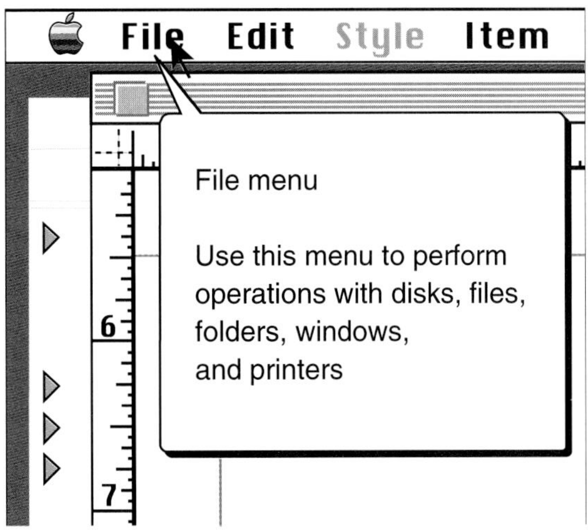

Balloon Help is built into your Macintosh. It is also built into many software programs that are available for your PC—although on your PC, the help is usually in a box instead of a balloon.

"Balloon Help" is a trademark that is owned by Apple Computers. That means that no other company is allowed to use the words "Balloon Help" in their manuals. For this reason, you will not see the term "Balloon Help" in any of the manuals for your PC. But you can call the feature "Balloon Help" no matter what kind of computer you own.

bar chart A *bar chart* is a graph that has long rectangular blocks on it called bars. Each bar on the chart represents one group or thing. Suppose you wanted to make a bar chart showing how much of each popular snack is eaten each year by the kids at your school. Each bar on the bar chart shows a different snack (such as chocolate bars, ice cream, cake, fruit, and popcorn). The length of each bar shows how much of that snack is eaten each year by the kids at your school. The more popular the snack, the longer the bar on the bar chart.

Look up *pie chart.*

bar code If you look on the back of a bag of potato chips, a box of cereal, or your favorite game or magazine, you will see a little box that contains a bunch of vertical (up and down) lines with some numbers underneath. This vertical bunch of lines (or bars) is called a *bar code.*

When a company makes a product, it can't give the product any bar code it wants since there may be another company using the same bar code. What would happen if two food companies used the same bar code? You might get to the checkout line in your supermarket and your Rice Krispies could get rung up as pickled beets.

Who assigns the bar code numbers? When a company wants to place a bar code on their products, the company contacts the Uniform Code Council. The council gives the company specific bar codes to use. These special bar codes are called universal product codes or UPCs. Once the council has given a company UPCs to use on their products, those bar codes are now reserved and are not used for other products that are made by other companies.

Why are there numbers underneath the bar codes? Each set of lines in the bar code represents a number from zero to nine. The number underneath each set of lines is there just in case the scanner that reads the codes has a problem. If the scanner stops working, the store checkout clerk can enter the numbers under the UPC into the cash register by hand. Can you imagine how long it would take to get through the checkout line if the person behind the counter had to figure out the number for each little group of lines in the UPC? Look up *bar code reader.*

Why do stores use the bar code system? Stores have many reasons for using bar codes. A few of the major reasons are listed below. As an example, suppose you were buying a Tazmanian Devil mouse pad as a birthday gift for your friend. Let's just call the mouse pad Taz.

1. Stores use bar codes to help you (the customer) get through the checkout line more quickly. It is faster for the cashier to slide Taz over a scanner than to key Taz's price into the cash register.
2. Bar codes also help to prevent cashier errors. Since the cashier does not key Taz's price into the register, there is less chance for the cashier to make a mistake.
3. If Taz in on sale, the bar code gets you the sale price—even if you didn't know Taz was on sale. When the storc decides to put their mouse pads on sale, the price for Taz and the other mouse pads is changed in the computer. When Taz's bar code is scanned, you get the sale price automatically. Neither you nor the cashier has to remember that mouse pads are on sale.
4. Bar codes help stop dishonest customers from changing the price stickers. Some sneaky customers take a less expensive price sticker from another item and place it on the mouse pad they want to buy. They do this to trick the store into giving them a lower price. But since the cashier doesn't use the price sticker to key the price of the mouse pad into the register, the bar code on the mouse pad shows the computer the correct price—even when the price stickers have been switched.
5. Bar codes also help the store to keep track of how many Taz mouse pads have been sold and how many Taz mouse pads are left on the shelves. When Taz is scanned by the cashier, the inventory for the item is changed to show that the store now has one less Taz in stock.

bar code reader Does your family use a supermarket where the checkout clerk rings up your purchases by moving each item over an opening in the counter? If so, the glass-covered opening in the counter contains a machine called an optical laser scanner—or scanner, for short. The scanner reads the bunches of little black lines that appear on most food items, magazines, toys, and other products. The scanner is often called a *bar code reader* because the collection of little black lines on the back of the food and other products is called a bar code.

The optical laser scanner is connected to the cash register that the clerk is using, and to the store computer. As the clerk scans your purchase, the computer looks up the price, rings it up on the register, and adjusts the store's inventory record so that the manager of the store will know how many of the item have been sold and how many need to be ordered for next week. If your parents have a club card for the supermarket, the computer also records which products your parents are purchasing. The supermarket uses the club card to learn the buying habits of your family and send your family coupons for the types of products that your family uses. Look up *bar code* and *universal product code.*

baseline Each line of text on your computer screen sits on an invisible line called a *baseline.* Think of a baseline as a line on your notebook paper. The baseline is used as a starting point for measuring the point size (the vertical height) of a font. Look up *font* and *point.*

BASIC *BASIC* is the name of a computer language. It is an acronym for beginner's all-purpose symbolic instruction code. BASIC is a good programming language for kids to learn because many of the instructions read like English. For example, to have the computer display "Computers are cool!" you would use the following command in your BASIC program:

```
PRINT "Computers are cool!"
```

Look up *acronym* and *computer language.*

baud rate If your computer has a modem, it can send and receive information through the telephone lines by connecting to another computer. How quickly your modem sends and receives information over the phone lines is called the *baud rate.*

Baud is a speed measurement that equals one bit per second. Since it takes eight (8) bits to make one letter or character, a modem sending (or receiving) data at 8 baud can send (or receive) one letter every second—which is *very* slow.

Most modems can send information at the speeds 300, 1200, 2400, 9600, 14,400 (pronounced 14-4), or 28,800 (pronounced 28-8). The higher the number, the quicker information can be sent or received. The abbreviation for baud is b, as in 9600b.

Your modem and the modem in the computer you are calling must both be operating at the same speed—so most modems can use a slower baud rate if the computers they call cannot send or receive information as quickly as they can. Look up *modem.*

What's the baud? Can you figure out how many letters these modems can send each second? (**Hint:** Divide the baud rate by 8.) *Answers appear in the Answer Section in the back of the book.*

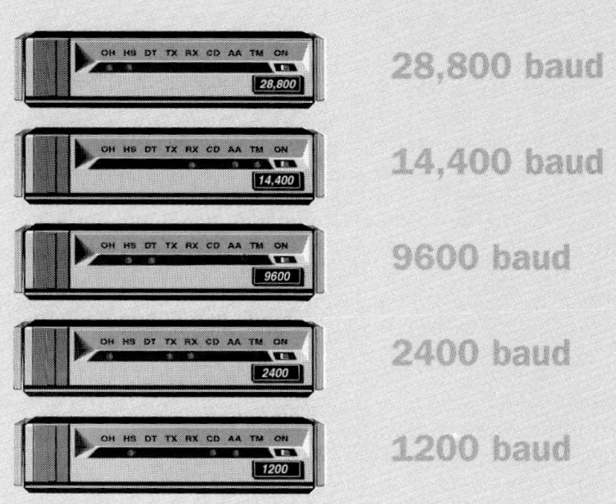

BBS *BBS* is an abbreviation for bulletin board system, a special type of club that you join and participate in by using your computer and a modem. Look up *bulletin board system.*

BEEP *BEEP* is a DOS command that tells your computer to make a beeping sound. Programmers sometimes use BEEP when they want your computer to make a sound. The sound gets your attention and makes you look at the screen.

How do I use the BEEP command? To use the BEEP command, type the following command at the DOS prompt.

```
BEEP [Enter]
```

Look up *DOS prompt.*

bells & whistles When a software program has *bells & whistles,* it has some cool extra features that make the program more fun to use. Bells & whistles is a term that is

used to refer to features that are nice to have but do not make a big difference in the way the software works. A computer game that begins with an animation may be said to have some bells & whistles. The animation may be neat to look at but doesn't make playing the game any better.

> *"Have you played that new computer game that Duncan got?" asked Zoe.*
>
> *"Yeah. It has a lot of* **bells & whistles** *but I really didn't like it," replied Amanda.*

beta test A *beta test* is a series of tests that are made on a software program before it is sold in stores. Look up *alpha test.*

beta test site The place where the beta test is done is called the *beta test site.* Look up *alpha test.*

David is beta testing the new Super Keen Commando VII game for a software company. David is testing the software at home, on his family's computer. David's house is a **beta test site** *for the new game software.*

beta tester A *beta tester* is a person who tests software programs before the software is sold in stores. Look up *alpha test.*

David wrote to his favorite software company and asked if he could help test new software before it is available in stores. The company was impressed with David's letter and told him that he could be a **beta tester** *for their new computer game.*

binary numbers A *binary number* is a number that is shown as a combination of zeros and ones. But before looking at binary numbers, let's review how our normal number system works.

The number system that you use every day is called a base 10 number system. In a base 10 number system you can count from zero to nine (0-1-2-3-4-5-6-7-8-9) in the ones column. After nine, you place a "1" in the tens column and "0" in the ones column.

Tens Column	Ones Column
1	0

After placing a "1" in the tens column, you count up to nine again in the ones column—making the numbers 11-12-13-14-15-16-17-18-19. After the number 19, you must add one to the tens column and place " 0" in the ones column—making the number twenty.

Tens Column	Ones Column
2	0

In a binary system you cannot use the numbers 2, 3, 4, 5, 6, 7, 8, or 9. "Bi" means two. In a binary number system you can only use two numbers, 0 and 1. When you reach the number two, you show it as "1" two and "0" ones. A binary number system is also called a base 2 number system.

Twos Column	Ones Column
1	0

After placing a "1" in the twos column, you can only count up to one again before having to move to the next column. In the base 10 number system, the third column is for hundreds, which is 10×10. What do you think is the third column in a binary system? It is 2×2, or 4. The number four is shown as "1" four, "0" twos, and "0" ones.

Fours Column	Twos Column	Ones Column
1	0	0

In the base 10 number system, the fourth column is for thousands, which is $10 \times 10 \times 10$. What do you think is the fourth column in a binary system? It is $2 \times 2 \times 2$, or 8. The number eight is shown as "1" eight, "0" fours, "0" twos, and "0" ones.

Eights Column	Fours Column	Twos Column	Ones Column
1	0	0	0

What are binary numbers used for? Binary numbers are how a computer understands information. Your computer at its most basic level understands information in the form of zeros (0) and ones (1). A zero means "no" and a one means "yes." So when you get right down to it, the only thing your computer really understands is a complicated combination of yes and no. Look up *bit, byte,* and *character.*

Can you count in binary? Counting in binary is very different than the way you are used to counting. What number would be represented by binary 11? Well, you have one "2" and one "1"; 2 + 1 = 3. **Can you figure out** what numbers are represented by the binary numbers shown below? *Answers appear in the Answer Section in the back of the book.*

1. 1
2. **111**
3. 101
4. **100**
5. 1100
6. **1001**
7. 1010
8. **1111**
9. 10000
10. **10100**
11. 10101
12. **11111**

bit A *bit* is the smallest piece of information that your computer can understand. Your computer, at its most basic level, understands information in the form of zeros (0) and ones (1). A zero means "no" and a one means "yes." A bit is either a zero or a one.

It takes eight bits to make a byte, the amount of disk space that it takes to store one character of information (such as the letter "A"). Look up *binary numbers, bitmap, byte, character,* and *file.*

bitmap A *bitmap* is a computer drawing that is made up of tiny dots called pixels. By arranging the pixels in a grid—a screen display that looks like graph paper—you can make a very colorful and detailed picture.

Arranging your pixels on the screen is like mapping out where you want to put each color in your picture.

Each pixel is made up of one or more bits, depending on whether the pixel is black, white, gray, or a color. Colored pixels are made up of more bits than black, white, or gray pixels.

If you have a paint program, you can create a detailed picture by zooming in on (enlarging) the screen until you see a grid. You can place a colored dot in each box to create your bitmap picture. When you zoom out, you will see a picture. Look up *bit, grid, Microsoft Windows, pixel, zoom in,* and *zoom out.*

You can draw these pictures on your computer screen by using a paint program like Corel Paint, MacPaint, Paintbrush (which is included in Microsoft Windows), Painter, PC Paintbrush, and others. Use the Zoom In option to make the screen so big that you see a grid. Then fill in the dots on your screen using one of the patterns shown below. When you zoom out, you will see a picture similar to one of the drawings below.

blink rate The keyboard cursor is a blinking line (_), blinking box (▮), or blinking vertical line (|) that shows you where on the screen your next keypress will appear. The cursor blinks so you can find it more easily. (If the cursor didn't blink, it could get lost in all the characters on your screen.)

The *blink rate* is the speed at which your keyboard cursor blinks on and off. Some software programs allow you to change the blink rate—so you can make the cursor blink faster or slower so it is easier for you to see. Look up *character* and *cursor.*

board **(1)** A *board* is an accessory that plugs into a slot inside your CPU (central processing unit) to give your computer extra abilities, such as sound or video. Look up *CPU* and *computer board.* **(2)** A *board* is a short name for bulletin board system or BBS, a special type of club that you can join and participate in with your computer and modem. Look up *bulletin board system* and *modem.*

bold *Bold* is a type of font weight. The letters of a bold font are darker than the normal font weight. A bold font is sometimes called boldface. Look up *bold italic, font, font weight,* and *italic.*

Normal fonts blend into the crowd.
Bold fonts stand out and are noticed.

bold italic *Bold italic* is a type of font weight. The letters of a bold italic font are different from a normal font in two ways. First, the letters are darker than the normal font weight. Second, the letters of a bold italic font are slanted. Look up *bold, font, font weight,* and *italic.*

Normal fonts blend into the crowd.
Bold fonts stand out and are noticed.
Italic fonts take on a slant.
Bold italic fonts stand out with a slant.

bomb When you are using a software program and your keyboard stops responding to your keypresses and your mouse no longer makes selections in your software program, or the program just suddenly stops or shuts down your computer, your software program has *bombed* or crashed.

When your software bombs, the only thing you can do is reboot your computer (if necessary) and try the program again. If you can remember the selections that you made before the software bombed, try not to repeat that combination (if you can help it). If the program bombs over and over again, ask your mom or dad to call the software company. Sometimes the company will send you a free diskette that corrects the problem. Look up *reboot.*

boot To *boot* (or boot up) your computer is to turn your computer on. Each time you use the on-off switch, you are starting your computer from a cold boot. If your computer is already on, and you start it up again (due to a problem with a software program or some other reason), you are rebooting or restarting your computer. Look up *reboot* and *restart.*

boot disk A *boot disk* is a diskette that you can use to start (boot) your computer. Your computer needs special files to get your computer running. Normally, those files are stored on the hard disk inside your computer. The boot disk contains the files that are needed to start your computer.

Why do I need a boot disk? You need to have a boot disk on hand in case there is ever a problem with your hard disk (which can happen when the battery inside your computer runs out). The boot disk can be used to start your computer and get to the information on the hard disk.

Where do I get a boot disk?
Mac The Disk Tools disk that comes with your Mac OS is a boot disk. To make another boot disk, follow the instructions in your manual.

PC You can make a boot disk by using the DOS FORMAT command in a special way. You must use a diskette that will fit in your "A" drive. You cannot boot your computer from the "B" drive. To create a boot disk, follow the instructions below.
1. Place a blank diskette in drive "A."
2. Type the following command at the DOS prompt.

FORMAT A:/S Enter

It is a good idea to make a new boot disk each time you upgrade to a new version of DOS.

How do I start my computer with a boot disk? To start your computer with a boot disk, follow the instructions below

Mac Put the boot disk in the drive. Then turn on your computer.

PC Place the boot disk in drive "A." Then turn on your computer.

Look up *DOS command* and *DOS prompt.*

bootleg A *bootleg* copy of a software program is a copy of the software that is not official. Computer software is protected by laws that make it illegal for anyone to make a copy of a software program and give it away or sell it. Look up *software piracy.*

"Francis, can you make me a copy of your Amazon Trail game?" asked Corey.

"You don't want a **bootleg** *copy. Besides, it's illegal," replied Francis. "Ask your mom to buy you one for your birthday."*

bug A *bug* is an error or problem in a software program. Every software program has bugs. If you find one that keeps you from using the software, ask your mom or dad to contact the software company. Sometimes the company will send you a free diskette that corrects the problem.

Don't confuse bug with virus. A bug is in the program because someone made a mistake. A virus gets into a program because someone put it there on purpose.

Look up *debug* and *virus.*

bulletin board system The bulletin boards in your classroom at school are used to display notices, artwork, and other information that your teacher wants everyone to see.

A *bulletin board system*, called a BBS, is a special type of club that you go to by using your computer and modem. When your computer calls the BBS, you are greeted with an opening message and given a menu of choices. One of the most popular features of most BBS's is the message area. The message area works somewhat like a regular bulletin board in that people place messages and notices that they want other people to see.

Many kids join a BBS to communicate with other kids for fun. Some messages are very funny. You can get into all types of silly or serious discussions by asking a question, stating your opinion, or responding to a question or statement that someone else made in another message. Some BBS's also have a file area where you can upload or download shareware games and other files.

You join the BBS by calling the BBS with the modem in your computer and giving the BBS a handle (your code name) and a password. Most BBS's are free, other than the telephone call you make with your computer. Many BBS's are run by teenagers and college students who run them from their bedrooms at home or dorm rooms at school. A few BBS's have an age that you must be in order to join the BBS, but most allow anyone to join and participate. Some even have parties and special events that you can attend in person.

How do I find a BBS in my area? If you live in a city or large town, there are probably dozens of BBS's nearby. But since BBS's don't make any money, they usually don't spend any money by advertising. The best place to find a BBS in your area is to ask someone who belongs to the local computer club or user group.

Look up *download, handle, modem, password, upload,* and *user group.*

burn-in If you leave your computer on for hours or days at a time, it is a good idea to protect your computer screen from a problem called *burn-in.* When you walk away from your computer and leave the text or a picture on the screen for hours at a time, it is possible that you will see a ghostly image of the same picture or text when you finally turn off your monitor. The ghostly image is called burn-in.

Many monitors today are made in a way that protects them from burn-in, but it is still a good idea not to leave the same image on your screen for hours at a time. Many companies make a type of software program called a screen saver that saves your monitor from burn-in. The screen saver displays an attractive, changing picture on your screen. Since the picture changes, no single picture has the time to burn-in to your monitor. Look up *screen saver.*

butterfly key The *butterfly key* is the key on your keyboard with the ⌘ symbol. The technical name for this key is command key. The command key is sometimes called the butterfly key, propeller key, or flower key because many people think that the symbol on the key looks like a butterfly, flower, or propeller.

The command key can be used in many programs to give an alternate (or different) meaning to another key. To use the command key, you hold it down while you press another key. Look up *command key.*

buzzword A computer *buzzword* is any term or phrase that refers to a computer subject that is very new or very popular. Some of the popular buzzwords of 1995 and 1996 are client server, cyberspace, information superhighway, multimedia, surf the net, and world wide web. Look up *computer jargon.*

byte A *byte* (pronounced "bite") is the amount of space, on your diskette or hard disk, that it takes to store one character of information (such as the letter "A"). A byte is made up of eight bits. A bit is the smallest piece of information your computer can understand. Byte is abbreviated as "b."

When we talk about the size of a computer file, and whether or not there is enough space on a diskette to store the file, we are talking about how many bytes of storage space the file takes up. Since file sizes can get very large, it is sometimes useful to talk about files and disk storage space in terms of kilobytes, megabytes, and gigabytes.

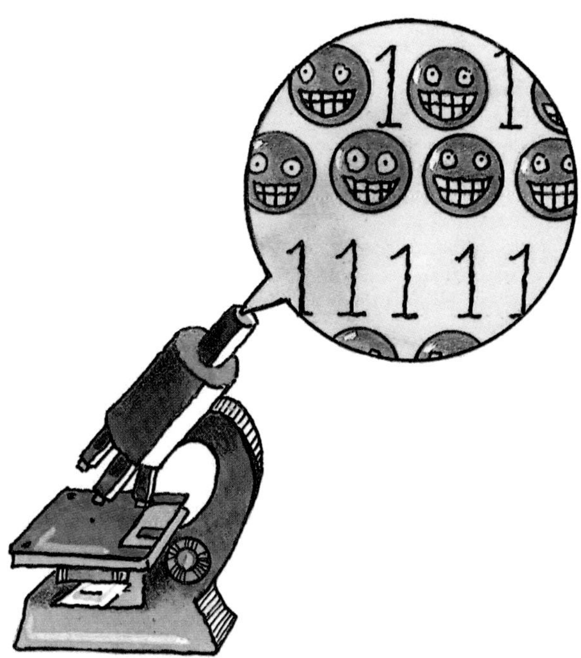

How many bytes are there in a kilobyte, megabyte, and gigabyte? We say that there are about 1,000 (one thousand) bytes in a kilobyte, or "K," 1,000,000 (one million) bytes in a megabyte, or "Mb," and 1,000,000,000 (one billion) bytes in a gigabyte, or "Gb." The chart below shows you the actual number of bytes in a kilobyte, megabyte, and gigabyte. Look up *binary numbers, bit, character, file,* and *storage.*

1,024 bytes	=	1 K
1,048,576 bytes	=	1 Mb
1,024 Kilobytes	=	1 Mb
1,073,741,824 bytes	=	1 Gb
1,048,576 Kilobytes	=	1 Gb
1,024 Megabytes	=	1 Gb

cable All those cords and wires in a big tangle behind your computer are called *cables.* A cable is an electrical cord that connects one piece of computer equipment to another piece of computer equipment (or to your power strip). You have a cable that goes from your computer to your monitor, your computer to your printer, your computer to your power strip (the electric plugs), your monitor to your power strip...well, you get the idea. Look up *monitor* and *power strip.*

Wow! These cables really are in a tangle. Can you follow the **cord** and plug it into the **socket**? *The answer appears in the Answer Section in the back of the book.*

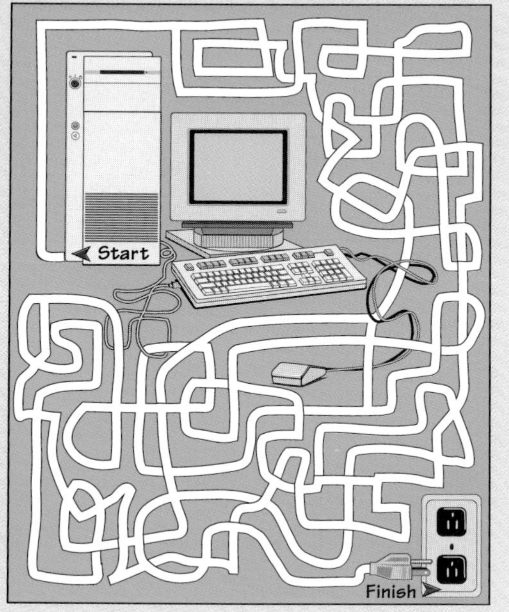

caddy Some CD-ROM drives need you to place your CD in a *caddy* before inserting it into the CD-ROM drive. The caddy is a special type of rectangular-shaped holder for your CD. The caddy holds the CD while it is in the CD-ROM drive. Look up *CD-ROM* and *CD-ROM drive.*

cancel When you make plans to go to the movies with your friends and then can't go for some reason, you *cancel* your plans. When you cancel, you make a decision not to do something you had planned.

When you give a command to your computer, and then stop your computer from performing the task, you have canceled the command. Many software programs give you a chance to cancel certain selections that you make (such as deleting a file) before the program actually does what you asked.

Caps Lock When the Caps Lock key is pressed, *Caps Lock* is turned on and all the letters that you type are capital letters. Many keyboards have a red or green light (called an indicator light) that lets you know that Caps Lock is on. Caps Lock is short for "capitals locked."

When you write a story or report, most of the letters in each sentence (except the first letter) are in lower case letters. When you need an occasional capital letter, you can hold down the Shift key (before pressing a letter) and the letter that you press is capitalized. The Caps Lock key is useful on the rare occasions when you need to type a lot of text that is all capital letters.

On the PC, you can type a lower case letter while the Caps Lock is on by holding down the Shift key before typing the letter. (This feature does not exist on the Mac.) Look up *acronym*, *cursor movement keys*, and *numeric keypad*.

card A *card* (or expansion card) is another name for a computer board. A card is an accessory that gives your computer extra capabilities such as sound, better video, or more memory. The card plugs into one of the expansion slots inside your computer's CPU. Look up *computer board*, *CPU*, and *expansion slot*.

card slot *Card slot* is another term for expansion slot, a place inside your computer's CPU where you can add a card (also called a computer board). Look up *computer board*, *CPU*, and *expansion slot*.

carriage return The Enter key on your computer is sometimes called the return key or *carriage return*. Before there were computers, all letters and reports were typed on typewriters. The term carriage return comes from typewriters.

On a typewriter, the carriage return (on manual typewriters) or the return key (on electric typewriters) is used to move the paper to the beginning of the next blank line so you can continue typing.

Some computer keyboards still use the word "Return" on the keyboard rather than "Enter"—even though in word-processing programs you do not press Enter (or Return) until you reach the end of a paragraph. Look up *Enter key*.

carrier tone The *carrier tone* is a high-pitched sound that your modem makes when it has connected your computer to another computer over the phone lines. The sound comes out through the speaker that is built into your modem. Look up *modem*.

cartridge font Some printers can use a cartridge that plugs into a slot in your printer the way a game cartridge is plugged into a slot in the game system. Since the cartridge usually contains fonts, it is called a font cartridge. The fonts on the cartridge are called *cartridge fonts*. Look up *font* and *font cartridge*.

case sensitive Is the word "giggles" the same as the word "GIGGLES" or the word "Giggles"? Although the definition of all three words is the same, your computer may think of them as three different words depending on whether or not the software program you are using is *case sensitive*.

Case sensitive has to do with whether the letters in your words are upper case, lower case, or mixed. Upper case is another phrase for capital letters (such as A, B, and C). Lower case is another phrase for small letters (such as a, b, and c). Mixed means that both upper case and lower case letters are used.

When a software program is case sensitive, it treats words that have different cases (words that are spelled the same but have different capitalization) as different words.

When is case sensitivity useful? One of the times that case sensitivity is most useful is when you are searching for a word in a report or story. Look up *lower case* and *upper case*.

Ben was writing a term paper about life in the American West in the late 1800s. His great-grandfather had been a guide and trapper in the Rocky Mountains. As Ben was finishing the term paper, he asked his mom to proofread it.

"You know, Ben, your great-grandfather went by the name Mark," said Mom, "but his first name was actually Fred. He just preferred to use Mark, which was a nickname that he was given when he was a child."

"Okay. It should be easy to change mark to fred with my word-processing program," Ben replied.

Ben went back to his word-processing program, and entered the commands to replace every mark with fred. But look at the results!

Before	After
My great-grandfather **Mark** was a guide and trapper in the late 1800s.	My great-grandfather **fred** was a guide and trapper in the late 1800s.
Mark only went shopping for supplies once per month, since the nearest **mark**et was 20 miles away.	**fred** only went shopping for supplies once per month, since the nearest **fred**et was 20 miles away.
While guiding a hunting party, he would **mark** the trails with stones or cut several **mark**s in a tree trunk to show the way.	While guiding a hunting party, he would **fred** the trails with stones or cut several **fred**s in a tree trunk to show the way.
When he was not busy working as a guide and trapper, my great-grandfather would **mark** time by carving wooden figures shaped like animals.	When he was not busy working as a guide and trapper, my great-grandfather would **fred** time by carving wooden figures shaped like animals.
He had many re**mark**able experiences.	He had many re**fred**able experiences.

Can you figure out Ben's mistake? Can you figure out **what Ben could have done** so that the text would have been changed correctly? *Answers appear in the Answer Section in the back of the book.*

CD A *CD* is a flat, circular disk that can contain programs, graphics, video, and sound. CD is an abbreviation for compact disc. Although many people call a compact disc a CD, the full name for a compact disc is CD-ROM (compact disc, read-only memory).
Look up *CD-ROM* and *CD-ROM drive.*

CD command The *CD command* is a DOS command that means change directory. Files on your computer are stored in directories. You can move from directory to directory by using the CD command. Before you can use the CD command you need to know:

- Which directory you want to go to.
- How to get to the directory you want to go to. For example, say you wanted to go to the directory that has your Space Simulator game. All the files for the game are listed in the directory called SPACE. The SPACE directory is located in a directory called GAMES.

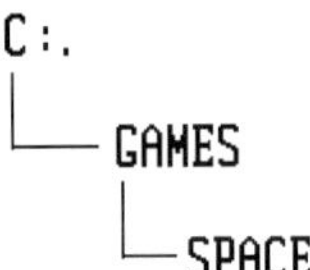

How do I know where a directory is located? If you do not know where on your hard disk the directory is located, use the TREE command. TREE is a DOS command that shows you where each directory is located.

How do I use the CD command? When you use the CD command, you must tell your computer which directory you want to go to. Type CD and the name of each directory you need to go through to get to the directory you want. You must separate the CD command and each directory name with a backslash (\).

To go to the SPACE directory, which is located in the GAMES directory, you type the following instruction at the DOS prompt.

```
CD\ GAMES\SPACE [Enter]
```

To go to the top directory (called the root directory), just type the CD command, a backslash, and no directory name.

Look up *backslash, directory, DOS command, DOS prompt,* and *TREE command.*

CD-ROM A *CD-ROM* is a flat, circular disk that can contain programs, graphics, video, and sound. A CD-ROM is usually just called a CD, like the music CDs you may have at home. As a matter of fact, a computer CD and a music CD look identical. Music CDs can even be played in most computer CD-ROM drives, although a computer CD cannot usually be played in your stereo.

CDs are about five inches in diameter and have a shiny surface. The back of the CD is so shiny that you can use it as a mirror! The mirrored side of the CD contains the data or music. The other side usually has writing, such as the name of the CD.

Your computer can read the data on the CD in any order, but the beginning of the CD is in the center, and the end is at the outer edge—unlike a record for a record player, where the beginning is at the outer edge and the end is in the middle.

CD-ROM stands for compact disc, read-only memory. Notice that the term "disc" in "compact disc" is spelled with a "c." This is a different spelling than the term "disk," which means "diskette" or "hard disk." Both "disc" and "disk" are pronounced the same way.

Unlike a diskette, where you can store (write) information, a CD-ROM is read-only—in other words, you can use (read) the information that is on the CD, but you cannot erase or change any of the information that is stored on the CD.

How much information can a CD store? CDs can hold a whole bunch of information—650 megabytes worth. That's more information than most people can store on the hard disk in their computer!

Can you figure out how many 3½-inch diskettes it takes to hold the same information as one CD? (Hint: A high-density, 3½-diskette on a PC can hold 1.4 megabytes of information. A high-density, 3½-diskette on a Mac can hold 1.2 megabytes of information.) *Answers appear in the Answer Section in the back of the book.*

Never put your fingers directly on a CD-ROM. Hold the CD by the edges. Fingerprints can cause your computer to have trouble reading the information that is stored on the CD.

Look up *3½-inch diskette*, *CD-ROM drive*, and *hard disk*.

Can you find the rainbow hidden in your CDs? This trick works with both the CDs from your computer and the ones from your stereo. Hold a CD on its edge, with the blank side facing you. Now tilt the CD just a little bit. Can you see a colorful rainbow move around the CD as you tilt it back and forth? Hint: This trick works best if you point the CD toward a light.

CD-ROM drive A *CD-ROM drive* is a computer accessory that is used to play computer (and music) CDs. Most computers can use either an internal or an external CD-ROM drive. An internal CD-ROM drive is installed inside your computer. An external CD-ROM drive is a small rectangular box that is installed outside your computer. An external CD-ROM drive looks similar to a portable CD player that you might use to play music CDs.

When you play a computer game that is stored on your hard disk, your computer responds very quickly to your selections within the game. That's because the speed at which your computer can get the information is very quick. Unfortunately, CD-ROM drives do not allow your computer to get information as quickly as hard drives. CD-ROM drives are usually 10 to 20 times slower than a hard disk drive.

When you and your parents go shopping for a CD-ROM drive, there are two technical things to check out. One is access time, the other is data transfer rate. The access time of a CD-ROM drive is the amount of time it takes your computer to find information on a CD in the drive. The shorter (lower) the access time, the faster the CD-ROM drive can find the information on a CD.

The data transfer rate is how much information the CD-ROM drive can send to your computer every second. The higher the data transfer rate, the faster your computer will have the information from the CD-ROM drive. Both the access time and data transfer rate can usually be found on the box containing the CD-ROM drive. Look for "specifications" (the section of the box with the technical details). Look up *access speed, CD, data transfer rate,* and *Photo CD.*

centered text *Centered text* is a phrase that describes how words, or the lines in a paragraph, are formatted. When the text is centered, the same amount of unused space appears on the left side of the line as on the right side of the line. Each line of the paragraph is centered separately. Look up *flush left, flush right, full justification, ragged left,* and *ragged right.*

When a paragraph is centered, each line is centered so the white space on each side of the paragraph varies from line to line. Neither side forms a smooth straight line as it does in most paragraphs.

central processing unit The *central processing unit* is the actual computer part of your computer setup. It is the box that contains your computer's hard disk, memory, diskette drives, and sound card. The central processing unit is usually just called by its abbreviation, CPU. Look up *computer.*

change directory Files on your computer are stored in directories. You can move from one directory to another by using a DOS command that tells your computer you want to *change directory.* The DOS command for change directory is CD (or CHDIR). Look up *CD command* and *DOS command.*

character A *character* is any letter or symbol that can be displayed on your screen or printed on your printer. All the letters of the alphabet are characters—so are all the numbers and symbols on your keyboard. There are hundreds of other characters that do not even appear on your keyboard (such as ☞, ❦, ♡, ✂, ☎, ▲, ¥, ®, and ©). Some programs let you use these special characters by selecting them from a chart or using a special combination of keyboard keys.

character recognition Can you recognize each of the characters in the alphabet? Of course you can. If you didn't recognize every letter, you would not be able to read! *Character recognition* is a combination of software and computer equipment that gets your computer to recognize each of the letters in the alphabet. Character recognition is also called OCR or optical character recognition. Look up *character* and *optical character recognition.*

How many characters per inch? Can you measure the **fixed-space fonts** below and figure out their **cpi**? (Hint: Be sure to count the spaces.) *Answers appear in the Answer Section in the back of the book.*

1. Computers are cool!
2. Computers are cool!
3. Computers are cool!
4. Computers are cool!

characters per inch Some fonts are called fixed-space fonts because each letter takes up the same amount of space on the line. When you have a fixed-space font, you can count the number of characters that will fit on one inch of the line. The number of characters that will fit in one inch of line is called the *characters per inch.*

To measure characters per inch you first need a ruler so you can measure one inch across. Next, place the ruler under one line of letters. Count the number of characters along one inch of line—be sure to count any spaces as a character. The number you counted is the font's characters per inch. Characters per inch is abbreviated cpi. Look up *character, fixed-space font,* and *proportionally spaced font.*

characters per second *Characters per second* is a measurement of the number of letters, spaces, and symbols (in other words, characters) that a dot-matrix printer can print each second. The abbreviation for characters per second is cps. The higher the cps, the faster the printer. Look up *dot-matrix printer.*

CHDIR *CHDIR* (pronounced "change-der" or "C—H—D—I—R") is a DOS command that means change directory. A shorter (and more popular) DOS command for changing directory is the CD command. Look up *CD command* and *DOS command.*

Chooser At school (or at home) you may be allowed to use more than one printer to print your papers and reports. The *Chooser* is a program that lets you pick which printer you want to use. To use the Chooser, select it from the Apple menu. Look up *Apple menu.*

chronological order *Chronological order* means in order by date. When you put a list of words in alphabetical order, you place them in order based on the letters in the alphabet, starting with "A." When you place a list of dates in chronological order, you place them in order beginning with the oldest date. The older the date, the closer it is to the top of the list. The more recent the date, the closer it is to the bottom of the list. Look up *ascending order, descending order, numerical order,* and *sort.*

Kito's history teacher, Mr. Jensen, gave Kito and his classmates a **chronological** list of years in which important inventions and events took place. **Can you match the inventions and events to the year?** (Hint: More than one invention or event occurring during the same years is marked with an asterisk (*).) *Answers appear in the Answer Section in the back of the book.*

Years Include:		Inventions & Events Include:	
1450	1877	Air conditioning	Phonograph
1492	1879*	Airplane	Polaroid camera
1776	1893*	Bicycle	Polio vaccine
1793	1903	Cash register	Printing press
1787	1911	Color television	Revolver
1796	1925	Columbus' arrival in North America	Sewing machine
1816	1948	Cotton gin	Smallpox vaccine
1835	1950	Declaration of Independence was signed	Steamboat
1837	1954	First astronaut launched into space	Telegraph
1845	1956	First astronaut walked on the moon	Telephone
1860	1961	Gas engine	Television
1876	1969	Light bulb	Videotape
		Movie projector	Zipper

clean When you *clean* a diskette or your hard disk, you use an anti-virus program to remove any computer viruses that exist in your files. Look up *anti-virus program, scan, Trojan horse,* and *virus.*

click To *click* the mouse is to press a mouse button one time. Most Macs have a mouse with only one button, so click means to press the button. Most PCs have a mouse with two or three buttons. On a PC, click means to click the left mouse button. When the right mouse button needs to be clicked, you are usually asked to right-click the mouse. The center button (on a three- button mouse) is not used in most software programs. Look up *mouse button.*

client *Client* is another word for customer. Many professional people, such as architects, lawyers, and programmers, call their customers clients.

A client program is a computer program that goes to another program to get its information—just like a customer goes to a store. A client computer is a computer that is controlled by another computer. Look up *client server.*

client server When you go to a restaurant and place your order, you are the customer (or client). The waiter or waitress who take takes your order, gets the food from the kitchen, gives the food to you, and keeps things running smoothly, is the server. The server serves you and several other customers too. Sometimes the server tells you where to find other items that you want, such as the salad bar or a self-service soft-drink machine. When the server can't give you an item right away, you are asked to wait a few minutes.

Imagine what it would be like if everyone who went into a restaurant had to go into the kitchen and get their own food. Or what would happen if 100 customers all reached for the last hamburger at the same time!

In some ways, a restaurant is like a *client server* computer setup. Client server is a way that some computer programs interact with each other. The server program controls information that is needed by the client (customer) programs. The server program controls programs, files, printers, and other items that are needed by other client programs.

Back to the restaurant to finish our lunch. Let's say that you ordered french fries as part of your meal. The server tries to get fries for you, but discovers that they aren't ready. All the fries are still being cooked. The server comes back to your table and says that your fries are not ready,

but will be ready soon. You—the client—wait for a few minutes, and then ask the server to check again. You repeat this process until you get your fries. Sending the waiter or waitress back to the kitchen to check on your fries is how client programs and server programs interact with each other. The server program tells a client program when a resource (a printer, program, or file) can't be used. The client program will wait for a while and then ask the server program to try again.

Client server is also the way that computers on a network interact with each other. The server computer has hard disks with lots of programs on them. The client computers are like the personal computers you use at home and at school. The client computers use the programs that are located on the hard disks on the server. When you ask the server computer to run a program that someone else is using, you get a message that asks you to try again later.

clip *Clip* is short for video clip, a short movie that you can insert into your projects that are created on a computer. Look up *video clip*.

clip-art Before you were able to buy artwork on diskettes and CD-ROMs, companies sold books of pictures that could be cut out (clipped) and pasted into your projects. These pictures are called *clip-art*. Even though clip-art in book form is not used very much any more, many companies still use the term clip-art for their computer artwork—even though you no longer have to clip the artwork from a book. (Other companies call computer artwork graphics or electronic art.) Clip-art can be used in any of the following programs:

- Word Processing.
- Paint.
- Draw.
- Desktop Publishing.

Clip-art comes in many different types of file formats. A few of these formats are BMP, CDR, EPS, Paint, PCX, PICT, TIFF, TIF, TGA, and WPG. Before you buy clip-art, make sure that you are buying it in a format that your software program can use. Otherwise, you will have beautiful pictures that you will not be able to use in your project.

clock speed *Clock speed* indicates how fast your computer processes information. The speed of most computers is measured in megahertz. (Megahertz is abbreviated MHz.) When you play a strategy game (like chess) against the computer, a computer with a fast clock speed (such at 100 MHz) makes its next move much faster than a computer with a slow clock speed (such as 8 MHz). Look up *megahertz* and *microprocessor*.

clockwise Do you know which way the hands of a clock move? The direction that the hands of a clock move is called *clockwise*. When you are instructed to move or turn something in a clockwise direction, you turn it the same direction that the hands of the clock move.

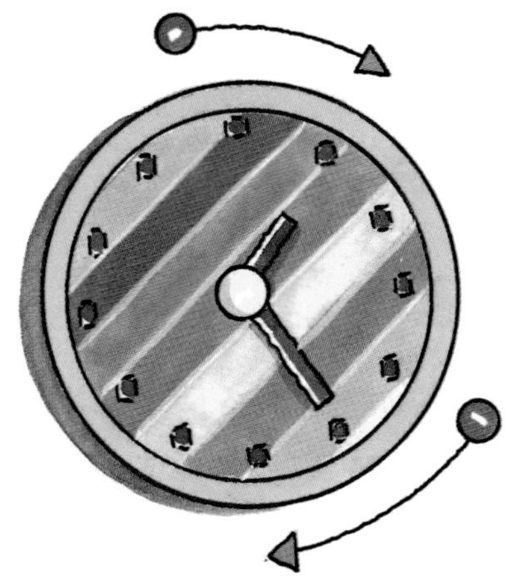

clone In science fiction, a *clone* is someone who is a copy of another person—sort of like having a twin. If the science fiction clone was a copy of you, your clone would look like you, talk like you, think like you, and may even have your memories—from the time you were born until the time the clone was made.

In computers, the word clone has a slightly different meaning. Most of the computers manufactured today are IBM-compatibles. The term clone has come to mean a computer that was not made by IBM Corporation but will run all the software that will run on a personal computer made by IBM Corporation.

Are there Mac clones? Yes. There are some manufacturers (other than Apple Computer) that build Mac-compatible computers. But Mac clones are usually called "Mac clones." The term clone, when used by itself, means an IBM-compatible (not a Mac-compatible) computer.

Can you find the clones? Two of the computers below are **clones.** The other four look alike, but are not exactly the same. *Answers appear in the Answer Section in the back of the book.*

close box On the top left-hand corner of every window is a small box. This box is called the *close box.* Click on this box to close (put away) the window or document that is displayed on your screen.

"It is my turn to use the computer but Alina left her report on the screen," complained Lia. "How do I get it off the screen?"

"Just hit the **close box**, *" responded Vittorio. "It's that little box at the top of her report."*

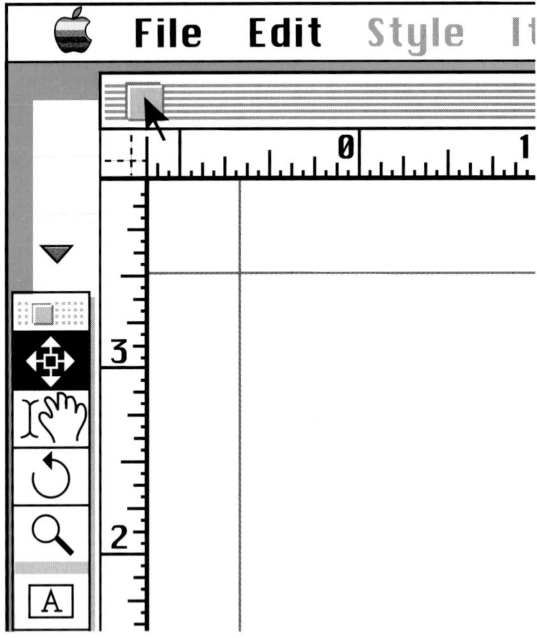

CLS *CLS* is a DOS command that means clear screen. When you use CLS from the DOS prompt, all the information that is displayed on your screen disappears. It is as though your screen were a blackboard you erased. After you use the CLS command your DOS prompt reappears on the screen.

How do I use the CLS command? To use CLS to clear your screen, type the following command at the DOS prompt.

CLS [Enter]

Look up *DOS command* and *DOS prompt.*

code When a programmer writes a software program, he or she writes instructions to the computer in a special language that the computer can understand. The special instructions to the computer are called *code* or source code.

"In junior high they have a course in BASIC programming," Willa told her little sister. "When I go there next year, Jenine, I'm going to learn how to write BASIC **code**—*just like Mama does."*

"Can I learn to write **code** *too?" asked Jenine.*

"Sure, I'll teach you," replied Willa.

coder *Coder* is another word for programmer. Look up *programmer.*

cold boot To *cold boot* your computer is to start your computer using the on-off switch. Look up *boot.*

cold start To *cold start* your computer is to start your computer using the on-off switch. Starting your computer with the on-off switch is often called cold booting your computer. Look up *boot.*

color printer A *color printer* is a printer that can produce pictures and text in color, rather than in just black and white. Many color printers can produce printouts that look very close to the original artwork you create on your computer. Look up *printer* and *printout*.

column A *column* is a list of information that is organized in a vertical line. Most tables (like your multiplication tables) are made up of rows and columns. The rows are made up of information you read from left to right across the line. A column is the line of information you read up and down, from the top row to the bottom row. Look up *row*.

2	3	4	5	6	7
4	6	8	10	12	14
6	9	12	15	18	21
8	12	16	20	24	28
10	15	20	25	30	35
12	18	24	30	36	42
14	21	28	35	42	49
16	24	32	40	48	56

command A *command* is an order or instruction you give to your computer. When you give a command to a puppy, you might tell it to sit, stay, or come. When you give a command to your computer, you might tell it to start a software program, show you a file, copy a file from one place to another, or delete a file that you no longer need.

There are different types of commands that you can tell your computer. If you are using DOS, you can type your command at the DOS prompt or select it from a menu (if you are using Windows or a shell program). If you are using a Mac, a command can be selected from a menu or used by pressing a special combination of keys on your keyboard. Look up *command key, DOS command,* and *DOS prompt.*

command key The *command key* is the key on your keyboard with the ⌘ symbol. As a matter of fact, most computers have two command keys, one on either side of the spacebar. The command key is sometimes called the propeller key, butterfly key, or flower key because many people think that the symbol on the key looks like a propeller, butterfly, or flower.

What does the command key do? Selecting a command from a menu is not always the fastest way to do something. The command key is the keyboard shortcut key. Do you ever take a shortcut on your way home from school? Shortcuts save time. The command key can also help you save time because you can use it to select a command without using the menus.

How do I use the command key? Do you know how to use the SHIFT key? You hold down SHIFT while you press another key. The command key is used the same way. You hold down the command key while you press another key.

How do I know which key to use with the command key? If you look at the commands on your menus, you will see ⌘ and a letter to the right of the commands. If you hold down ⌘ and press the letter, you can use the same command from the keyboard—without having to open a menu.

Does the PC have a command key? No, PCs do not have a command key. But PCs do have other keys (called Alt and Ctrl) that are used to do the same job. Look up *ALT key, CTRL key,* and *function key.*

communications software *Communications software* is a type of software program that lets your modem connect and talk to other computers over the phone lines. Communications software—which is not always included when you buy a modem—is used to dial another computer, type messages, send files (upload), and receive files (download). Many communications software programs allow you to be the host so that your friends who have a modem in their computer can call you on your computer.

compact disc, read-only memory *Compact disc, read-only memory* is the full name for CD-ROM, a flat, circular disk that can contain programs, graphics, video, and sound. A CD-ROM is usually just called a CD. Look up *CD-ROM.*

compatible When two people are *compatible,* they work together well. When two computers are compatible, it means that the computers can use many of the same components and can run the same software programs. For example, many personal computers are called IBM-compatible because they are not made by IBM Corporation but will run all the software that will run on a personal computer made by IBM Corporation. Look up *clone* and *component.*

Which one is not compatible? Look at each group and pick out the **one thing** that is not compatible with the **other things** in the same group. *Answers appear in the Answer Section in the back of the book.*

component *Component* is a fancy word for a part. A computer component is any of the many parts of your computer system such as the central processing unit (CPU), monitor, printer, CD-ROM drive, sound card, modem, and so on.

An internal component is a part that belongs inside your CPU, such as the sound card or video board. An external component is a part that connects to your computer system from the outside, such as a monitor or printer. Look up *CPU.*

compress Have you ever had to pack your clothes in a suitcase? Sometimes the only way to fit everything into your suitcase is to squeeze or *compress* everything so that it takes up as little space as possible.

Computer files are sometimes compressed too. Compressing computer files makes them smaller so they take up less space. When the files are smaller, you can fit more files on your hard disk or diskette. Compressed files also take less time to upload and download than files that are not compressed. Compressed files must be decompressed (made full size) before they can be used. Look up *decompress, download, upload,* and *zip.*

computer Although a keyboard, mouse, monitor, modem, printer, sound card, and other accessories make up your computer system, the *computer* itself is the plastic or metal box that contains your computer's hard disk, memory, microprocessor, diskette drives, and motherboard. A more specific term for your computer is central processing unit or CPU, since the term "computer" is often used to mean computer system. Look up *CPU, microprocessor,* and *motherboard.*

computer accessory A *computer accessory* is any item that is not necessary in order to use your computer, but makes your computer better or more fun to use. Look up *accessory.*

computer board A *computer board* is an accessory that plugs into one of the expansion slots inside your computer's CPU. The computer board gives your computer extra capabilities such as sound, better video, or more memory. Another name for a computer board is card or expansion card.

A computer board is called an internal component because it goes inside your CPU rather than connecting to your computer from the outside. Some accessories (such as a modem) that are available as a computer board can also be purchased as an external component. There are advantages and disadvantages to selecting a computer board over an external accessory.

The advantages of a computer board are that it is typically less expensive than an external accessory and does not take up any space on your desk—since it goes inside the CPU. The disadvantages of a computer board is that it is more difficult to install since your CPU has to be opened up in order to insert the computer board. A computer board also takes up one of the few expansion slots that you have in your computer. (Most computers come with three to six expansion slots that are not being used.) Look up *CPU, component,* and *install.*

Be sure to remind your mom or dad to unplug all your computer equipment before opening the CPU to install a new computer card. **Never open a computer yourself without your parent's permission.** You and your computer can both get hurt if you go poking around inside it.

computer camp A *computer camp* is a summer camp where one of the main activities is learning about and using computers. Many computer camps advertise in large town newspapers. If you can't find an ad for a computer camp, try looking under "Camps" in the yellow pages of your phone book. Or, ask your school or town librarian to help you locate one.

computer center In a school, the *computer center* (or computer lab) is usually a classroom where students use computers to do their work. In a business, the computer center is a big room (or rooms) where large computer equipment is kept and important computer programs are run. Since many businesses have computer programs that take days or weeks to run, businesses have employees watching the computer equipment 24 hours a day, even on weekends and holidays.

computer game A *computer game* is any game that can be played on a personal computer or video gaming system—such as 3DO, Sega, or Super Nintendo. Unlike traditional games such as board games, card games, and sport-type games, many computer games are designed to be played by one person.

The computer automates most of the traditional game-playing tasks such as rolling the dice, moving any markers, keeping score, and paying the bank. Unlike traditional games, many computer games have sound, music, animation, and video clips.

There are many different types of computer games. Some games are electronic versions of popular board games (such as Monopoly and Scrabble) and television games (such as *Wheel of Fortune* and *Jeopardy*). Some games let you pilot your own plane or spaceship and engage computer-pilots in air combat.

There are adventure games where you have to solve puzzles, find your way through a dungeon or mansion, and rescue a captive or save the world. There are fighting and warlike games where you have to fight or kill all the bad guys in an attempt to get the highest score. There are sporting games where you can play baseball, football, basketball, go bowling, fish, race cars, or participate in any sporting event you can dream of. There are dozens of different types of games, and thousands of game titles. New ones are released every week. There are so many games that you could play a different one every day for the next twenty years and still have more to play. Look up *animation* and *video clip*.

computer jargon Jargon is a collection of special words that are used to discuss a particular subject. *Computer jargon* is the collection of technical words that are used to discuss computers. Once you learn a few of the terms in this book, you too will be speaking computer jargon.

computer language Programmers tell computers what they want the computers to do by communicating with them using a *computer language*. Natural languages such as English, Spanish, French, and Russian are used to talk to people. Computer languages are called artificial languages because they have been specially created to talk to machines.

Computer languages are written languages, and are not spoken out loud. Just as there are many natural languages, there are many computer languages. Examples of popular computer languages include Assembly, ADA, BASIC, C, COBOL, FORTRAN, and PASCAL. Look up *artificial language, natural language,* and *programmer.*

Juan's father works for the State Department, so Juan and his family have lived in many foreign countries. When Juan lived in France, he learned how to speak French. Now that Juan is back in the States and taking a class in computer programming, he is learning BASIC. BASIC is a **computer language** *that is used to talk to computers.*

computer literate When you have completed school and can read, write, and speak with correct grammar, you are considered a literate person. When you have learned to use a computer and understand some of the basics of making a computer do what you want, you will be *computer literate.* If you learn the computer terms in this book, you will become computer literate.

Can you find the hidden computer terms? Twenty computer terms are hidden in the puzzle below. How many of their **meanings** do you know? *Answers appear in the Answer Section in the back of the book.*

WORD LIST

acronym	byte	DOS	mouse	text
android	CPU	drag	pixel	virtual reality
animation	data	hidden file	run	virus
Apple	destination disk	jewel case	surf the net	wildcard

J	E	E	L	I	F	N	E	D	D	I	H	A	T	R	T	Y
A	J	A	R	G	O	N	L	I	T	T	T	E	E	E	M	O
R	E	L	W	Y	S	I	W	Y	G	A	I	S	N	X	X	G
I	W	H	A	N	D	R	O	I	D	A	S	C	E	I	R	T
S	E	L	F	W	O	B	L	O	S	O	S	P	H	A	W	S
O	L	M	Y	T	I	L	A	E	R	L	A	U	T	R	I	V
Z	C	O	I	N	S	P	O	P	G	R	E	A	F	L	L	I
I	A	S	P	O	E	C	O	M	P	U	T	E	R	E	D	R
P	S	K	G	C	Z	R	R	A	I	L	U	I	U	S	C	U
S	E	A	A	A	C	R	O	N	Y	M	E	T	S	U	A	S
A	R	N	R	I	H	Q	U	I	O	N	A	X	Z	O	R	B
D	C	L	M	C	Y	U	U	N	S	F	T	I	I	M	D	Y
D	O	A	A	N	I	M	A	T	I	O	N	G	B	P	A	T
D	E	S	T	I	N	A	T	I	O	N	D	I	S	K	Y	E

computer program A *computer program* is another name for a software program. The computer program gives your computer instructions that make it play a game, display a graphic, run an animation, edit text, send e-mail, and all the other activities that make your computer useful and fun. Look up *software program.*

"When I grow up I want to be a programmer so I can design some really neat game software," said Shara.

"Yeah, I want to study **computer science** *too," said Owen. "Maybe we'll be able to work at the same company."*

"Maybe we could even start our own company!" replied Shara.

computer science The field of computers, software, programming, virtual reality, video games, and anything else having to do with computers is called *computer science.*

The term computer science is usually used when talking about studying computers and programming in college. If you decide that you want to go to college to study computers, you will major in computer science and graduate with a degree in computer science.

computer screen Your *computer screen* is the part of your monitor that looks like the picture portion of a television set. It is here that your computer displays text, graphics, and information. Look up *monitor.*

computer store A *computer store* is a place where you can buy computers, software, diskettes, and other items for your computers.

What a weird computer store! There are lots of things in this **computer store** that do not belong. Can you find them? *Answers appear in the Answer Section in the back of the book.*

computer system A *computer system* is all the parts that make up a complete and usable computer setup, such as the computer (CPU) itself, monitor, keyboard, mouse, diskette drives, hard disk, modem, printer, and any other accessory that happens to be attached. Look up *computer* and *CPU*.

computer user *A computer user* is someone who uses a computer—someone like you.

computer user group A *computer user group* is a computer club. The members of the user group have meetings (usually once a month) where a guest speaker demonstrates a new software program or discusses a new idea or topic having to do with computers. Your school might even have a computer club or user group. Look up *user group*.

computer virus Just like you, a computer can get sick with a virus. But where your virus is caused by germs, a *computer virus* is caused by a bad computer program. The virus will not damage your computer equipment, but it can damage or erase all the software on your hard disk. Look up *anti-virus program, Trojan horse,* and *virus*.

CONFIG.SYS *CONFIG.SYS* (pronounced "con—fig—dot—sis") is a file in the root directory of your hard disk that contains a lot of technical information that is used by your computer. CONFIG.SYS is used by your computer each time you turn it on.

Never delete the CONFIG.SYS file from your computer or you could have trouble using your computer or the accessories that are connected to your computer (like your mouse or sound card). Look up *root directory*.

connect When you call a friend on the phone and he or she answers the phone, you have *connected* with your friend. The same term is used when one computer calls another computer over the phone line or a computer network. You connect when your computer calls another computer and the other computer answers.

connect time Your *connect time* is the length of time your computer is communicating with another computer over the phone line or a network. If you are connected to a computer service (like America Online, CompuServe, GEnie, Prodigy, and many others), you may be charged for the length of your connect time. Be sure to check with your parents as to how long you are allowed to stay connected to a specific online service. Look up *connect, online,* and *online service.*

context-sensitive help When a software program has instructions that you can look at while you are using the software, it has online help. Online help lets you search through a list of help subjects that you can read about.

Context-sensitive help is online help with an extra feature. Context-sensitive help gives you help with the last feature you were using when you asked for help. Context-sensitive help can save time because it shows you the information you need immediately—without you having to look for it.

continuous paper Something that is continuous goes on and on without any breaks. *Continuous paper* is a special kind of printer paper that comes in one very long sheet that is divided into pages. Each page is separated from the next page with a line of small cuts (called perforations) like a roll of paper towels. The perforations make it easy to tear apart the pages after you print.

Continuous paper usually has small holes punched in the edges. The holes are used by a part of the printer called a tractor feed. The tractor feed helps keep each page straight as it goes through the printer. The edges of the paper are also perforated so that the strip of paper with the holes can also be easily removed after you print. Continuous paper is usually used with dot-matrix printers—it is particularly good for making banners. (Ink jet and laser printers use single sheets of paper.)

Did you ever make a paper fan by folding a piece of paper back and forth? The perforations in continuous paper make it easy to fold up the paper into a nice neat stack—just like you fold a paper fan. This is why continuous paper is sometimes called fanfold paper. Look up *dot matrix-printer* and *tractor feed.*

control key The *control key* on a PC keyboard usually just has the letters C-T-R-L. The control key is pressed along with another key to change the meaning of the other key.

Most Mac keyboards also have a control key, but it is seldom (if ever) used. When you want to change the meaning of a key on a Mac keyboard, you press the command key. Look up *command key* and *CTRL key.*

control panel A *control panel* is a special software program that lets you customize the way your computer works. The control panel lets you change the date, time, screen saver, screen colors, sounds, and many other features.

Where can I find the control panel(s)?

PC Microsoft Windows has one control panel. It is located in the Main window of the Program Manager. As you get more programs and accessories for your PC, more icons (settings) appear on the control panel.

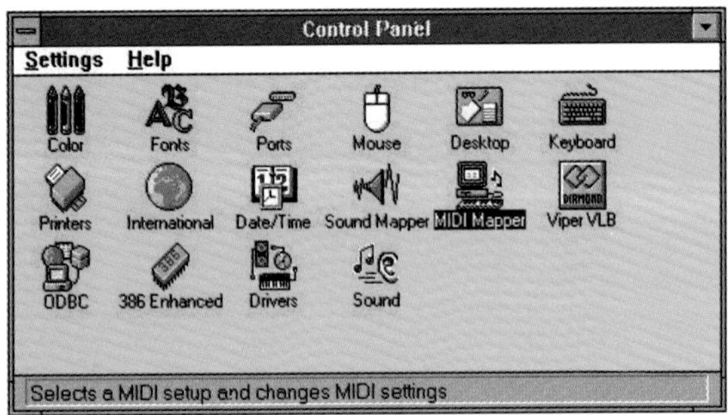

Mac The Mac has several control panels. The control panels are located in the control panels folder. You can get to the control panels folder by selecting it from the Apple menu. As you get more programs and accessories for your Mac, more control panels are put in the control panels folder. You can even buy extra control panels that add features to your computer (such as more sounds).

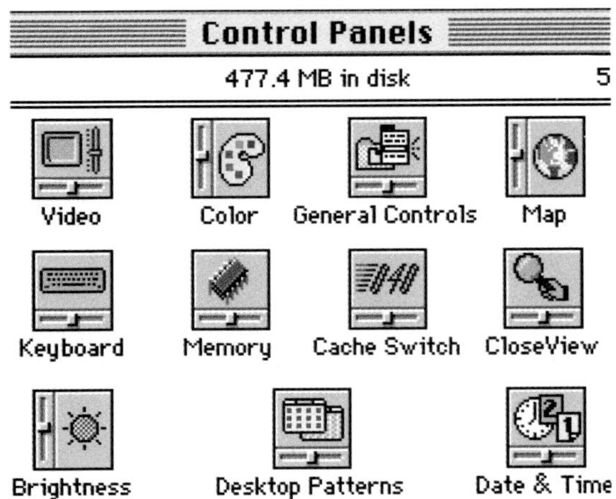

copy When you *copy* a file you create a second file. The original file and the copy of the files are exactly alike. If you want the copy to have the same name as the original file, you must put the copy in a different directory. If you want both files to stay in the same directory, the files must each have a different name. You can copy files from:

- One directory on your hard disk to another directory on your hard disk.
- Your hard disk to a diskette.
- A diskette to your hard disk.
- One diskette to another diskette.
- A CD-ROM to a diskette or your hard disk.

COPY command The *COPY command* is a DOS command that you can use to make a copy of one or more computer files.

Unless you tell it otherwise, your computer thinks that you want to copy the files from the directory you are in (the current directory).

How do I use the COPY command?

1. Use the CD command to move to the directory where the files you want to copy are located.
2. Type the COPY command. Then type:
   a. The name of the file you want to copy. (You can use wildcards if you want.)
   b. The destination drive and directory (the drive and directory where you want the copy to go).

For example, if you wanted to copy a file called REPORT1.DOC to a directory on your drive C called \SCHOOL\REPORTS you would type the following command:

```
COPY REPORT1.DOC C:\SCHOOL\REPORTS\*.* [Enter]
```

If your file has an extension, be sure to include the extension or your file won't get copied.

*The *.* tells the computer to keep the same filename (REPORT1.DOC). If you want to change the name of the file in the new location, you can type a filename instead of typing *.*.*

Look up *CD command, current directory, extension,* and *wildcard.*

Can you make an exact copy? Use a piece of graph paper and see if you can make an exact **copy** of the picture shown below.

copy-protected When a software program is *copy-protected,* the software has a shield that prevents you from making an illegal copy of the software. The shield is not a metal shield like a knight's suit of armor—it is a software shield. There are many types of software shields that programmers use, but they all prevent you from making a usable copy of the software. When a software program is copy-protected, you may be able to copy most of the program's files using the COPY command, but you will not be able to run the newly made copy of the software. Look up *software piracy.*

corrupt When a computer file has been damaged in some way, it is said to be *corrupt.*

counterclockwise If you had a clock that ran backwards, that is the hands of the clock moved in the opposite direction that they should move, your clock would be running *counterclockwise*, or opposite the way that a normal clock runs.

When you are instructed to turn something in a counterclockwise direction, you turn it opposite the direction that the hands of a clock move.

cpi *Cpi* is an abbreviation for characters per inch, the number of letters (or characters) that will fit on just one inch of line when you are using a fixed-space font. Look up *character, characters per inch,* and *fixed-space font.*

cps *Cps* is an abbreviation for characters per second, the number of letters (or characters) a dot-matrix printer can print in one second. Look up *characters per second* and *dot-matrix printer.*

CPU *CPU* (pronounced C—P—U) is the actual computer part of your computer setup. It is the box that contains your computer's hard disk, memory, diskette drives, and sound card. CPU is an abbreviation for central processing unit. Look up *computer.*

crash When you are using a software program and your keyboard stops responding to your keypresses, and your mouse no longer makes selections in your software

program, you have *crashed.* Other terms for crash are bomb and down. There are two types of crashes: hardware crashes and software crashes—in either case, you have a problem.

Software crashes are the most common. When you are using your computer and your software program stops working or shuts down the computer, you have a software crash. When your software crashes, the only thing you can do is to restart your computer and try the program again. Any work that was not saved will have to be done over. Any game that you were playing will have to be restarted. It is likely that the problem will not bother you again.

Save your word-processing files often. That way, you won't lose too much of your work if your computer crashes.

A hardware crash is much more serious. A hardware crash means that something has gone wrong with a major piece of your computer equipment such as your computer, hard disk, or monitor. If you have a hardware crash you need to ask your mom or dad to look at the computer. The problem could be as simple as a loose cable or as complicated as a defective computer. If the problem is not something your parents can fix, the problem part (or piece of equipment) will need to be replaced or taken to a computer repair shop. Look up *down* and *downtime.*

CRT *CRT* (pronounced C—R—T) is an abbreviation for cathode ray tube. CRT is a technical way of referring to a monitor or computer screen on a desktop computer. CRT is not used when talking about the screen that is connected to a portable computer. Look up *desktop computer* and *portable computer.*

> *"Do you all see a blinking cursor on your* **CRT***?" Mr. Dugan asked the class. "Good, now let's begin by typing a short paragraph that describes the video we just saw."*

CTRL key The *CTRL key* (pronounced "control key") is the key on your keyboard with the letters C-T-R-L. As a matter of fact, most computers have two [Ctrl] keys, one on either side of the spacebar. The [Ctrl] key can be used in many programs to give a different meaning to another key (usually a function key). Do you know how to use the [Shift] key? You hold down [Shift] while you press another key. The [Ctrl] key is used the same way. You hold down [Ctrl] while you press another key.

What does the [Ctrl] key on a PC do? It depends on the program you are using. Just as each program has a different use for each function key (those programs that use function keys), different programs also have a different use for each [Ctrl] key combination. The manual that comes with your software program tells you whether or not the [Ctrl] key is used, and if so, what it is used for.

Do Macs have a [Ctrl] key? The control key on a Mac is seldom (if ever) used. However, the control key can be used to run macros. A macro is a miniprogram that you create yourself. To make a macro, you must have special macro software such as Tempo or QuicKeys. Look up *command key* and *function key.*

> *"Dad, I was trying to run a BASIC program I made, but I can't get it to stop. How do I turn it off?" asked Todd.*
>
> *"Press* **CTRL***-C."*
>
> *"It worked! Does* **CTRL***-C always stop a program?" asked Todd.*
>
> *"It will often work if you are running a program in DOS, but it depends on the program," replied Dad.*

Ctrl-Alt-Del *Ctrl-Alt-Del* (pronounced "control, alt, delete") is a command that you can use to reboot your PC. Ctrl-Alt-Del can be used when your computer locks up and you cannot exit your game or other software program the usual way. Pressing Ctrl-Alt-Del is similar to pressing your computer's reset button.

Ctrl-Alt-Del works from within any software program, but it is better to exit your program normally. To reboot your computer using Ctrl-Alt-Del,

1. Hold down the [Ctrl] key.
2. Hold down the [Alt] key.
3. Press the [Del] key.

Look up *boot, lock up,* and *reset button.*

current directory Current means now. All the games and software on your computer's hard disk are organized into groups called directories. The *current directory* is the directory you are using now.

When you want to move a file from place to place in Windows, OS/2, or on the Mac, you drag it from one place to another using the mouse. In DOS it's different. In DOS, you must type the name of each file you want to move, copy, or delete.

DOS always looks in the current directory for the file you want to move, copy, or delete (unless you tell your computer otherwise). Since DOS is using the current directory to look for your files, it is important that you know:

1. Which directory is the current directory.
2. How to use DOS to move from one directory to another. You can move from one directory to another using the change directory (CD) command.

Look up *CD command, command,* and *directory.*

current drive Current means now. The *current drive* is the drive you are using now. Most computer systems today have at least two drives: a diskette drive and a hard drive (or hard disk). The diskette drive is called the "A drive." The hard drive is usually called the "C drive." If you are using the A drive, then the current drive is A. If you are using the C drive, then the current drive is C.

How do I change the current drive? When you want to change the current drive in Windows, OS/2, or on the Mac, you simply click on the icon (the picture) of another drive. In DOS it's different. In DOS, you must type the letter of the new current drive.

To change the current drive in DOS,

1. You must be at the DOS prompt.
2. Type the letter of the new current drive.
3. Type a colon (:).
4. Press [Enter].

For example, to change to the A drive, type the following command at the DOS prompt.

```
A: [Enter]
```

Look up *DOS prompt.*

cursor Remember when you were first learning to read and you kept your finger next to the line you were reading so you wouldn't lose your place? Well the *cursor* takes the place of your finger when it comes to keeping your place on a computer screen.

If you use a keyboard with the software program, the software has a keyboard cursor. If you use a mouse with the software program, the program has a mouse cursor. If the software program can be used with both a keyboard and a mouse then the program has two cursors: one for the mouse, and one for the keyboard.

What is a keyboard cursor? The keyboard cursor is a blinking horizontal line (_), blinking vertical line (|), or blinking box (▮). The keyboard cursor shows you where your next keypress will appear. You can move the keyboard cursor by pressing an arrow key or one of the other cursor movement keys that are located on your keyboard. The keyboard cursor is particularly useful in keeping track of your place in a word-processing program. Without it, you would never know where your next keypress was going to appear.

What is a mouse cursor? The mouse cursor is usually shown on the screen as a pointer (↗) or cross hair (+). As you move your mouse on your desk (or mouse pad), the mouse cursor on your screen moves in the same direction.

Can I use the keyboard to move the mouse cursor? No, the mouse cursor can only be moved by the mouse. You cannot move the mouse cursor with the keyboard keys, but you can sometimes get the mouse cursor to disappear by pressing Esc. (You can get the mouse cursor to reappear by moving it.)

Can I use the mouse to move the keyboard cursor? Yes, you can use the mouse to move the keyboard cursor to another place in your text. To do this,

1. Move the mouse to the place in your text where you want to move your keyboard cursor.
2. Click the left (or the only) mouse button. Your keyboard cursor moves to the same place.

Look up *blink rate, click, cursor movement keys, keyboard, keypress,* and *mouse.*

---

cursor movement keys The *cursor movement keys* are the keys on your keyboard that move the keyboard cursor around your screen and from place to place within your text.

Some of the cursor movement keys perform a different job depending on which software program you are using. If you press Alt or Ctrl in combination with a cursor movement key, the cursor may move to a different place in your text than when you just press the cursor movement key itself. Check the manuals that came with your software programs to find out the cursor movement key combinations that can be used with your software.

Look up *ALT key, CTRL key,* and *keyboard cursor.*

Key	Name	Job
↑	Up Arrow	Moves your cursor up one line.
↓	Down Arrow	Moves your cursor down one line.
→	Right Arrow	Moves your cursor one space to the right.
←	Left Arrow	Moves your cursor one space to the left.
Home	Home key	Moves your cursor to the top of your text, the top of your screen, or the beginning of the line.
End	End key	Moves your cursor to the bottom of your text, the bottom of your screen, or the end of the line.
Pg Up	Page Up	Moves your cursor to the top of the current screen, the top of the previous screen, or the top of the previous page.
Pg Dn	Page Down	Moves your cursor to the bottom of the current screen, the top of the next screen, or the top of the next page.

cyberspace Outer space is not one single place, but an infinite number of places that are outside the planet Earth. Like outer space, *cyberspace* is not one particular place, but all the places inside your computer and every other computer that your computer is connected to with your modem. The term "cyberspace" is usually used when talking about the different places you can go inside a computer network, an online service, or the Internet. Look up *cybersurfing, Internet, modem, network,* and *online service.*

cybersurfing When you go looking around cyberspace with no particular goal in mind, you are said to be *cybersurfing*. Another name for cybersurfing is information surfing. Look up *cyberspace.*

daisy-chain Have you ever watched someone plug extension cords together? The first cord is plugged into the second cord. The second cord is plugged into the third cord, and so on until the cord is long enough to reach whatever needs to be plugged in. It is easy to plug extension cords together because at the end of each cord is a connector that plugs into the next extension cord. Connecting things together, one right after the other, is called daisy-chaining.

In computers, *daisy-chain* is a term that describes how some computer equipment is connected to a computer. When the equipment is daisy-chained, the items are plugged into each other to form a chain. The neat thing about daisy-chaining is that only one of the items has to be connected to your computer for all of the items to work.

Can all computer equipment be daisy-chained? No. Only computer equipment that has a special kind of connector can be daisy-chained. For example, hard drives, CD-ROM drives, and scanners that have a SCSI connection can be daisy-chained to each other. Also, Macintosh keyboards, mice, and joysticks that have an ADB connection can be daisy-chained to each other. (PCs do not use ADB connections.)

Look up *ADB, CD-ROM drive, hard drive, scanner,* and *SCSI.*

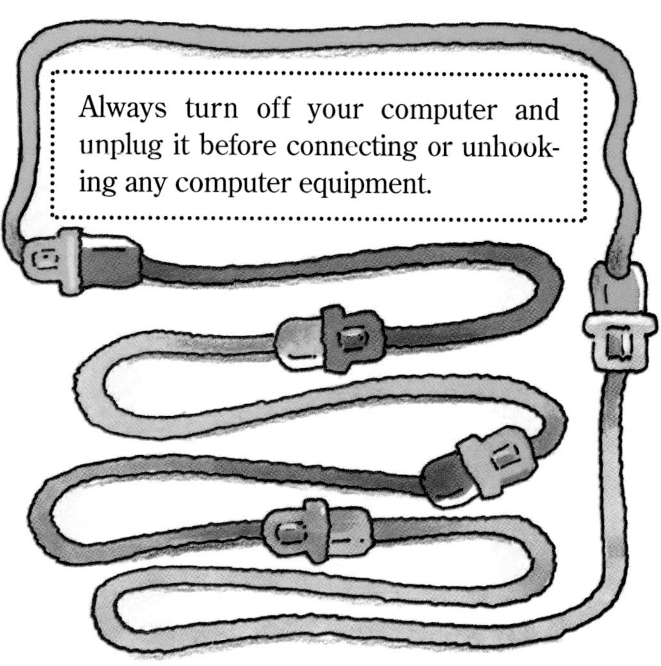

data *Data* means information. Unlike other words in the English language, data is both singular and plural. Data can mean one piece of information or many pieces of information.

Often, data is meaningless unless it is organized in some way. Below is some data that has not been organized.

Marie 100 Paul 95 Candice 71 Bob 75 Rose 87 Charles 90

The data above does not seem to have any meaning. Below is the same data organized in a way that makes sense.

Name	Science Test Score
Marie	100
Paul	95
Charles	90
Rose	87
Bob	75
Candice	71

We keep data on computer disks, paper, and even in our heads. We use the computer to help us look at data in different ways, or to make the data easier to work with. If we have a lot of data that we need to organize (for example, putting the names of everyone in our class into alphabetical order), the computer can usually make the job go faster. Look up *database.*

Can you identify the data? Below are several sets of **data**. Can you tell what **each set of data** has in common? *Answers appear in the Answer Section in the back of the book.*

1. red, pink, blue, yellow, orange, green
2. 2, 8, 10, 12, 18
3. Harrisburg, Philadelphia, Scranton, Pittsburgh, Gettysburg
4. rock, jazz, rap, blues, New Age, classical
5. rain, ice, snow, sleet, hail
6. Sim City 2000, XWing, Space Simulator, Master of Orion, Wing Commander
7. Clinton, Harding, Cleveland, Washington, Jefferson, Monroe (Hint: These are not only the names of people.)

data center A *data center* is another term for a computer center, the place where large computer equipment is kept and important computer programs are run. Look up *computer center.*

data entry Have you or your family ever filled out an order form to buy something from a mail-order catalog? After your order arrives at the mail-order company, your name, address, and each item you ordered is typed into a database on a computer. The process of entering information into a database is called *data entry.*

Does your family ever get mail where the name is spelled incorrectly? The reason you may get mail with an incorrect name is that a data entry person made a mistake when typing the name into the database. Look up *data* and *database.*

data field A *data field* is the place in a database where you can enter and change the information that lives in the database. A data field is usually just called a field. Look up *database* and *field.*

data file All the information on your computer is organized into files. Some files are called program files. Program files contain instructions for the computer. Other files contain pieces of information that programs will use; these are called *data files.*

For example, many computer games keep track of the highest scores in a data file. Each time you play the game, the game program looks in this data file to find the high scores. If your score is high enough, the game program changes the information in the high score data file, adding your high score and name. Look up *data* and *file.*

data processing *Data processing* is all the activities that get information into the computer (such as data entry), all the activities that change data (such as editing, sorting, and calculating), and all the activities that print and store data. Basically, any activity that involves working with data in a database is considered data processing. Look up *data, data entry,* and *database.*

data transfer rate The *data transfer rate* is a measurement of how much information can be sent from one place to another in one second. The information may be going from one computer's memory to another computer's memory, or back and forth from your computer's memory to a hard disk, diskette, or CD-ROM.

You will want to check the data transfer rate if you and your parents go shopping for a CD-ROM drive. Since CD-ROM drives are much slower than hard disks, you will want to buy the fastest CD-ROM drive that is within your budget. The fastest CD-ROM drive is one with the largest data transfer rate.

Suppose you had to gather up all the laundry and bring it into the laundry room. The more laundry you could carry at one time, the less trips you would have to make. The data transfer rate of a CD-ROM drive is similar to how much laundry you can carry at one time. The larger the data transfer rate, the more data the CD-ROM drive can carry at one time, the less trips it has to make to get the data.

When you play a game or search for information on a CD in your CD-ROM drive, information is sent to your computer memory in pieces. The fewer times the CD-ROM drive has to get information from the CD, the faster your game will respond.

Data transfer rate is measured in kilobytes per second (K/sec). CD-ROM drives are called "single speed," "double speed," "triple speed," or "quad speed," depending on the drive's access speed and data transfer rate. Each type is described below.

- **Single Speed.** A single speed CD-ROM drive usually has a data transfer rate of about 150 K/sec.
- **Double Speed.** A double speed CD-ROM drive (also called a 2X drive) usually has a data transfer rate of about 300 K/sec.
- **Triple Speed.** A triple speed CD-ROM drive (also called a 3X drive) usually has a data transfer rate of about 450 K/sec.
- **Quad Speed.** A quad speed CD-ROM drive (also called a 4X drive) usually has a data transfer rate of about 600 K/sec.

The data transfer rate can usually be found on the box containing the CD-ROM drive. Look for "Specifications" (the section of the box with the technical details). Look up *access speed, CD-ROM, CD-ROM drive,* and *kilobyte.*

database A *database* is a way to store and organize data that is alike in some way.

How can I design a database? First, you have to decide what it is that you want to keep track of. For example, suppose you want a database that has information about every kid in your class. Each student will be a record in your database.

Next, you need to decide exactly what data (pieces of information) you want to keep about each person. To keep it simple, let's just use last name, first name, and birthday. Each piece of information that you collect in the database is a field. Below is some data for our database.

Last Name	First Name	Birthday
Ronderos	Pete	March 3
Harrison	Judy	October 26
Franklin	George	July 15
Nguyen	Frances	September 7
Goldman	Adelle	April 22
King	Carmen	February 1

A database is a group of records that have been organized in a way to make them useful. A database can organize information any way you like. Suppose you wanted an alphabetical list of the kids in your class. The database could organize the information as shown below.

Last Name	First Name	Birthday
Franklin	George	July 15
Goldman	Adelle	April 22
Harrison	Judy	October 26
King	Carmen	February 1
Nguyen	Frances	September 7
Ronderos	Pete	March 3

Suppose rather than an alphabetical list, what you really want is a list of everyone's birthday in chronological order. That list would look like the one below. Remember, the trick to designing a good database is to create fields that will allow you to organize the data in a way that is useful to you.

Last Name	First Name	Birthday
King	Carmen	February 1
Ronderos	Pete	March 3
Goldman	Adelle	April 22
Franklin	George	July 15
Nguyen	Frances	September 7
Harrison	Judy	October 26

Look up *chronological order, data,* and *field.*

database administrator A *database administrator* is the person who is responsible for making sure that information in the database is entered completely and correctly. The abbreviation for a database administrator is DBA.

The DBA knows what kind of information should be in the database, and what fields are part of each record. Suppose that your school has a database called STUDENTS that contains the first and last name of each student (beside some other useful information). The DBA would know the rules for the FIRST NAME field and the LAST NAME field. For example, the following are sample rules for a LAST NAME field.

- LAST NAME can be no longer than 20 characters.
- LAST NAME can never be blank.
- LAST NAME cannot contain any spaces.
- LAST NAME must always start with a letter.
- LAST NAME can contain letters, an apostrophe ('), and a hyphen (-) (for names like O'Brien or Able-Baker).

The DBA also answers questions from people who need to use the data in the database (like the school principal or your teacher) and makes sure that a backup copy of the database is made once a day or each time a major change is made to the database. Look up *backup copy* and *database.*

date Most computers have a little clock inside them that keeps track of the *date* and time. When you get a new computer, you may need to set the date. After that, your computer will probably be able to remember the date on its own—even when you unplug it—since most computers have a built-in battery.

How can I set the date on my computer?

PC If you are using DOS, you use the DATE command. If you are using Microsoft Windows, you open the control panel and select the Date/Time icon.

Mac Use the Apple menu to open the Control Panels Folder. Then open the folder called General Control Panel.

Look up *Apple menu, control panel, DATE command, folder, icon,* and *TIME command.*

DATE command The *DATE command* is a DOS command that lets you see the date. The DATE command can also be used to change the date.

How do I use the DATE command?

1. Type the following command at the DOS prompt.

   ```
   DATE [Enter]
   ```

   Your computer displays the date on your screen and asks you to type a new date.
2. If you do not want to change the date press [Enter]. If you do want to change the date, type today's date before pressing Enter.

> The computer prompts you to type the date in "mm-dd-yy" format.
>
> mm The number of the month (January is 01, March is 03, October is 10).
> dd The day of the month (such as 05 for the 5th).
> yy The last two numbers of the year (such as 96 for 1996).
>
> But even though the computer asks for the date to be typed 03-25-96 (for example), you can type it 3/25/96 or 3-25-96 or 3.25.96 and your computer will still understand.

Look up *date, DOS command, DOS prompt,* and *TIME command.*

debug When a programmer *debugs* a software program, the programmer looks for and fixes bugs in the software program.

Bugs are errors in a software program. Many software programs take longer to debug than they take to create.

Do not confuse a bug with a virus. A bug is a mistake made by the programmer. A virus is a nasty trick that a programmer did on purpose. Look up *bug* and *virus.*

decompress Computer files are sometimes compressed so they take up less space. You *decompress* a file when you make a compressed file full-size again. Compressed files must be decompressed before they can be used. Look up *compress* and *unzip.*

decrypt To *decrypt* a file means to use a software program to decode a file that was written in a secret code. Only someone who knows the password and how the file information was encrypted (put into secret code) can decrypt the file. Computer programs that encrypt and decrypt data are often used by governments to protect top secret information.

Can you decrypt the message below? Look at the secret code. To **decrypt** the message, change each letter in the message to the corresponding letter in the secret code. For example, the letter **"c"** in the message is decrypted to the letter **"w."** *The answer appears in the Answer Section in the back of the book.*

Secret Code

A = R	F = H	K = S	P = U	U = X
B = E	G = J	L = D	Q = I	V = C
C = W	H = K	M = F	R = O	W = V
D = Q	I = L	N = T	S = P	X = M
E = G	J = A	O = Y	T = Z	Y = B
				Z = N

"Cfr lql orp sjkk rz nfb arjl?" nfb Hqze cbzn rz, frilqze
rpn fqk fjzl nr nfb Xbkkbzeba mra krxb fjo.
"Zryrlo," kjql nfb Xbkkbzeba.
"Dpqnb aqefn," kjql nfb Hqze: "nfqk orpze ijlo kjc fqx nrr.
Kr rm vrpakb Zryrlo cjihk kircba nfjz orp."
—Ibcqk Vjaarii, *Nfarpef nfb Irrhqze Eijkk*

default Sometimes the computer asks you a question that most people answer a certain way. To make it easier for you to respond to the question, the computer will make a selection for you. This selection is called the *default*. To use the default, you usually just press [Enter]. If you do not want to use the default, make another choice from the ones you are given.

> *Toby was using Microsoft Word to type a report on South America for school. When he went to exit the program, he was asked if he wanted to save his report. Although Toby could have answered Yes or No, he decided to press* [Enter] *to select the* **default** *answer (which was Yes).*

DBA *DBA* is an abbreviation for database administrator. The DBA is the person who is responsible for making sure that information in the database is entered in completely and correctly. Look up *database administrator.*

DEL command *DEL* is a DOS command that you use when you want to delete one or more files from your hard disk or diskette.

How do I use the DEL command?

1. From the DOS prompt, change to the drive letter that contains the files you want to delete.
   a. To delete files from your hard disk, you will probably need to change to the C drive.
   b. To delete files from a diskette drive, you will need to change to the A or B drive, depending on which drive contains the diskette where the files are located. To change drives, type the letter of the drive and a colon (:). For example,

   `C:` [Enter]

2. Use the CD command to change to the directory that contains the files you want to delete.

> **Warning!** If you are deleting files from your C drive, do not skip Step #2. If you accidentally delete the files in your root directory (C:\), you will not be able to use your computer the next time you turn it on!

3. Type the DEL command.
   a. Then type the name of the file you want to delete. For example, to delete the file named REPORT2.OLD, type the following command.

   `DEL REPORT2.OLD` [Enter]

   b. If you want to delete all of the files in the directory, you can use the asterisk wildcard as shown below.

   `DEL *.*` [Enter]

   Your computer responds:

```
All files in directory will be deleted!
Are you sure (Y/N)?
```

4. If you used wildcards to tell your computer to delete all of the files in the directory, you now have a chance to change your mind.
   a. Press [Y] to erase all the files. Then press [Enter].

b. Press N if you don't want to erase all the files. Then press Enter.

Look up *CD command, directory, DOS prompt, file, UNDELETE command,* and *wildcard.*

delete key The *delete key* is the key on your keyboard with the word Delete or the letters D-E-L on it. The delete key is used to remove text, an icon, a file, or other items that you have selected with your keyboard or mouse. Since it is not always an easy task to get back what you delete, the Delete key should be used with caution.

The Delete keys on a PC and a Mac are located in different places and work differently. Many PCs have two Delete keys, one to the right of the letter keys, and one in the numeric keypad. The Delete key on the Mac is above the Enter key.

What does Delete do on the PC? If you are using a program in DOS, pressing Delete erases the character on (or under) the keyboard cursor. If you are using Microsoft Windows, or another program with a graphical display, pressing Delete removes

- The character to the right of the cursor.
- Any text you have highlighted.
- An icon, file, or other item you have selected with your cursor.

What does Delete do on the Mac? On the Mac, Delete works like a Backspace key. It removes

- The character to the left of the cursor.
- Any text you have highlighted.

The ⌦ on a Mac works similar to Delete on a PC.

Look up *backspace, keyboard cursor, Microsoft Windows, UNDELETE command,* and *undo.*

demagnetize The magnetic material on diskettes is what allows the diskette to store computer programs and files. When the diskette becomes *demagnetized,* some or all of the information on the diskette is erased. Never store your diskettes under or near a magnet or the information on your diskettes could get demagnetized.

Look up *diskette.*

"Blair, don't put the diskette under a magnet!" cried Wayne.

"Why?" asked Blair.

"You'll **demagnetize** *it."*

"So?"

"Diskettes are made of magnetized material. When you place it next to a magnet, or hang it on your locker door with a magnet like you were going to do, you can erase some or all of the information on the diskette."

"Wow! I could have lost all my notes for my term paper!" exclaimed Blair.

"Better copy those notes to your hard disk before something happens to them."

"Gee, thanks."

density Diskettes come in two *densities*: double-density and high-density. Both double-density and high-density diskettes are the same size. So density doesn't indicate how big the diskette is but how close together information is placed on the diskette.

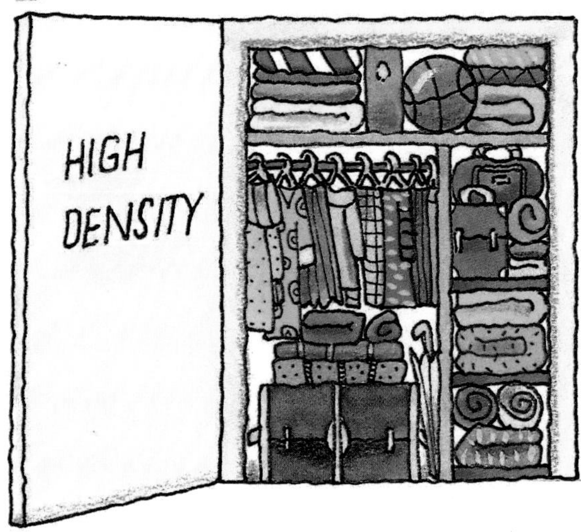

Think of density as your closet space. Your closet is a certain size, but you can pack more things into the closet by placing items closer together (otherwise known as jamming stuff into your closet). A high-density diskette lets you pack more information into the same amount of space as a double-density diskette. (In case you were wondering, there used to be a single-density size, but they're no longer used.)

Look up *diskette* and *diskette drive.*

descender A *descender* is a lower case letter of the alphabet whose tail or bottom portion of the letter reaches below the bottom of the line. If you look at the illustration below, you will notice that the all the descenders reach below the bottom of the baseline. The descenders include the letters g, j, p, q, and y.

Look up *ascender* and *font.*

Happy

descending order *Descending order* is very similar to alphabetical order—only in reverse. When you put a list of words in alphabetical order, you place them in order based on the letters of the alphabet, starting with "A." When you place a list of words in descending order, the list begins with the "Z" words followed by the "Y" words, and so on up to letter "A."

Numbers can also be put in descending order. A descending list of numbers is like counting backwards. You count from the highest number to the lowest number. For example, the numbers 1–10 in descending order are 10, 9, 8, 7, 6, 5, 4, 3, 2, 1. Look up *ascending order, chronological order, numerical order,* and *sort.*

Can you change the roll call?
Madeline Zubrowski was tired of being the last student on the list every time attendance was taken. When Madeline's teacher heard of Madeline's disappointment in always being last she said, "Madeline, if you make up a **descending** class list, I will use it during the next roll call." Below are some of the students in Madeline's class. Can you help her put this list of students in **descending order** so that *Madeline Zubrowski* is the first name to be called every morning? *Answers appear in the Answer Section in the back of the book.*

Madeline Zubrowski	Kenneth Brown
Kiki Hahn	Leah Cohen
Myra Josephs	David Tang
Brenna Sinclair	Charlie Jewel
Robert Stern	Jarik Quinn

desktop Your desk at home or at school has many of the things you need to do your schoolwork, such as books, paper, pencils, a protractor or compass, and a calculator. You can arrange your desk anyway you like so that things are easy to find. You can put new things on your desk and get rid of old things you don't need.

The *desktop* on your computer works the same way. When you turn on your Macintosh, or fire up Microsoft Windows or OS/2 on your PC, the first thing you see is your desktop. A computer desktop has many of the things that you may want to use while you are working or playing on your computer. It has programs, files, a clock, a calculator, a trash can (Mac) and other items that you may need. You can change the colors of your desktop so it is more attractive. You can also move things around so the items that you use most often are easy to find. The desktop keeps your computer organized so you can keep things running smoothly.

desktop computer Computers come in many sizes. There are computers that sit on the floor, computers that sit on your desk, and computers that can fit in your lap and are lightweight enough to carry. Of the three types just mentioned, which type do you think is the desktop computer? Of course—the one that sits on your desk. A *desktop computer* is a computer that must sit on a desk or table because it is too big to carry around or sit on your lap, and is not designed to sit on the floor.

desktop publishing *Desktop publishing* means using a personal computer and a high-quality printer to produce newsletters, stories, reports, invitations, announcements, and other printouts that look like they were printed (published) by a professional print shop. Documents that have been desktop published usually have different size letters for headings. They can also have charts, tables, photographs, or graphics. Desktop publishing is abbreviated DTP.

To do desktop publishing, all you need is a computer, a printer, and a word-processing program. Desktop publishing gets its name from the fact that everything you need to create published documents can fit on a desk. A desk is much less space than you need for a printing press! Desktop publishing is one of the most popular uses of a personal computer.

Do I need a special program to do desktop publishing? There are programs that are made for desktop publishing. However, these "special" programs often do not have any more features than your word-processing program! All you really need to do desktop publishing is a good word-processing program.

What kind of printer do I need to do desktop publishing? Laser printers are the printers most often used for desktop publishing. But as the quality of ink jet printers continues to improve, they are being selected more and more for desktop publishing. Dot-matrix printers are not used for desktop publishing. Look up *document* and *word processing.*

destination disk When you copy files from one diskette to another diskette, the *destination disk* is the diskette that receives the information. Another name for a destination disk is target disk. The diskette that contains the information you are going to use is called the source disk.

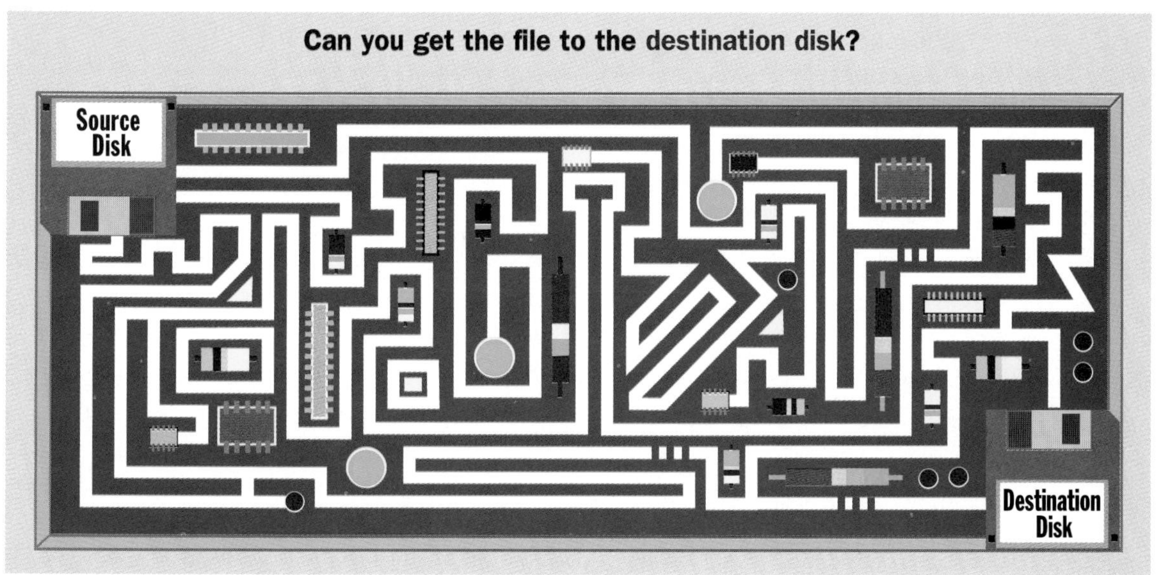

device A *device* is a piece of computer equipment that is added to a computer (inside or outside) to give the computer more capabilities. Computer devices include a disk drive, printer, mouse, monitor, or CD-ROM. Devices that go inside your computer, like a hard disk, are called internal devices. Devices that connect to the outside of your computer, like a printer, are called external devices.

Before your computer can work with a device, it has to know how to use the device! When you add a device—like a CD-ROM drive—to your computer, you usually have to install some software that tells your computer how to use the device. The software program that comes with a device is called a device driver. Look up *install.*

dialog box A conversation between two people is called a dialog. When your computer needs to ask you a question it may display a *dialog box.* A dialog box is your computer's way of communicating.

Suppose you are using a program and you select the print command. The program may display a dialog box like the one below.

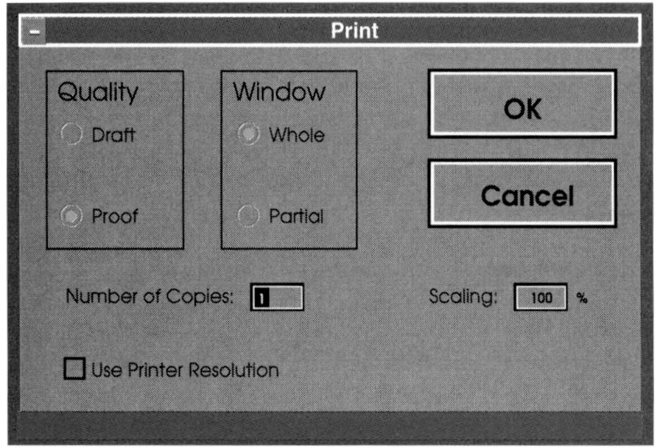

Many dialog boxes preselected the choices that most people make. These choices are called the defaults. To use the defaults, just press [Enter] or select [OK]. Otherwise, change any setting you want (such as the number of copies to print) and then press [Enter] or select [OK].

DIR command The *DIR command* is a DOS command that tells your computer to show you all the files in the current directory. The easiest way to see the files in a directory is to go to the directory where the files are located. Use the CD command to move from one directory to another.

How do I use the DIR command?

1. Use the CD command to move to the directory where the files are located.
2. Type the following command at the DOS prompt.

```
DIR [Enter]
```

What do all the numbers mean? When you use the DIR command you see the name of your files along with some columns of numbers. Each part of the DIR listing is explained in the illustration on the next page. (Note: The DIR listing that you get on your computer may look a bit different, depending on which version of DOS is on your computer.) Look up *CD command, current directory, DOS command, DOS prompt,* and *file size.*

directory All the games and software programs on your computer's hard disk are organized into groups called *directories.*

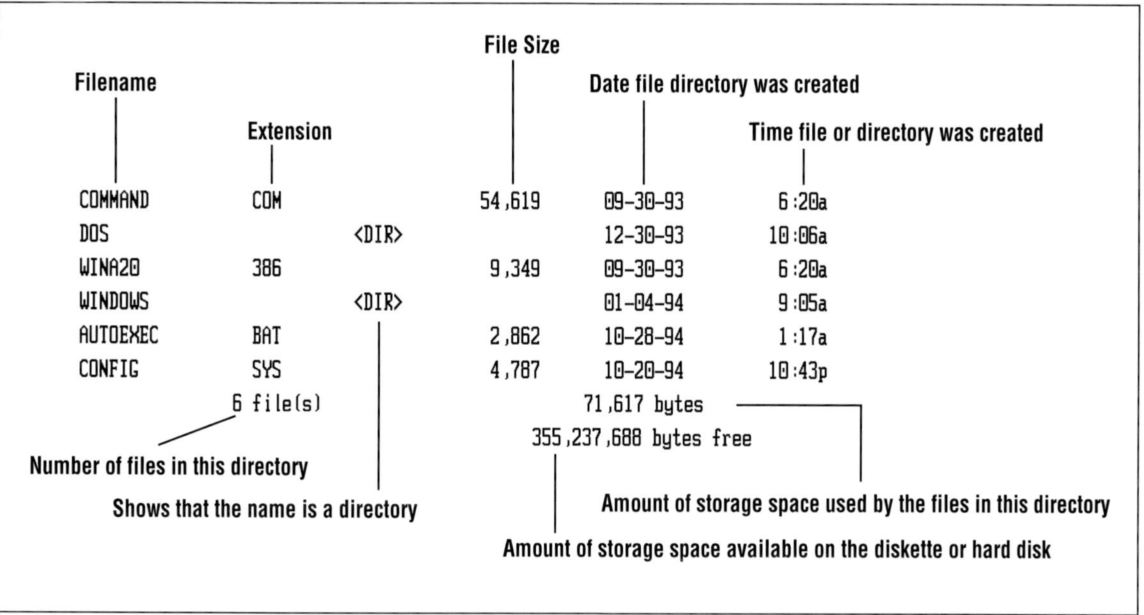

When a new game or software program is installed on your computer, the software's installation program usually creates a new directory on your computer. The installation program then copies the files that make up the program into the directory it created.

You may think that all the directories on your hard disk are arranged into one big list, but in fact, the directories are organized like a tree. The first directory on your hard disk is called the root directory. Think of the root directory as the trunk of the tree. The root directory can hold many other directories.

When a directory is located inside another directory, it is called a subdirectory. Think of the branches of the tree as subdirectories off the root directory. When the branch has leaves, think of each leaf as a file that is located in the subdirectory.

Just as the branches of a tree continue to split into more branches, each subdirectory on your hard disk can have additional subdirectories. When a subdirectory is located inside another subdirectory, it is called a nested subdirectory.

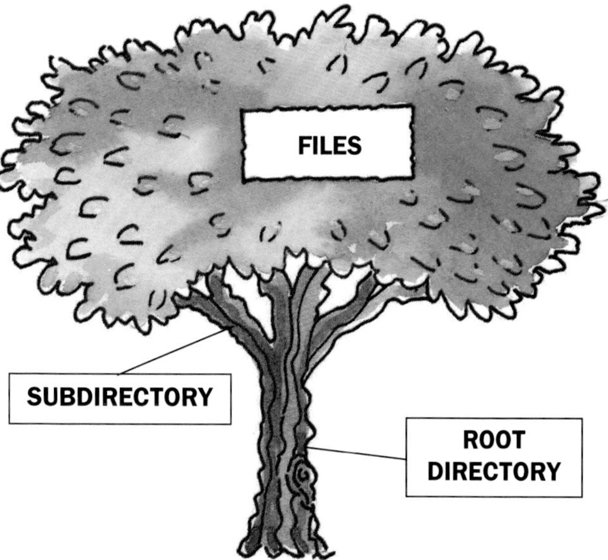

A directory structure is the way that directories are organized on your hard disk. Your computer's directory structure is different than anyone else's because your family has a different collection of software programs than other families.

On a PC, there are different commands and programs that you can use to view your directories and directory structure. In DOS, you can use the DIR and TREE commands. In Microsoft Windows, you can use the File Manager.

On a Mac, each folder is a directory. Each folder inside a folder is a subdirectory.

Look up *DIR command, directory structure, DOS, hard disk, TREE command,* and *Microsoft Windows.*

---

directory structure All the games and software programs on your computer's hard disk are organized into groups called directories. The *directory structure* is a picture or explanation of how those directories are organized on your hard disk.

What does a directory structure look like in Microsoft Windows? If you are using Microsoft Windows, you can see your directory structure by clicking on the File Manager icon.

Let's take a look at the various parts of the directory structure.

1. Since we are looking at the directory structure of a hard disk, the root directory is the C drive. Windows uses the symbol `C:\` to represent the root directory.
2. There is one subdirectory off the root directory. The name of the subdirectory is `games`.

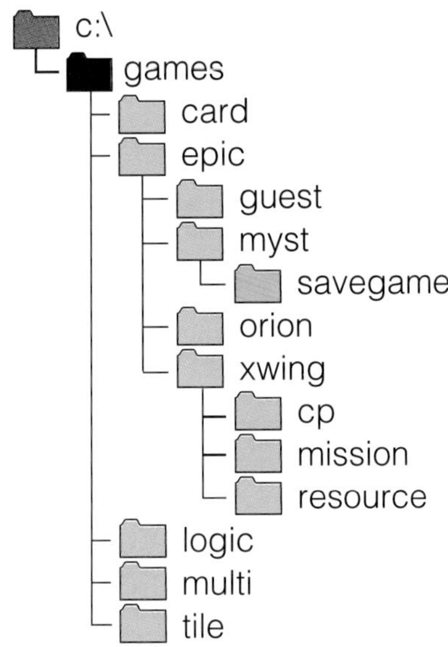

3. There are five subdirectories off the `games` directory. Those directories are `card`, `epic`, `logic`, `multi`, and `tile`. Notice that the directories and subdirectories are listed in alphabetical order.
4. There are four subdirectories off the `epic` directory. Those directories are `guest`, `myst`, `orion`, and `xwing`.
5. The `myst` and `xwing` directories each have additional subdirectories.

What does a directory structure look like in DOS? If you are using DOS, you can see a picture of your directory structure by using the TREE command. Let's take a look at the various parts of the directory structure.

1. Since we are looking at the directory structure of a hard disk, the root directory is the C drive. DOS uses the symbol `C:`. to represent the root directory.
2. There is one subdirectory off the root directory. The name of the subdirectory is `games`.
3. There are five subdirectories off the

`games` directory. Those directories are `card`, `epic`, `logic`, `multi`, and `tile`. Notice that the directories and subdirectories are not listed in alphabetical order.

4. There are four subdirectories off the `epic` directory. Those directories are `guest`, `myst`, `orion`, and `xwing`.
5. The `myst` and `xwing` directories each have additional subdirectories.

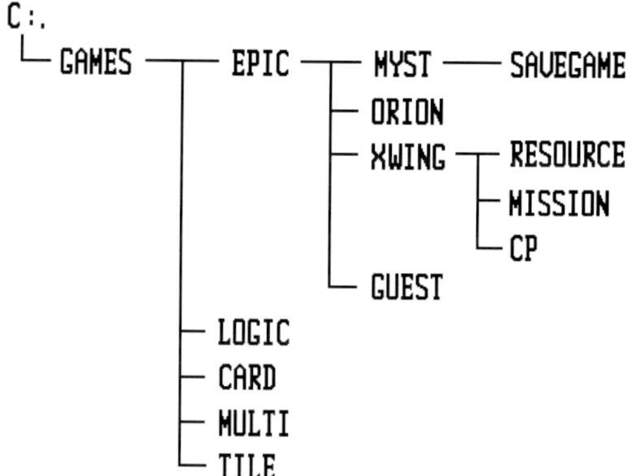

Look up *directory, DIR command, DOS, icon, Microsoft Windows, pipe, root directory,* and *TREE command.*

disable When a programmer turns off a feature of a software program on purpose, it is known as *disabling* the feature or disabling the software. Disabled features of a software program cannot be used.

Why do programmers disable software? Have you ever played the demo version of a software game? Some companies give out free copies of their software for you to try. The free copy is called a demo version because it demonstrates how the game is played. In most demo software, some features are disabled so you cannot use part of the program. The software company hopes that you will like the game so much that you will go to a computer store and pay money for the full version game—a copy of the game that has not been disabled.

Is disabled software different from a bug in the software? Yes. When software is disabled, the programmers have turned off certain features on purpose. When a bug exists in the software, there is a problem that the programmers need to find and fix. The programmers did not intend to make the bug part of the software. Look up *feature* and *programmer.*

disc *Disc* is a short name for compact disc (also called a CD or CD-ROM). Look up *CD-ROM.*

disk *Disk* is a short name for diskette and hard disk. Look up *diskette* and *hard disk.*

disk drive *Disk drive* is another term for diskette drive. Look up *diskette drive.*

Disk First Aid When you get a cut or scrape you go to your mom, dad, or the school nurse for a bandage or a little first aid. When your computer can't read your diskette or can't display your icons or folders, you should turn to *Disk First Aid.*

How do I use Disk First Aid? Disk First Aid is a program that comes with your Mac system software. It is located on the Disk Tools disk. Disk First Aid checks your diskette and repairs the problems automat-

ically. To use Disk First Aid, double-click on the Disk First Aid icon.
Look up *folder*, *icon*, and *system software*.

disk jacket A *disk jacket* is an envelope that slides onto a 5¼-inch diskette to help keep it clean. All 5¼-inch diskettes have an open center like a doughnut. If the center area gets scratched or really dirty, you may not be able to use any of the information that was saved on the diskette (like your high scores for a great game).

Some 3½-inch diskettes come with a clear, plastic disk jacket. But you don't have to use a disk jacket with 3½-inch diskettes since they are totally enclosed and do not have the doughnut hole in the middle. A disk jacket is also called a disk sleeve.

disk shutter The *disk shutter* is the sliding metal bar you see on all 3½-inch diskettes. The disk shutter protects the layer of plastic inside the diskette that holds your information. Look up *diskette*.

disk sleeve A *disk sleeve* is an envelope that covers a diskette. A disk sleeve is also called a disk jacket. Look up *disk jacket*.

DISKCOPY command The *DISKCOPY command* is a DOS command that you use when you want to copy all the files on one diskette to another diskette. (When you only want to copy one or two files, you should use the COPY command.)

How do I use DISKCOPY when I have two diskette drives?

1. Place the source diskette (the diskette with the files you want to copy) in one drive.
2. Place the target diskette (the blank disk) in your second drive. Any files that are on this diskette will be erased when you use the DISKCOPY command, so do not use a target diskette that has files you want to keep.

If you are using DOS version 5.0 or higher, you can copy the files from a 3½-inch diskette to a 5¼-inch diskette (or vice versa). Otherwise, both your diskettes must be 3½-inch or both must be 5¼-inch.

You can check which version of DOS your computer is using by using the VER command.

3. Type the DISKCOPY command. Then type:
   a. The letter of the drive that contains your source diskette.
   b. A colon (:).
   c. The letter of the drive that contains your target diskette, and another colon.

For example, if your source diskette is in your drive A and your target diskette is in your drive B, type the following command:

```
DISKCOPY A: B:
```

It is important that you do not mix up which diskette is your source diskette and which is your target diskette or your files will not get copied correctly.

How do I use DISKCOPY when I have <u>one</u> diskette drive?

1. Place the source diskette (the diskette with the files you want to copy) in the diskette drive.
2. Type the DISKCOPY command. Then type the letter of the drive that contains your source diskette, and a colon (:). For example, if your source diskette is in your drive A, type the following command.

```
DISKCOPY A:
```

3. When DOS asks you to insert the target diskette, take the source diskette out of the diskette drive and put the blank diskette in the diskette drive. Follow the instructions that your computer displays on the screen. You may need to take the diskettes in and out of the diskette drive several times until all the files are copied.

As before, it is important that you do not mix up which diskette is your source diskette and which is your target diskette or your files will not get copied correctly.

Look up *3½-inch diskette, 5¼-inch diskette, DOS command, DOS prompt, source disk, target disk,* and *VER command.*

diskette A *diskette* (also called a floppy disk and just plain disk) is a thin, magnetic sandwich that is used to hold software programs and computer files. The outside of the sandwich is square and made of plastic. The inside of the sandwich is round and looks like a flat, black pancake. It is here, on the magnetic-coated center, that your computer files are stored.

Diskettes come in two sizes: 5¼-inch and 3½-inch. Diskettes also come in two densities: double-density and high-density. The density indicates how close together information is placed on the diskette. High-density diskettes can store more information than double-density diskettes.

The 5¼-inch double-density and high-density diskettes look exactly like each other. Sometimes the company that makes the diskette will put a label on the diskette to let you know whether it is a double- or high-density diskette. But unless there is a label on the diskette, you cannot tell the difference.

The 3½-inch double-density and high-density diskettes look almost identical. However, the high-density diskette

- Has the letters HD (for high density) in the upper right-hand corner of the diskette.
- Has a hole in the bottom right-hand corner of the diskette.

How much information can fit on a diskette? Even though the 5¼-inch diskette is bigger than a 3½-inch, the 3½-inch diskette can hold more information. The chart below shows you how much information each diskette size can hold.

Diskette Size	Diskette Density	
	Double-Density	High-Density
3½ PC	720K	1.44M (1440K)
3½ Mac	800K	1.2M (1200K)
5¼ (PC only)	360K	1.2M (1200K)

K = kilobytes / M = megabytes

Can all computers use all sizes of diskettes? No. Although some computers have a single diskette drive that can read both 5¼-inch and 3½-inch diskettes, most computers have a diskette drive that can only read one size diskette. Many computers have two diskette drives: one for 3½-inch diskettes and one for 5¼-inch diskettes. Look up *density*, *kilobyte*, and *megabyte*.

diskette drive The *diskette drive* (also called a disk drive) is the part of your computer that can use diskettes. The drive itself is located inside your computer. All you see is a thin slot into which you can slide the diskette. Many diskette drives also have a light that turns on when the diskette is being used. The diskette is being used when the diskette drive reads information from a diskette or writes information to a diskette.

> Do not remove a diskette from the diskette drive while the light is on or you could damage your diskette.

The diskette drive reads from the diskette when you install a new software program or copy files to your hard disk. The diskette drive writes to the diskette when you copy a file from your hard disk to the diskette.

Although some computers have a single diskette drive that can read both 5¼-inch and 3½-inch diskettes, most computers have a diskette drive that can only read one size diskette. Many computers have two diskette drives: one for 3½-inch diskettes and one for 5¼-inch diskettes.

Can all diskette drives read both double-density and high-density diskettes? No. All new computers come with a high-density diskette drive that can read both high-density and double-density diskettes. But some older computers have a double-density diskette drive that cannot read high-density diskettes. The chart below shows you what type of drive can read what type of diskettes.

Drive	Type of Diskette	
	Double-Density	High-Density
Double-Density	*yes*	*no*
High-Density	*yes*	*yes*

Are diskette drives for the PC and Mac different? All diskettes must be formatted before they can be used. The PC and the Mac each need their diskettes formatted in a different way. So the diskette drives for the PC and the Mac are also different.

As a general rule, a PC cannot read a diskette that has been used on a Macintosh. However, most Macs are able to read a diskette that has been used by a PC. In order to use the PC diskette in your Mac, you have to have a special software program such as DOS Mounter Plus or Mac/PC Exchange. A Macintosh drive that can read both Mac and PC diskettes is called a Superdrive.

What kind of diskettes does software come on? When you go to buy software, it is important to know what size and what density diskettes your diskette drive can use. Most software comes on 3½-inch, high-density diskettes.

Some PC software can be purchased on 3½ or 5¼-inch diskettes right at the store. Other software has both 3½ and 5¼-inch diskettes in the box—so you can use whichever size you need. Still other software only comes on 3½-inch diskettes and includes a coupon for 5¼-inch or low-density 3½-inch diskettes. If your diskette drive cannot read high-density, 3½-inch diskettes, you may have to purchase software on 3½-inch diskettes and send away for the 5¼-inch ones. The software package will tell you what size diskettes are included.

Can a diskette get stuck in my drive? It is extremely rare for a disk to get stuck in the diskette drive on your PC. But from time to time you may find that a disk gets stuck in the diskette drive on your Mac. Some of the reasons that a diskette can get stuck in the drive are

- The diskette is damaged.
- The electricity to your Mac goes out (or is accidentally turned off).
- You put a PC diskette in a Mac drive and do not have the special software program that lets you use PC diskettes.

How can I eject a diskette that is stuck in my Mac? If you can see the icon for the diskette on your desktop, the diskette is not stuck, it is just mounted. To eject the diskette, drag the diskette icon to the trash can.

If you cannot see the icon for the diskette on your desktop and you know there is a disk in your diskette drive, the diskette is stuck. There are three ways to eject a disk. Only use the third solution as a last resort—after trying the first two solutions.

1. Press [⌘]-[E]. This will usually eject the diskette.

2. Try rebooting. Each time you start your computer, it checks to see if a system diskette is in the diskette drive. Your Mac will automatically eject any diskette that is not a system disk.
3. If ⌘-E doesn't eject your diskette, follow the steps below.
   a. **Turn off your Mac.**
   b. Find a large paper-clip and unfold it until you have a straight piece of metal.
   c. Look for a small hole to the right of the diskette drive.
   d. Push the paper clip into the hole. The paper clip will push a button that ejects the diskette.
   e. Remove the paper clip.

Look up *access, demagnetize, diskette,* and *installation program.*

---

docking station Although *docking station* sounds like a place to park your spaceship, it is an accessory for a portable computer. The docking station has features that are not built in to the computer, such as a CD-ROM drive, sound, speakers, video, or other features. When the computer is docked (sitting on top of the docking station), it can use any of the features that are provided by the docking station. Look up *accessory* and *portable computer.*

---

document *Document* is a very general term that refers to any kind of writing that has been created in a word-processing program. A document can be a newsletter, report, love letter, story, poem, invitation, announcement, or greeting card. Basically, any type of file that you (or anyone else) can create in your word-processing program is a document. Look up *word processing.*

---

documentation *Documentation* is the set of printed instructions that come with a software program. Documentation can include user manuals, a card that explains how to install the program on your computer, and other useful information.

> *"Wow, you sure have a lot of books about computers," Bob said to his friend Peggy.*
>
> *"That's just the* **documentation** *that came with all our software," replied Peggy.*

DOS *DOS* (rhymes with "boss") is an acronym for disk operating system. DOS is the software that controls your computer's basic functions such as how information is stored on your hard disk. MS-DOS (Microsoft DOS) is the operating system used on most IBM-compatible computers. PC-DOS (personal computer DOS) is the operating system used on most IBM personal computers.

DOS does not have graphical user interface (GUI) like Microsoft Windows, OS/2, and Mac OS. To communicate with DOS you must type commands at a special location called the DOS prompt. Look up *acronym, DOS command, DOS prompt,* and *operating system.*

DOS command *DOS commands* are a way of communicating with your IBM or IBM-compatible computer. A DOS command can be used to tell your computer to start a software program, show you a file, copy a file from one place to another, delete a file that you no longer need, and a variety of other tasks.

A DOS command can be given to any computer that is using DOS. You can find out whether or not your computer is using DOS by typing a command that tells your computer to show you which version of DOS it is using. Try typing the following DOS command at the DOS prompt.

```
ver [Enter]
```

If your computer responds with one of the messages shown below—or even responds with a message that looks just a little like one of the messages shown below—your computer is using DOS.

```
MS DOS Version 6.2
Compaq DOS Version 5.0
PC DOS Version 3.3
```

Where do I use a DOS command? You usually type a DOS command at the DOS prompt—although some software programs let you type a DOS command from inside them. The easiest way to get to the DOS prompt is to exit Microsoft Windows or any other programs you are using. You can recognize the DOS prompt because it has a letter (usually A, B, or C) which is followed by a greater-than sign (>) and one or more directory names with backslashes (\) between them. For example,

```
C>\WINDOWS
C>\GAMES\OUTPOST
A>\
```

This dictionary includes explanations for the following DOS commands:

CD	ERASE	RD
CHDIR	FORMAT	RENAME
CLS	HELP	RMDIR
COPY	MD	TIME
DATE	MKDIR	TREE
DEL	MORE	TYPE
DIR	PATH	UNDELETE
DISKCOPY	PRINT	VER
DOSKEY	PROMPT	

To find out more information about a command, just look it up in this book. Look up *command* and *DOS prompt.*

DOS prompt A prompt is your computer's way of letting you know that it is ready for your next command or instruction. Since most computers can't talk, your computer usually signals you by typing words or symbols on your screen.

The *DOS prompt* is a special kind of prompt. It is your computer's way of letting you know that it is ready for your next DOS command. Although some software programs allow you to use DOS commands, most programs make you go to a DOS prompt to give DOS commands to your computer.

The easiest way to get to the DOS prompt is to exit Microsoft Windows or any other programs you are using. You can recognize the DOS prompt because it has a letter (usually A, B, or C) which is followed by a greater-than sign (>) and one or more directory names with backslashes between (\) them. For example,

```
C>\WINDOWS
C>\GAMES\OUTPOST
A>\
```

You can change what information is shown at the DOS prompt by using the PROMPT command. PROMPT is a DOS command that lets you tell your computer what look you would like for the DOS prompt. Look up *DOS command* and *PROMPT command.*

DOSKEY *DOSKEY* (pronounced "doss-key") is a DOS program that you can use so that you do not have to type the same commands over and over again. After you start DOSKEY, it remembers all the DOS commands you type.

How do I use DOSKEY?

1. Type the following command at the DOS prompt.

   DOSKEY Enter

2. Use any DOS commands you want to use.
3. Press ↑ or ↓ to display the last DOS command you typed. Press the arrow key again, and again, to display all the DOS commands you have typed since you began the DOSKEY program.
4. When you find the DOS command you want to use, you can either
   a. Press Enter to use the same DOS command again.
   b. Make changes to the DOS command by editing any information that is different (such as the name of a file to COPY). Then press Enter.

Look up *DOS command and DOS prompt.*

dot-matrix printer A *dot-matrix printer* has small metal pins that press against a printer ribbon to make each letter. As the pins hit the ribbon, they form a pattern of little dots in a matrix (a graph) on the paper. The pattern of little dots make up each letter. If you look very closely at the printout from a dot matrix printer, you will see that each letter is made up of tiny little dots.

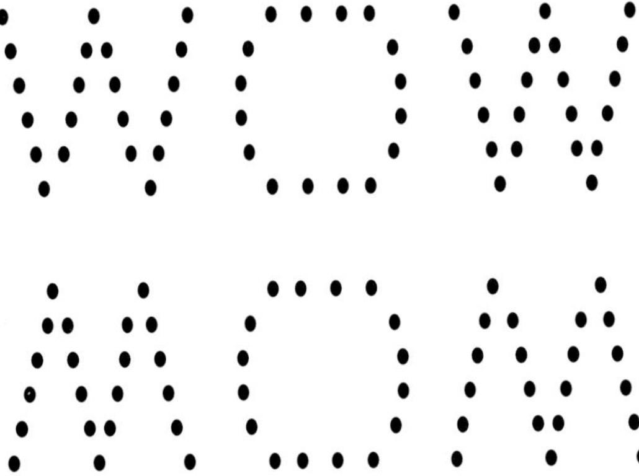

A dot-matrix printer is called an impact printer, because the pins impact (hit) the ribbon against the paper to form each letter on the paper. Dot-matrix printers are usually less expensive than ink jet and laser printers but they have some disadvantages.

First, the printouts from a dot-matrix printer are typically not as dark or easy to read as the printouts from an ink jet or laser printer. Second, a dot-matrix printer does not have as many fonts to choose from as the other printers, so it is not a good choice if you want to do desktop publishing. Third, it does not print as fast as ink jet or laser printers.

However, in spite of its shortcomings, a dot-matrix can be a good buy when you just need basic printouts of text and graphics at an affordable price. Look up *desktop publishing, font, ink jet printer,* and *laser printer.*

dot pitch If you were to examine your computer screen with a magnifying glass, you would see that each letter, picture, and color is made up of red, green, and blue dots. If you had an instrument that could measure just one of those tiny little dots you would be measuring the *dot pitch* of your monitor. The dot pitch is the size of the smallest dot that your monitor can display on its screen.

Dot pitch is measured in millimeters. The smaller the dot pitch, the better the picture quality you will get on your screen. Most color monitors have a dot pitch of .31 millimeters or smaller. A better quality monitor has a dot pitch of .28 millimeters or smaller.

When you and your parents go shopping for a monitor, dot pitch is one of the features that helps you judge the quality of the monitor. The dot pitch can usually be found on the box containing the monitor. Look for "Specifications" (the section of the box with the technical details). Look up *millimeter, monitor,* and *resolution.*

The illustration below helps you see why a smaller dot makes for a better picture.

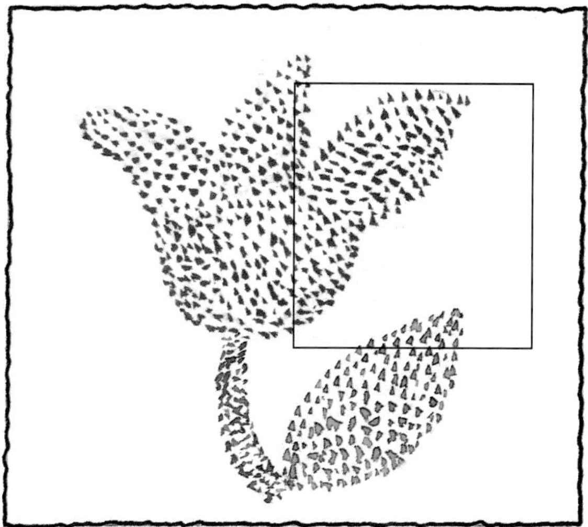

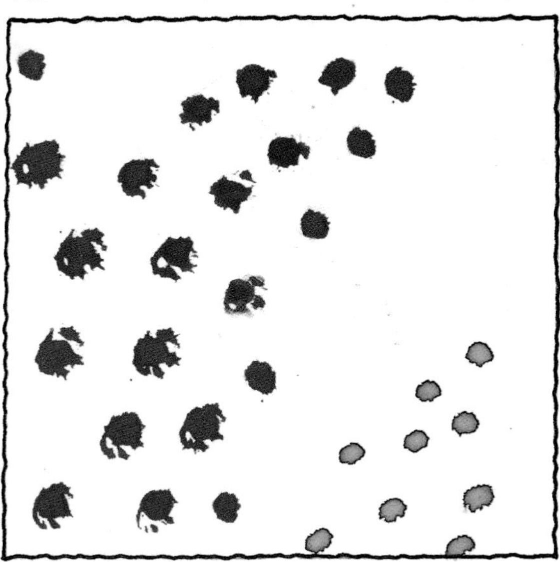

dots per inch The quality of the printouts from a laser or ink jet printer is measured in *dots per inch*. Dots per inch is abbreviated dpi.

Many laser and ink jet printers have a printout quality of 300 dpi. This means that if you printed a solid black square that was one-inch long on each every side, the box would contain 300 × 300 dots (for a total of 90,000 dots). A 400 dpi printer would print a one inch box with 400 × 400 dots (for a total of 160,000 dots). The higher the dpi, the more dots per each inch, and the better the quality of your printouts. Look up *ink jet printer* and *laser printer.*

double-click To *double-click* the mouse is to press a mouse button two times.

PC The mouse on your PC has two or three buttons. When you double-click the mouse on your PC, you press the left mouse button two times.

Mac The mouse on your Mac usually has only one mouse button, so you press that button two times.

Double-clicking must be done quickly or the computer may think that you made two single clicks instead.

What is double-click used for? One use of double-click is to start a software program. When you double-click an icon on your desktop, the program begins. Many software programs have a special use for the double-click. You need to check the manuals that come with your software to see if there is a special use for double-click. If your software has no special use for a double-click, your computer usually responds to a double-click the same as it would to a single-click. Look up *mouse button* and *single click.*

double-density Diskettes come in two densities: *double-density* and high-density. The density indicates how close together information is placed on the diskette. Double-density diskettes store less information than high-density diskettes.

The 5¼-inch double-density and high density diskettes look exactly like each other. Sometimes the company that makes the diskette puts a label on the diskette to let you know whether it is a double- or high-density diskette. But unless there is a label on the diskette, you cannot tell the difference.

The 3½-inch double-density and high-density diskettes look almost identical. However, the high density diskette

- Has the letters HD (for high density) in the upper right-hand corner of the diskette, and
- Has a hole in the bottom right-hand corner of the diskette.

How much information can fit on a double-density diskette? Even though the 5¼-inch diskette is bigger than a 3½-inch, the 3½-inch diskette can hold more information. The chart below shows you how much information each diskette size can hold. (Note: K = kilobytes.)

Diskette Size	Double Density
3½ PC	720K
3½ Mac	800K
5¼ (PC only)	360K

Look up *3½-inch diskette, 5¼-inch diskette, diskette, diskette drive, high-density,* and *kilobyte.*

down When a boxer gets hit really hard, he falls down and is unable to continue the match. He may be down for a few seconds and get right back into the fight or he may be down for the count—and lose the match. When your computer goes *down*, it too is out of the game.

A computer is a very complex piece of equipment and can go down (or crash) for many reasons. It may go down for a few seconds or down for the count—in which case you will need to wait for your mom or dad to look at it so they can fix it or have it serviced by a computer professional. Look up *crash* and *downtime.*

down arrow key The *down arrow key* moves the keyboard cursor down one line. The down arrow key is the key on your keyboard that looks like [↓].

download When you *download* a file to your printer, you send the file (usually fonts) to your printer's memory.

When you are using the modem in your computer to talk to another computer, you can download a file from the other computer. You download a file when you ask the other computer to send you a file over the phone lines. Look up *modem* and *upload.*

"Where did you get that beautiful graphic of a horse for your report?" Mrs. Cantor asked Nathan.

"I **downloaded** *it from CompuServe, an online computer service," replied Nathan.*

downtime *Downtime* is the amount of time that you are not able to use your computer because it is being fixed (or waiting to be fixed). When a computer crashes, it can take minutes, hours, or days to get the computer working again—depending on what caused it to crash in the first place. The period of time between the crash and when you are able to use the computer again is called downtime because it is the time that the computer is down and unusable. Look up *crash* and *down*.

dpi The printout quality of an inkjet or laser printer is measured in dots per inch. Dots per inch is abbreviated *dpi*. Look up *dots per inch*.

draft quality Does it take your printer a long time to print out pictures that you draw on your computer screen? Most printers can print in more than one level of quality.

Some software programs have a selection called *draft quality* or draft mode that lets you print out your drawing or text more quickly. The draft quality setting does not make as nice a printout as the normal setting, but if you have not completed your drawing and just want to get an idea of what it will look like when it prints out, draft quality is the way to go. Unfortunately, not all software programs have a draft quality selection, and some printers will just ignore the draft quality selection you make in a software program. The best way to find out if your software and printer can print in draft quality is to try it.

drag *Drag* means to hold down a mouse button as you move the mouse from one place to another across the screen.

PC The mouse on your PC has two or three buttons. When you drag the mouse on your PC, you hold down the left mouse button.

Mac The mouse on your Mac usually has only one mouse button. When you drag the mouse you hold down the only mouse button.

What is drag used for? In many computer programs, to move a picture or object from one place to another, you first click on the object (to select it) and then drag it to another location on the screen. When the object is where you want it, you let go of the mouse button and the object stays in place.

draw program A *draw program* is a software program that is designed for drawing pictures, greeting cards, advertisements, invitations, notices, illustrations for your school reports, and any other artistic type printout. Most draw programs come with lots of clip-art that you can use in your artwork. Look up *clip-art* and *paint program*.

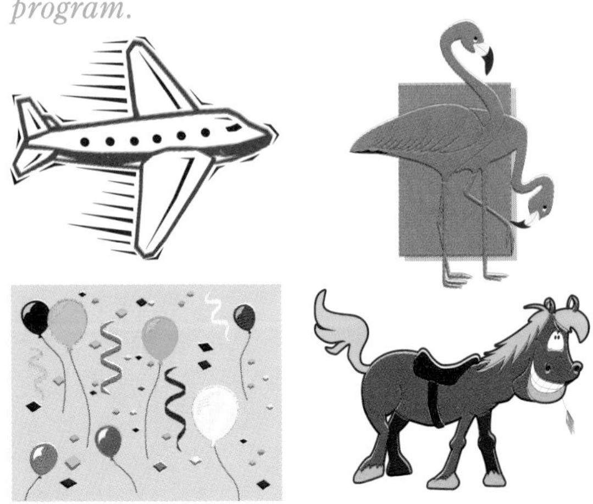

drive *Drive* is another term for both a diskette drive and a hard disk. 👁 Look up *diskette drive* and *hard disk.*

drop-down menu When you use a software program that has a menu bar across the top of the screen, the menu bar will have drop-down or pull-down menus. A *drop-down menu* is a menu that pops open when you click on it.

Drop down menus are easy to use. If you want to make a selection, click on it. To close the menu without making a selection, click anywhere else on your desktop. 👁 Look up *menu, menu bar,* and *pull-down menu.*

drop shadow Do you ever form your fingers into a rabbit or another shape and make shadow puppets on the wall? How about when you are walking outside on a sunny day—do you ever try to avoid stepping on your shadow? A *drop shadow* is a set of dark lines next to a box to make it look like the box is casting a shadow.

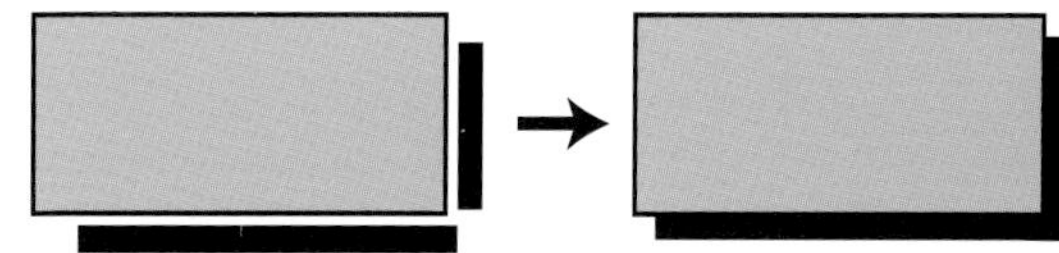

DTP *DTP* is an abbreviation for desktop publishing, which means using your personal computer and a high-quality printer to produce newsletters, stories, reports, invitations, announcements, and other printouts that look like they were printed (published) by a professional print shop. 👁 Look up *desktop publishing.*

duplex printing *Duplex printing* is a fancy name for printing on both sides of a piece of a paper. To get most printers to print on two sides of a piece of paper, you have to let the printer print on one side of the paper, then remove the paper and flip it over so that the printer can print on the second side. In a duplex printer, the printer can print on both sides of the paper without you having to turn the paper over.

dust cover A *dust cover* is a thin, plastic cover that you can put over your keyboard, monitor, and printer to protect your computer equipment from dust, animal fur (cats love to walk on your keyboard), and other hazards. Dust covers should only be used when your computer equipment is turned off.

e-mail *E-mail* is an acronym for electronic mail. E-mail has two meanings. **(1)** E-mail is a type of software program that lets you send a note, file, or message from your computer to a friend on another computer. **(2)** E-mail is what an electronic message is called. Look up *electronic mail.*

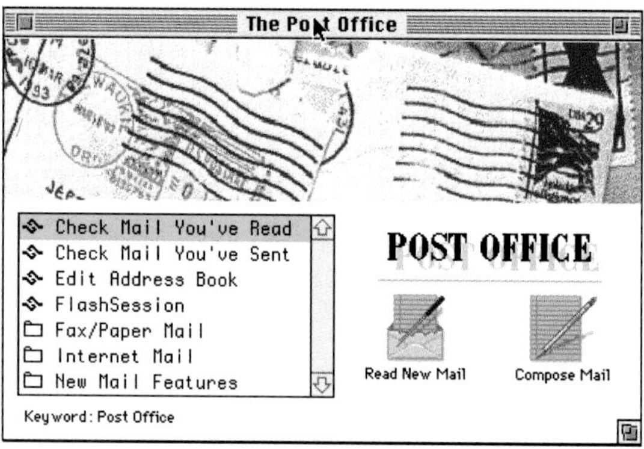

edit When you *edit* text, you look it over to make sure it is correct, make some changes to make the text better, and fix any problems (such as spelling errors) that you find.

EDIT command The *EDIT command* is a DOS command that lets you create, change, and print text files. The EDIT command starts up a text editor called EDIT.

EDIT is built in to newer versions of DOS (version 5.0 and higher). A text editor is different from a word-processing program in that a text editor has no special features that let you change fonts, add page numbers, insert graphics, or use any other features that format the text.

EDIT cannot be used with files that were created in a word-processing program such as Ami Pro, Microsoft Word, or WordPerfect. If you try to use EDIT to change a word-processing file, you will probably see garbage on your screen and your computer will beep at you.

How do I use the EDIT command? To use the EDIT command to create or edit a file, just type EDIT and the name of the file at the DOS prompt. If the file already exists, EDIT displays the file for you to edit. If the file does not exist, EDIT creates a new file with the name you entered. It then places your cursor in the edit screen. From there, you begin to type your text or commands.

For example, suppose you want to use EDIT to create or change a list of chores you have to do this week. At the DOS prompt you would type the following command.

```
EDIT CHORES [Enter]
```

The file called CHORES would be created (if you didn't have one) or displayed on your screen (if you already had one.) Enter new text (or change existing text) by moving the cursor anywhere on the screen and begin typing.

Be sure to save any changes to your file by selecting the FILE menu and the SAVE command. You can print your file by selecting the FILE menu and the PRINT command. Look up *DOS command, DOS prompt, edit, garbage, text file, VER command,* and *version number.*

electronic art There are companies that sell artwork that you can use inside your greeting cards, pictures, reports, and other projects that you create on your computer. The art is called *electronic art* because it comes on diskettes and CD-ROMs (electronically) rather than on paper—the way that art used to be sold. Electronic art is also called clip-art or graphics.

Electronic art comes in many different types of file formats (such as BMP, CDR, EPS, Paint, PCX, PICT, TIFF, TIF, TGA, and WPG—to name only a few). Before you buy electronic art, make sure that you are buying it in a format that your paint or drawing program can use, otherwise you will have beautiful pictures that you will not be able to use in your project.

electronic bulletin board *Electronic bulletin board* is another name for a bulletin board system, a special type of club that you join and participate in by using your computer and a modem. Look up *bulletin board system.*

electronic mail **(1)** *Electronic mail* is a type of software program that lets you send a note, file, or message from your computer to a friend on another computer. You must have a modem or be connected to a network in order to send and receive electronic mail. Electronic mail is usually called e-mail.

For you to correspond with your friend through e-mail, you must both belong to the same BBS, online service, or network. Your friend does not need to be logged on to the service when you send the message. The message will sit in your friend's e-mail mailbox until your friend logs onto the service and sees the message. Look up *bulletin board system, log on, network,* and *online service.*

(2) *Electronic mail* (or e-mail) is also what an electronic message is called. In other words, you use e-mail to send e-mail.

> *"Nick, did you get my* **e-mail** *message about the party?" asked Donna.*
>
> *"Yeah. I'll be there." replied Nick.*

electronic mailbox If you can receive electronic mail—called e-mail—then you already have an *electronic mailbox*! Your electronic mailbox is the place on a network or online service where your e-mail is stored. Just like your mailbox at home, your electronic mailbox is just usually called a mailbox (rather than electronic mailbox). Look up *mailbox.*

emoticon Emote means to express your feelings. An icon is a small picture. An *emoticon* is a simple cartoon picture that you can use to express your feelings. Smiley faces :-) and sad faces :-(are two emoticons that you have seen many times.

Why use emoticons? When you talk with someone in person or on the phone, your feelings come across by your laugh, the look on your face, the tone of your voice, how you are standing, and so on. In a conversation, you provide a lot of nonverbal information—information that is not found in your words.

When you talk to someone on an online service, or in an e-mail message, the only thing that you can use to communicate is the text that you type. The other person can't see your face or hear your voice. This can make it difficult for the other person to understand the real meaning of what you are saying. But by adding a few well-placed emoticons, you can liven up the conversation, and make yourself clear.

You can use emoticons in your e-mail messages, online chats that you have with other kids, or even in the written notes that you pass to your friends.

How do I make an emoticon? Unlike the smiley and sad faces, most emoticons are eyes or small faces that you can make using the punctuation marks on your keyboard. Some emoticons face you. Others are turned to the side. Below are some emoticons to try yourself. To test them out on your computer, just type them into any word-processing program or text editor.

These emoticons of eyes are looking at you.

<o> <->	wink
<0><0>	awake
<+> <+>	unconscious
<-> <->	asleep

Turn your head to see these emoticon faces.

:-)	smiley face
:-(	sad face
:-o	surprised
;-)	wink
I-(	sleeping / bored
:-}	smirk
B-)	glasses
:-P	sticking tongue out
:-D	laughing
:Y	pucker up
=:-)	nerd
:-)x	snappy dresser
(:-)	bald head

Look up *e-mail, icon, online service, text editor*, and *word processing.*

The examples below show how you can liven up your conversations with emoticons. Use the emoticons shown above, or make up your own!

Here is a sample online conversation without emoticons.

> *CAP: I missed you in class today.*
> *JEN: Get real.*
> *CAP: Mr. Clark said that anyone who wasn't in class has to take a quiz tomorrow.*
> *JEN: Really?*
> *CAP: No. But he did say to finish Chapter 3.*
> *JEN: I read that stuff last week.*

Here is the same online conversation with emoticons.

> *CAP: I missed you in class today* :Y .
> *JEN:* :-P.
> *CAP: Mr. Clark* (:-) *said that anyone who wasn't in class has to take a quiz tomorrow* :-}.
> *JEN:* :-o
> *CAP:* <o><-> *Just finish Chapter 3.*
> *JEN: I read that stuff last week* <-><->.

encrypt Did you ever talk to your friends using a secret code? To *encrypt* a file means to use a special software program that puts the information in the file into a secret code. Once a file is encrypted, you can't read what is inside the file unless you have a password that can decode (decrypt) the information. Computer programs that encrypt and decrypt data are often used by governments to protect top secret information. Look up *decrypt.*

Can you encrypt a message? Sarita wants to **encrypt** the following poem so she can send it to her cousin Carmela. The poem is the password for a secret club. Can you help Sarita encrypt the poem? Just substitute each letter for the next letter of the alphabet. For example, "A" becomes "B," "C" becomes "D," "Z" becomes "A,"and so on. *The encrypted message is in the Answer Section in the back of the book.*

Mary had a little lamb,
His bed was by the heater.
But every time he tossed and turned,
He burnt his wooly seater.

End key The End *key* is a cursor movement key because many programs let you use it to move your cursor to the end of a line of text or to the bottom of your screen. Some game programs have a special use for the End key. Check the instruction manual that came with your game program to see whether or not the End key has a special purpose. Look up *cursor, cursor movement key,* and *text.*

"What are you working on?" Miranda asked her younger brother Tim.

"I'm working on a letter for English. I have to pretend I have a problem with a store and write a letter to the manager about the problem," replied Tim.

"What's the problem you're writing about?"

"That the cleaner shrunk my pants. I'm almost done; I am just editing the text."

"Why are you holding down the right arrow key to move across the line?" asked Miranda.

"How else can I move across the line?" asked Tim.

"Just press the **End key***."*

end user The *end user* is someone who uses a software program—someone like you.

Enter key The Enter *key* is a way to interact with your computer. It is a way of saying to your computer, I'm done, now I want you to do something. Enter is used a lot when working on a computer. For example, in many word-processing programs, you press Enter when you're finished typing a paragraph. The word-processing program then knows to move to a new line, go to the left margin, and get ready to start the next paragraph.

The Enter key is larger than all the other keys on your keyboard—except the spacebar. Usually the Enter key has the word "Enter" on it and/or the ↵ arrow. Some keyboards have "Return" instead of "Enter" on the key. "Return" is a term that comes from electric typewriter keyboards. Electric typewriters have a key marked Return that moves the paper in the typewriter to the beginning of the next line. Look up *carriage return* and *word-processing program.*

erase When you are writing a story on notebook paper and make a mistake, you can *erase* the mistake with your pencil eraser. When you erase a file on your computer, you remove it from your diskette or hard disk.

When you erase text from your notebook paper you can use that space over again. The same is true of computer files. When you erase files, you can use the space on the diskette or hard disk over again.

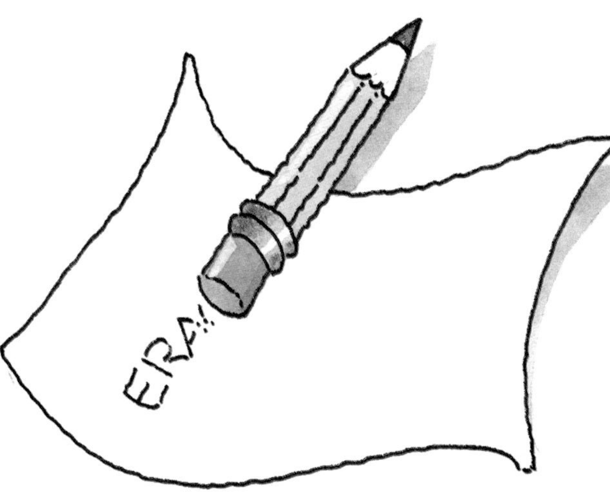

ERASE command The *ERASE command* is a DOS command that you use when you want to erase (delete) one or more files from your hard disk or diskette. The ERASE command and the DEL command do the same job.

How do I use the ERASE command?

1. From the DOS prompt, change to the drive letter that contains the files you want to erase.
   a. To erase files from your hard disk, you will probably need to type a `C:`.
   b. To erase files from a diskette in a diskette drive, you type `A:` or `B:`,

depending on which drive contains the diskette.

To change to your C drive, type the following command at the DOS prompt.

```
C: [Enter]
```

2. Use the CD command to change to the directory that contains the files you want to erase.

> **Warning!** If you are erasing files from your C drive, do not skip Step #2. If you accidentally erase the files in your root directory (C:\), you will not be able to use your computer the next time you turn it on!

3. Type the ERASE command.
   a. Then type the name of the file you want to erase. For example, to erase the file named REPORT2.OLD, type the following command.

```
ERASE REPORT2.OLD [Enter]
```

   b. If you want to erase all of the files in the directory, you can use the asterisk wildcard as shown below.

```
ERASE *.* [Enter]
```

Your computer responds:

```
All files in directory will be deleted!
Are you sure (Y/N)?
```

4. If you used wildcards to tell your computer to erase all of the files in the directory, you now have a chance to change your mind.
   a. Press [Y] to erase all the files. Then press [Enter].
   b. Press [N] if you don't want to erase all the files. Then press [Enter].

Look up *CD command, directory, DOS command, DOS prompt, file, UNDELETE command,* and *wildcard.*

---

error message An *error message* is a note that your software displays on your computer screen when something has gone wrong. When you read certain error messages you will know what to do right away (like that you forgot to put a diskette in the drive). Other times you will see the error message and not have a clue as to what is causing the problem.

When your computer displays an error message that you don't understand, STOP! Don't panic, but do NOT continue to use your computer. Wait until your mom or dad has read the message before you continue, reboot, or turn off your computer. Look up *fatal error, general failure error, non-system disk error,* and *not ready reading error.*

Esc key If you found yourself in trouble, you would want to escape from it. In many software programs, the [Esc] *key* on your keyboard does just that—it helps you escape from trouble! Esc is short for <u>esc</u>ape.

[Esc] (or [Escape]) is located on the left-hand side of the keyboard, near the top. Depending on which software program you are using, the Esc key can be used to

- Make a program stop what it is doing,
- Cancel a choice that you highlighted on a menu, or

- Close the top window and go back to the last window you were using.

Almost every software program on your PC uses the Esc key in some way. But this is not true on your Mac. Some Mac software uses Esc and some Mac software doesn't. Many programs for your Mac use ⌘-. to cancel or escape your last command. Look up *menu* and *window*.

Jill was using her dad's word-processing program to write a letter to her grandmother. She had been working on the letter for a while and remembered that she should save it. She selected Save from the menu, and gave the file the name GRANDMA.LTR. Then she continued to work on the letter.

When she was all finished, she went to save the letter again but accidentally chose Save As from the menu. A window appeared asking her to give the file a new name.

"Uh oh," Jill said. "I didn't want to do that."

"Why not?" asked her brother John, who had been looking over Jill's shoulder the whole time. "You need to save the letter, don't you?"

"Yes, but I want to keep the same name, not give it a new name," Jill replied. "Watch what I do now."

Jill pressed Esc *and the Save As window disappeared. She then chose Save, and the letter was saved using the name that Jill had been using all along.*

"I get it," said John. "You used the **Esc key** *to cancel Save As, so you could go back and start the Save all over again."*

"Right! Now all we have to do is print the letter, and then we can mail it."

escape The key on your keyboard marked Esc (or Escape) is called the *escape* key. The escape key is used to cancel or stop an activity. Look up *Esc key.*

.EXE Both you and your computer can figure out which files on the computer are the program files by looking at the extension that comes after the filename. The *.EXE* extension means that a file contains a software program (the instructions that the computer needs to play a game, display a picture, run an animation, edit text, send an e-mail, or any other activity). Look up *extension, file,* and *filename.*

expansion card An *expansion card* (or card) is another name for a computer board, an accessory that plugs into one of the expansion slots inside your computer's

CPU. The card gives your computer extra capabilities such as sound, better video, or more memory. Look up *computer board, CPU,* and *expansion slot.*

expansion slot An *expansion slot* is a place inside your computer's CPU where you can add computer boards that give your computer extra capabilities such as sound, better video, or more memory. Most computers come with three to six expansion slots that are not being used.

Each board that you add to your computer takes up one or two expansion slots. Usually a computer card only plugs into one expansion slot but may be so wide that it blocks a second expansion slot from being used. Look up *computer board.*

expert system An *expert system* is a special type of computer software that is designed to make the same choices that an expert—such as a doctor—would make. The expert system reviews all the information you give it and then calculates all the

possible answers based on the instructions that were programmed into it.

Although expert systems are designed to solve complicated problems, let's look at a simple example. Suppose you tell an expert medical system that you have been sneezing, coughing, have a runny nose, and have a fever. The expert system would review all the symptoms that you entered and probably diagnose that you have a cold, the flu, or some exotic (rare) illness.

The expert system might even indicate which of the possible illnesses is more likely, based on how often each illness is diagnosed. The expert system might tell you that it is more likely that you have the flu rather than the exotic illness because the exotic illness is very rare and the flu is very common. Look up *artificial intelligence.*

extension An *extension* is the last part of a filename. Filenames have three parts.

- The first part of the filename is the name of the file.
- The second part of the filename is a period (.) that separates the name of the file from the extension.
- The third part of the filename is the extension. An extension can be one, two, or three letters long—though most extensions are three letters long.

All software programs are made up of one or more files. Most programs have many files. The extension is used to describe the kind of information that is in the file.

Sometimes the extension only has meaning to the person who created the file. Other extensions have a standard meaning that everyone uses the same way. Below are a few extensions that you are likely to see on your files. The standard meaning for each extension is shown next to the extension.

.AVI	Movie file
.BAT	Software program
.BMP	Picture file
.COM	Software program
.DOC	Documents (letters, stories, notes, etc.)
.EXE	Software program
.ICO	Icon file
.PCX	Picture file
.WAV	Sound file

The most common extensions are made up of letters. But extensions can be made up of letters, numbers, and some symbols. The definition for *filename* has a table that lists the symbols you can use in filenames and extensions.

What is the extension used for? You recognize people by looking at their face or listening to their voice. The computer uses the extension to recognize a particular type of file. For example, suppose you write stories using your computer and save all the stories in a special directory called STORIES.

Suppose you also used the computer to draw pictures for all your stories. Each time you created a story or picture you would have to give it a filename. If you used the extension .DOC for all your stories and .PIC for all your pictures, you would be able to see a list of all your stories or a list of all your pictures by asking the computer to show you all the files that end with .DOC or all the files that end with .PIC.

For example, to see all the files that end in .DOC, you could type the following command at the DOS prompt.

```
DIR *.DOC [Enter]
```

How can an extension help me start a software program? If you can't remember what to type to start one of your games (or other software programs),

1. Look in the program's directory for files that have the extension .EXE, .COM, and .BAT (the extensions for a software program).
2. After you find the files with a software program extension, type the filename at the DOS prompt—you do not have to type the period or extension when the file has a software program extension. (**Hint:** Try typing the filename that ends with .EXE first.)
3. Press [Enter].

Look up *DOS, DOS prompt, DIR command, directory, file,* and *filename.*

WARNING: It is not a good idea to start software programs that you don't have permission to use (like your parents' programs). It's easy to mess up other people's settings when you go looking around programs that you don't know how to use or how to exit.

extensions *Extensions* are abilities that you can add to your computer. Some extensions are files that let your Mac work with different modems, printers, and CD-ROM drives. Another extension automatically makes your files smaller so you can fit more files on your hard disk.

How do I add an extension? To add an extension to your Mac, place the file in the "Extensions" folder. The Extensions folder is located inside the "System Folder." Then reboot your computer. You must reboot your Mac before it will use its new ability.

Look up *reboot* and *system folder.*

external device When something is external, it is on the outside. A device is a component (like your screen or keyboard) or accessory (like your mouse or CD-ROM drive) that attaches to your computer. An *external device* is a component or an accessory that does not go inside your computer but attaches to the outside of your computer.

Look up *accessory* and *component.*

external font Fonts that are not built in to your printer are called *external fonts*. Unlike built-in fonts (which are called internal fonts), external fonts are added to your printer and removed from your printer as needed. There are thousands of cxternal fonts. Some external fonts are basic fonts for everyday use—but many are very fancy, or have an unusual look.

Not all printers can use external fonts. Laser printers can use external fonts. Some inkjet and dot-matrix printers can use external fonts too. The manual that comes with your printer should tell you what kind of external fonts your printer can use.

There are two basic types of external fonts: soft fonts and cartridge fonts. Soft fonts are software that come on diskettes that are copied to your computer's hard disk. When you want to use the fonts, you run a special program that downloads (sends) the fonts to your printer. Cartridge fonts plug into a slot in your computer. Cartridge fonts look and work similar to the game cartridges for a Sega or Nintendo system. Look up *cartridge font, download, font, internal font,* and *run.*

Blippo Black

ENVIRO

Gill Sans

Goudy Bold

Palatino

fanfold paper Did you ever make a paper fan by folding a piece of paper back and forth? Continuous paper is sometimes called *fanfold paper* because you can fold the paper into a nice neat stack—just like you fold a paper fan. Look up *continuous paper.*

FAQ *FAQ* is an acronym for frequently asked questions. Many software programs and online services have an FAQ (or FAQ list). The FAQ lists questions and answers that are often asked about the software program or service. The FAQ is usually located in the Help menu of a software program or the help section of the online service. Look up *online service.*

fatal error A *fatal error* is a problem that is so severe that your software program crashes. When you find a fatal error, you often have to reboot your computer. A fatal error is usually caused by one or more bugs in a software program.

> *Chip and Daryl were playing a game on the computer when the screen suddenly froze and the sound went dead.*
>
> *"What happened? I was just about to get that guy!" cried Daryl.*
>
> *"It's the stupid software program," replied Chip. "My sister gave it to me. She warned me that it had a few* **fatal errors**. *I guess we just found one."*

feature The *features* of a software program are the things that a software program can do. Each task that the software program can do is called a feature, so some features are more important than others. Some of the features of a computer card game might include letting you select a pattern for the back of the cards, letting you save a game in progress, letting you play with just the computer or with another person, and giving you selections that allow you to change the rules of the games.

field Have you ever had to fill out a form or permission slip for school? The form has a place for your name, address, phone number, parent's signature, and whatever other information the form is designed to collect. Each of the places on the form where you write information is called a *field.*

Name Address Fields

Name:

Address:

City:

State:

Zip:

Phone:

In computers, a field is a place in a database where you can type and change the information that is in the database. In a name and address database, there are fields for NAME, STREET, CITY, STATE, and ZIP CODE. Look up *database* and *field name.*

field name Each field in a database has a name. The name of the field is called the *field name.* If you had a database of your music collection, sample field names might include ARTIST, ALBUM, BEST SONG, and TYPE OF MUSIC (if you listen to more than one type of music).

file All the software programs on your computer's hard disk are made up of files. A *file* contains information that your computer uses to run a program, display pictures on your screen, make a sound, or manage information. The files that make up a game program tell the computer how to play the game, what to display on the screen, and which high scores to use. You use files every time you turn on your computer, start a software program, or type a letter to your Uncle Bart.

When you or your parents install a new game on your computer, files are copied from the diskettes that came in the game box to the hard disk on your computer. If you have several software programs on your computer, you probably have over 1,000 files.

How does a computer keep track of a thousand files? Your computer can keep track of the files on your hard disk because they are organized into groups. On PCs the groups are called directories. On Macs the groups are called folders. When you install a new program on your computer, the installation program automatically makes a new directory or folder on your computer. The installation program then adds the program files to the new directory or folder. Look up *directory* and *folder.*

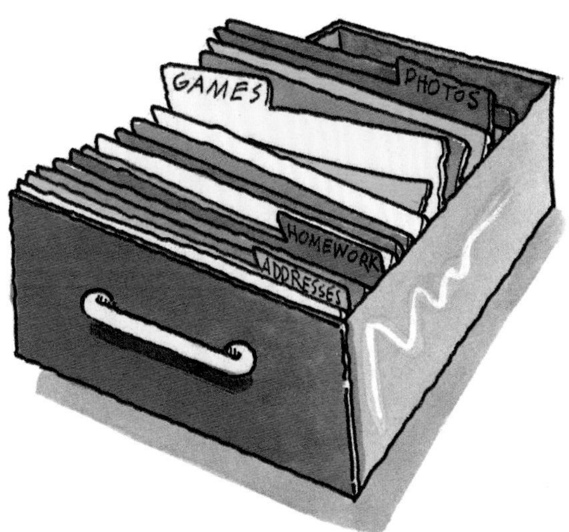

When Antonio's Aunt Catherine came to visit last summer, she brought him Return to Zork, an adventure game with animation, live action, and sound. "Does this game have many **files***?" asked Antonio.*

"Lots of **files***," replied Aunt Catherine. She showed Antonio the area of his computer that contained the new game. She typed D-I-R on the keyboard, and a list of* **files** *appeared on the screen.*

"All those **files** *make up the game Return to Zork," said Aunt Catherine.*

"You know," said Antonio, "I used

to think that a game was just one big **file**, *but now I know that computer games that have moving pictures and sound have many* **files**.*"*

"You're becoming quite a computer expert," said Aunt Catherine.

---

file size Files come in different sizes. The *file size* is the number of bytes that it takes to store the file on your diskette or hard disk. If you think that your hard disk or diskette may be getting full, it is a good idea to find out the size of the file before you actually copy it to your hard disk.

Where can I find the size of a file?

PC In DOS, you can use the DIR command to see the size of a file. In Microsoft Windows, click on the File Manager icon to locate and see the size of a file.

Mac Click on the file's icon to select the file. Then pull down the File menu and select the Get Info command. The Get Info command shows you the kind of file, its size, its location, and other details about the file.

Look up *3½-inch diskette*, *5¼-inch diskette*, *byte*, *DIR command*, *DOS*, *file*, *Microsoft Windows*, and *storage*.

---

file transfer When you send a file from your computer to another computer you are completing a *file transfer*. To perform a file transfer your computer must be connected to the other computer—either over the phone lines or through a network. Look up *modem* and *network*.

"You need to give me a copy of our report on a diskette so that I can add some pictures to it," Shara told her partner.

"Okay," replied Kito, "can you bring in a 3½-inch diskette tomorrow?"

"No. We only have a 5¼-inch diskette drive in our computer," said Shara.

"We only have a 3½-inch drive," said Kito.

"What are we going to do?" asked Shara.

"Do you have a modem?" asked Kito.

"Yes."

"Then we can do a **file transfer.** *I will come over and help you set up your computer. Then my computer can call your computer and give you the file."*

---

filename Every file has a name. A file's name is called its *filename*. Filenames on the PC and the Mac are very different.

How do I name files on a Mac? On the Mac, files are organized into groups called folders. No two files in the same folder can have exactly the same name. Files on the Mac are very easy to name. You can name a file anything you want. You can use up to thirty-one letters, spaces, numbers, and symbols to name your file. The only symbol you cannot use is a colon (:). If you try to type a colon, your Mac replaces it with a dash (-). Sample filenames are shown below.

Book report on Charlotte's Web
List of kids coming to my party
Chores I have to do

How do I name files on a PC? On the PC, files are organized into groups called directories. No two files in the same directory can have exactly the same name. Filenames on the PC are a bit more complicated than on the Mac. Filenames on a PC are a bit like people names.

Most people have names with three parts: a first name, a middle name, and a last name. For example, my name is **Jami Lynne Borman**. Just like people names, filenames also have three parts. The first part can be as short as one letter or as long as eight letters. The first part usually describes what is in the file. Do you think that you could describe what is inside a file in just eight letters?

The second part of the filename is a period (.). We will come back to the second part in a moment. The third part of the filename is called the extension. The extension can be one, two, or three letters long. Or it can be no letters long. No letters long means that you don't have to use an extension when you name a file—depending on what kind of information is inside the file. But most extensions are three letters long.

Now back to the second part, the period. The period separates the first part of the filename from the extension. When the filename doesn't have an extension, you do not need to use the period.

Can a PC filename use numbers and symbols? Yes. The filename does not need to be made up only of letters. A filename can be made up of letters, numbers, and the symbols in the chart below. No spaces are allowed in PC filenames.

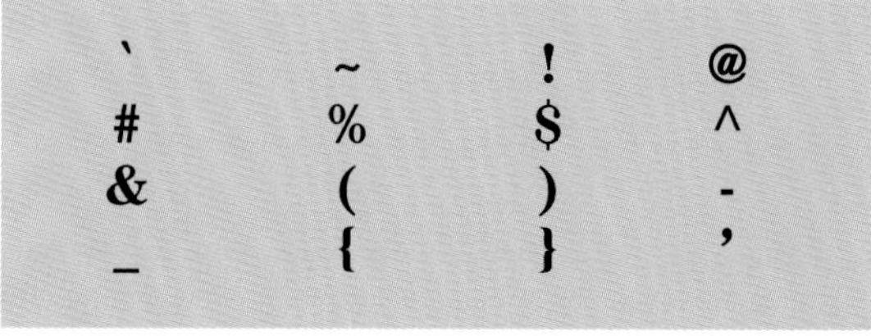

`	~	!	@
#	%	$	^
&	(	)	-
_	{	}	'

Look up *directory, extension, file,* and *folder.*

Sample PC Filenames			
Name	**Period**	**Extension**	**Filename**
XWING	.	EXE	XWING.EXE
007	.	COM	007.COM
$ALOWNCE	.		$ALOWNCE
MYCHORES	.	DO	MYCHORES.DO
DAD_NOTE	.		DAD_NOTE
READ	.	ME	READ.ME

filename extension Filenames on the PC have three parts. The extension is the last part of the filename. Look up *extension.*

Finder The *Finder* is the program that automatically starts each time you turn on your Macintosh. You may not even think of the Finder as a program because it is always ready and waiting for you.

What does the Finder do? The Finder manages your desktop and takes care of your computer's housekeeping chores. It lets you name, copy, open, close, and move around files and folders. The Finder is also the program that formats, erases, and ejects your diskettes. The Finder is a very important system program—and you can't use your Macintosh without it. Look up *desktop, file, folder,* and *systems program.*

fixed-space font If you look at the text in some of your books (including this one) you will see that different letters take up different amounts of space on a line. An "i" for example, takes up less space on the line than an "m."

Willows must whisper

In a *fixed-space font,* each letter takes the same amount of space on the line. When a letter such as "i" is too narrow to fill the space, there is just a gap between the narrow letter and the letter that is next to it. In the example above, see how there is lots of space next to the "i" and "l" and how the "m" and "w" looks squished. Another name for a fixed-space font is "mono-spaced font." Look up *font* and *proportionally spaced font.*

flight simulator A *flight simulator* is a type of computer game where you are the pilot of an aircraft. Some flight simulators allow you to fly missions, have dogfights (plane-to-plane combat) with other players, and bomb enemy targets. Other flight simulators are designed to give you the feeling and illusion of flying—they let you select an aircraft, take off, land, and view the surrounding scenery. Kids and adults agree that flight simulators are cool.

floppy disk *Floppy disk* is another name for a diskette. Look up *diskette.*

floppy drive *Floppy drive* is another name for a diskette drive. Look up *diskette drive.*

flower key The *flower key* is the key on your keyboard with the ⌘ symbol. The technical name for this key is command key. The command key is sometimes called the flower key, butterfly key, or propeller key because many people think that the symbol on the key looks like a flower, butterfly, or propeller.

The command key can be used in many programs to give an alternate (or different) meaning to another key. To use the command key, you hold it down while you press another key. Look up *command key.*

flush left *Flush left* is a phrase that describes how the left-hand side of a paragraph is formatted. When the text is flush left, the left-hand side of the paragraph forms a straight line. Every line in the paragraph begins at the same place on the page. Another term for flush left is left justified. Look up *flush right, full justification, ragged left,* and *ragged right.*

This is an example of text that is flush left. The left-hand side of the paragraph forms a straight line, while the right-hand side of the paragraph does not.

flush right *Flush right* is a phrase that describes how the right-hand side of a paragraph is formatted. When the text is flush right, the right-hand side of the paragraph forms a straight line. Every line in the paragraph ends at the same place on the page. Another term for flush right is right justified. Look up *flush left, full justification, ragged left,* and *ragged right.*

This is an example of text that is flush right. The right-hand side of the paragraph forms a straight line, while the left-hand side of the paragraph does not.

folder Does your teacher keep your papers, tests, and reports in a *folder*? If so, your teacher probably has a separate folder for you and each of the other kids in your class. Your Mac organizes information into folders too. Every folder is a directory. A folder that is inside another folder is a subdirectory.

What can I put in a folder? Each software program on your Mac has a separate folder. Each folder can hold as many computer files as you want. Each folder can also hold other folders.

How do I put a file or folder in a folder? To move a file or folder into another folder, just click on the file or folder to select it. Then drag it to whatever folder you want.

How do I know what is in a folder? To see what is inside a folder, double-click on it. The folder will open up and show you the files and other folders that are inside it. Look up *desktop, directory, double-click, drag,* and *subdirectory.*

font When you read a magazine, the ads, articles, and illustrations use different sizes and styles of text. A *font* is an alphabet that has the same size and style for each letter. Below are some examples of different fonts.

Benguiat Bold 14 pt.
Black Chancery 14 pt.
Dom Casual 14 pt.
Kaufmann 14 pt.
Mariage 14 pt.
Snell Roundhand 14 pt.

All fonts include all the letters of the alphabet. Most fonts also include the numbers from 0–9 and a variety of popular symbols. There are three basic things that separate one font from another: style, size, and weight. Look up *font style, font size,* and *font weight.*

font cartridge Did you ever play on a Sega Genesis or Super Nintendo video game system? Those systems use plug and play game cartridges. A game cartridge is a small, plastic container that contains a game written on a computer chip. When you want to play a game, you just plug the game's cartridge into a slot in the game system.

Since a game cartridge contains a game, what do you think a *font cartridge* contains? Fonts, of course! Most font cartridges contain many different fonts that can be used with a printer. The font cartridge is plugged into a slot in the printer just as a game cartridge is plugged into a slot in the game system. The fonts on the cartridge are called cartridge fonts.

Not all printers can use font cartridges. There are also different types of font cartridges that are made for the different types of printers. Just as you cannot use a Sega cartridge in a Nintendo system, you cannot use a font cartridge that was made for one type of printer in every other type of printer. Before you or your parents buy a font cartridge for your printer, be sure to look in the manual that came with your printer to see what kind of font cartridges your printer can use.

What if my printer can't use font cartridges? If your printer cannot use font cartridges it may be able to use soft fonts. Soft fonts must be downloaded (sent) from your hard disk to your printer's memory before they can be used. There are many more soft fonts to choose from than font cartridges, but soft fonts are more difficult to use. Look up *font.*

font size *Font size* is actually a measurement of font height (since fonts are not typically measured from side-to-side). When measuring the font size, you need to measure more than the height of just one letter. You must measure from the top of the tallest ascender to the bottom of lowest descender.

Ascenders are the letters that are taller than a lower case "x." These include the letters b, d, f, h, k, l, and t. Descenders are the letters that reach below the bottom of the line. These include the letters g, j, p, q, and y.

Font size is measured in points. A single point is very small. It is roughly 1/72 of an inch. That means that a 72-point font is one inch tall. One inch may not sound like a lot, but if you measure the text in some of your books, you'll find that there is very little text as tall as one inch. The text in most reading books is 10–12 points in size. Look up *ascender*, *descender*, and *font*.

The illustration below shows you some of the different point sizes that are used in books, magazines, and newspapers.

6 point
8 point
10 point
12 point
18 point
24 point
36 point
48 point
72 point

font style *Font style* is what makes one font look different than another; it is the design that makes the font unique. Some font styles are called serif. That means that the letters have little feet or edges on some ends. Other fonts are called sans serif. Sans is a French word that means without. Sans serif means without serifs—or without the little feet. Below are some samples of serif and sans serif letters. Look up *font*.

Can you tell which fonts are serif and which are sans serif? *Answers appear in the Answer Section in the back of the book.*

1. Cooper Black
2. Cheltenham
3. Tekton Bold
4. Chicago
5. Mariage
6. Ingenius
7. Kaufmann
8. CopperPlate
9. Impress
10. Garamond Ultra

font weight How much do you weigh? Do you have good posture? These are features that indicate whether you are thin, fat, stand up straight, slouch over, or are basically somewhere in the middle. *Font weight* indicates similar features about a font.

Font weight indicates whether a font is normal, thin, or fat and whether it stands up straight or slouches over. However, thin, fat, and slouching are words that are usually used to describe people—not fonts. When a font is fat (or dark) it may be called bold, demi, heavy, or black. When a font is thin, it may be called narrow or light. When a font is normal, it is called medium. When you are selecting a font and no font weight is given, you can assume that the font has a medium weight.

Fonts don't exactly have posture, so they can't slouch over—but they do lean. Fonts always lean to right, which is the direction you read. When a font is leaning, it may be called italic, oblique, or slanted. Fat and leaning fonts are used to draw your attention to a specific word, phrase, or heading. Below are some examples of fat and leaning fonts. You can find other examples by looking through this book. Look up *font*.

Century Light
Century Light Italic
Century Medium
Century Medium Italic
Century Bold
Century Bold Italic
Century Black
Century Black Italic

footer A *footer* is a line of text that appears at the bottom of each page in a book, magazine, manual, or other document. The footer may show the name of a book, the name of a chapter, the date of a magazine issue, the version of your software, and/or a page number. Sometimes the same footer appears at the bottom of every page. Sometimes a different footer appears on the even pages than on the odd pages.

Is a footnote a footer? If you use footnotes in your reports, you may be wondering if a footnote is a footer. It isn't. A footer repeats the same text over and over again across many pages. Even though you may have footnotes on many pages of your report, the footnotes themselves vary. Because the footnote text varies from one page to the next, it cannot be considered a footer. Look up *header*.

footprint Did you ever look at your *footprint* in the snow or sand? Your computer also has a footprint, although it isn't shaped at all like yours. A computer footprint is the amount of space that your computer takes up on your desk or table. The footprint refers to the amount of space the CPU takes, not the amount of space needed for your keyboard, mouse, monitor, and other components and accessories. Look up *accessory, CPU,* and *component.*

format Before you can use a new diskette for the first time, you must *format* it. Both 3½- and 5¼-inch diskettes must be formatted before they can be used. Formatting prepares the diskette for storing computer files.

PCs and Macs format diskettes differently. Before a 3½-inch disk has been formatted, it can be used in either a PC or a

Mac. But once formatted, the diskette must be used on the same type of machine that formatted it. In other words, a diskette that was formatted on a PC must be used on a PC, while a diskette that was formatted on a Mac must be used on a Mac. The 5¼-inch disks are only used on PCs.

Do all diskettes need to be formatted? Yes, but you can buy diskettes that are preformatted, which means the diskettes have already been formatted by the manufacturer. When you buy preformatted diskettes you do not have to format them again. Although preformatted diskettes are more convenient to use than formatting the diskettes yourself, preformatted diskettes are more expensive to purchase.

Does a hard disk have to be formatted? Yes. Every hard disk has to be formatted before it can be used. Your hard disk was probably formatted by the company who made your computer or at the store where you bought your computer.

> Do not format the hard disk on your family computer or you will erase every software program, file, and scrap of information that exists on your hard disk.

How do I know if a diskette for my PC has been formatted? The way you can tell varies, depending on whether you are using DOS or Microsoft Windows. In Microsoft Windows,

1. Select the File Manager icon.
2. Click on the icon for the drive that has the diskette. If the diskette is formatted it will show you all the files on the diskette. If not, a dialog box tells you that the diskette is not formatted. You are then asked whether or not you want to format the diskette.
3. Select [Yes] to format the diskette.

In DOS, you can tell whether or not a diskette is formatted by placing it in the diskette drive and typing DIR at the DOS prompt. If the diskette is formatted it will show you all the files on the diskette, or an empty file list if there are no files.

If the diskette is not formatted, your computer displays the following message on your screen.

```
General failure reading drive A (or B)
Abort, Retry, Fail?
```

When you get the message above,

1. Select the fail option by pressing [F] for fail. Your computer will respond with the following message.

```
Current drive is no longer valid=
```

2. To return to your C drive, type

   C: [Enter]

3. Use the FORMAT command to format the diskette.

How do I know if a diskette for my Mac has been formatted? When you place a diskette in the drive, your Mac automatically checks to see whether or not the diskette has been formatted. If it has been formatted, an icon for the diskette appears on your desktop. When the icon appears, your diskette has been "mounted."

If the diskette has not been formatted, a dialog box tells you that the diskette is not readable. You are then asked whether or not you want to initialize the diskette. (To initialize a diskette is the same as formatting it.) Click the button if you want to format the diskette. Look up *desktop, dialog box,* and *FORMAT command.*

FORMAT command All diskettes must be formatted before they can be used. The *FORMAT command* is a DOS command that can be used to format your new diskettes.

How do I use the FORMAT command?

1. Place the diskette you want to format in the diskette drive.
2. Type the FORMAT command, followed by the letter of the diskette drive. For example, to format the diskette in drive A, type the following command.

```
FORMAT A: [Enter]
```

Your computer responds:

```
Insert new diskette for drive A:
and press ENTER when ready...
```

3. Press [Enter]. Your computer shows you how much of the diskette has been formatted as it goes through the format. It takes about two minutes to format a high-density diskette. When your computer has completed the format, it displays the following message on your screen.

```
Volume label (11 characters,
ENTER for none)?
```

This message means you can give your diskette a name of up to eleven characters. The "volume label" is a term that means diskette name.

4. Press [Enter]. Your computer then displays some information about the diskette and asks you if you would like to format another diskette.
   a. To format another diskette, press [Y] [Enter]. Then follow these instructions again from step #1.
   b. If you do not want to format another diskette press [N] [Enter].

Look up *character, DIR command, diskette, DOS command,* and *format.*

forward slash (/) A *forward slash* is a symbol on your keyboard. The forward slash is often confused with the backslash.

/ Forward slash
\ Backslash

The forward slash points forward toward the rest of the sentence. Forward slashes are used in dates such as 10/31/96.

full justification *Full justification* is a phrase that describes how a paragraph is formatted. When text is fully justified, the paragraph is both flush left and flush right. In other words the left-hand and right-hand sides of the paragraph each form a straight line. Most newspapers print their paragraphs with full justification.

When a paragraph has full justification, your software adds spaces between the words so that the left and right-hand margins are straight. Since the spaces between the words are not even, a paragraph with full justification can be more difficult to read than a paragraph that is flush left. Look up *flush left.*

This is an example of text that has full justification. Both the left-hand side of the paragraph and the right-hand side of the paragraph form a straight line. Notice that in order to get a straight line on both the right and left sides of the paragraph, the spacing between words is not even.

function key The keys on your keyboard that begin with the letter *F* and are followed by a number (such as F1) are called *function keys.* Function keys get their name from the fact that software programs use those keys to perform a special purpose or function. For example, many programs use F1 as the help key. In those programs, pressing F1 displays a screen of help about the game or software program you are using.

Some games (and many application programs) give each function key four different jobs. One job is performed when you press the function key. Different jobs are performed when you hold down Shift, Alt, or Ctrl before pressing the function key.

Can you figure out the function of each key? Each function key or function key combination in the puzzle below stands for a special word. Use the chart below to figure out the meaning of each keypress. *The answer is in the Answer Section in the back of the book.*

F1 : Alt-F5 Ctrl-F2 F7 Alt-F8 Shift-F7 Ctrl-F4 Shift-F3 Alt-F1 ?

Shift-F8 : F9 Ctrl-F6 Shift-F5 F3 Ctrl-F9 .

	F1	F2	F3	F4	F5	F6	F7	F8	F9
	Question	can't	credit	New York	road	soup	you	fishing	Take
Alt	charging	said	bills	other	How	waiter	me	keep	but
Ctrl	clucked	can	drat	elephant	job	away	I	chicken	cards
Shift	giraffe	fly	from	side	his	please	an	Answer	can't

garbage Yuuuck! Just like a heap of left-over food that you can't identify, computer *garbage* is filled with strange text and symbols that don't make any sense. When your computer or software crashes, or you are using your computer to talk to another computer and you get disconnected, your screen can become filled with letters, symbols, and lines that don't make any sense. That's garbage.

How do I get rid of the garbage? You can usually get rid of the garbage on your screen by exiting whatever program you are using. You can always get rid of the garbage by rebooting your computer.

Look up *reboot.*

garbage-in, garbage-out *Garbage-in, garbage-out* is a computer expression that means that the information you get out of a computer is only as good as the information you put into a computer. The acronym for garbage-in, garbage-out is GIGO.

Suppose you wanted to keep a list of all the kids in your class, along with their names, addresses, and phone numbers. You begin to type the list and realize that you don't know all their last names, addresses, and phone numbers. The computer cannot fill in the missing information. If the information you give the computer is no good (garbage) then you are going to get garbage back when you ask the computer for information.

Gb *Gb* is an abbreviation for gigabyte. A gigabyte is the amount of space that it takes to store approximately 1,000,000,000 (one billion) letters, numbers, and symbols on your hard disk.

Gb is not a term that is spoken out loud. It is a term that is used when writing about gigabytes. For example, the computer has a 100Gb drive. Look up *byte, gigabyte,* and *megabyte.*

general failure error Sometimes your PC may display the *general failure error* shown below when you try to use a diskette.

```
General failure reading drive A (or B)
Abort, Retry, Fail?
```

There are two common problems that can cause this error to appear.

- The diskette is defective. If you think that the diskette is defective, have your mom or dad try to help you get any information that you can get off the diskette. Then throw the diskette away. Do not use an old diskette that has given you a general failure error.
- The diskette is not formatted. If you have a new diskette that has never been formatted, you will get a general failure error when you try to use the diskette. Use the FORMAT command to format the diskette.

How do I get back to my C drive after getting a general failure error? You can get back to your C drive by pressing F for fail. Your computer will respond with the following message.

```
Current drive is no longer valid=
```

Press C : Enter to return to your C drive. Look up *error message* and *FORMAT command.*

---

gig *Gig* (rhymes with "pig") is short for gigabyte, the amount of space that it takes to store approximately 1,000,000,000 (one billion) letters, numbers, and symbols on your hard disk.

Gig is not usually a term that is written. It is a term that is used when talking about gigabytes. For example, "At home we only have a 100 gig hard disk but at school we have a 250 gig drive." Look up *byte, gigabyte,* and *megabyte.*

---

gigabyte A *gigabyte* is a way of measuring space on your computer's hard disk. A gigabyte is the amount of space that it takes to store about 1,000,000,000 (one billion) letters, numbers, and symbols of information.

When you write gigabyte it is abbreviated "Gb." When you talk about gigabytes, you can call them gigs, for short. Look up *byte* and *storage.*

GIGO *GIGO* is an acronym for garbage-in, garbage-out. Look up *acronym* and *garbage-in, garbage-out.*

---

glare Is your computer near a window or a lamp? Did you ever see a reflection of the window or lamp in your computer screen that made it hard for you to see the screen? That reflection is called *glare.*

---

glitch A glitch is a temporary, unexplained problem that goes away on its own.

> *"Toby, did you see that flash on your computer screen?" asked Zane.*
>
> *"No. It was probably just a* **glitch**,*" replied Toby.*

---

graphic A *graphic* is a picture or illustration that you draw with a drawing program or buy from an art company. There are companies that sell artwork that you can use inside your greeting cards, pictures, reports, and other projects that you create on your computer. Some companies refer to their artwork as graphics, while others call it clip-art or electronic art. By any name it is still artwork that is available on diskettes and CD-ROMs.

Graphics come in many different types of file formats—such as BMP, CDR, EPS, Paint, PCX, PICT, TIFF, TIF, TGA, and WPG—to name only a few. Before you buy any graphics, make sure that you are buying them in a format that your paint or drawing program can use, otherwise you will have beautiful pictures that you will not be able to use in your project.

graphical user interface A *graphical user interface* lets you communicate with your computer by selecting and moving pictures (called icons) instead of typing commands. The acronym for graphical user interface is GUI (pronounced G—U—I or "gooey"). Look up *acronym* and *GUI.*

gray scale When you paint, you can get the color gray by mixing black and white paint together. Depending on how much black you use and how much white you use, you get different shades of gray. A *gray scale* includes all the shades of gray you can make. Most laser and inkjet printers cannot print more than five or six specific shades of gray. Look up *inkjet printer* and *laser printer.*

grid A *grid* is graph paper for your computer. Many drawing programs display a grid on the screen to make it easier for you to draw straight lines, squares, and other shapes. The grid does not print out with your drawing; it is only used to help you line things up on the screen.

group A *group* is a window that contains icons. You can organize your desktop by moving icons from one group to another. For example, you may want to put all your game icons in the same group. That way, when you look at the games group, all your game icons are in the same window. Look up *desktop, icon,* and *window.*

GUI *GUI* (pronounced G—U—I or "gooey") is an acronym for graphical user interface. The user interface is the part of a software program that allows you (the user) to work with the software. In every software program, there are actions that you take and selections that you make with the mouse or keyboard. Your keypresses and mouse clicks let you communicate with the software.

With GUI, you work with the software by selecting and moving pictures (little graphics or icons) rather than by typing words (as you do in DOS). Each software program on the computer has a little picture called an icon. To start a program, you just click on it with your mouse.

The Apple Macintosh was the first personal computer to use a graphical user interface. The most popular GUI on IBM-compatible computers is Microsoft Windows. Look up *acronym, icon, Macintosh, Microsoft Windows,* and *user interface.*

hack Did you ever see a scene in an adventure movie where the characters are trying to cut their way through a jungle by swinging machetes (very long, sharp knives) to cut through the bushes and underbrush that block their way? When they can't get through one part of the jungle growth, they try another area. These jungle adventurers are said to be hacking their way through the jungle. In computer terminology, *hack* has several different meanings.

(1) A *hack* is a computer program that solves a problem in an unusual or clever way.

(2) To *hack* at a computer program means to try to make the program work by trying a bunch of different things, rather than by planning out what you want the program to do and how you are going to approach that goal. Hacking at a computer program is one of the worst ways to work.

(3) To *hack* at a computer system means to try to get into a system, network, or online service without permission. This includes using someone else's log on ID, or by trying to guess at log on IDs and passwords until you find a combination that gets you into the system. Hacking a computer system is against federal law. If you hack a system you are committing a crime that can be punished with a jail sentence. Look up *ID, log on,* and *password.*

hacker A *hacker* is someone who tries to log on to a computer system, network, or online service using someone else's log on ID. A hacker may try to guess a log on ID and password for the system, or may try to break into a computer program by using a program that tries various log on ID and password

combinations. Hackers are committing a crime that can be punished with a jail sentence. Look up *ID, log on,* and *password.*

hand scanner A *hand scanner* is a scanner that is small enough to fit in your hand. Hand scanners can be used to scan small pictures or narrow columns of text. Look up *column* and *scanner.*

handle A *handle* is a fake name that you use for fun when you login to a BBS (bulletin board system). You can use any name you want, as long as it is not already being used by someone else. Look up *bulletin board system.*

> *"What* **handle** *do you use on the BBS?" asked Sharon.*
>
> *"Sam-the-Man," replied Samuel. "What do you use?"*
>
> *"Queen of Hearts," replied Sharon.*

Happy Mac The *Happy Mac* is the smiley face that greets you when you turn on your computer . The Happy Mac lets you know that your Mac has found the files it needs to start your computer. Look up *Sad Mac.*

hard copy Anything that has been printed on a printer that is connected to a computer is called a *hard copy.* For example, a printed copy of your history report is called a hard copy. Other terms for hard copy are output and printout.

hard disk A *hard disk* is a computer accessory that is used to hold lots of software programs and computer files. Depending on the size of your hard disk, it can hold from 10 to 9,000 times more information than can fit on a single floppy disk. A hard disk is also called a hard drive.

The inside of the hard disk has one or more round, metal platters called disks. The disks are where your data is kept. A part of the hard disk called the read/write head records the data onto the hard disk, and reads the data from the hard disk when you are ready to get it back.

The outside of the hard disk looks like a metal box that has been sealed. The hard disk is sealed to keep out dirt and dust that might damage the disk. The hard disk itself goes inside your computer. Many computers have a small light on the front that lights up when the disk is being used.

When you go to buy software, it is important to know if you have enough free space on your hard disk to store the new software program. If you don't have enough free space, you can choose not to buy the software, or you can remove enough files from your hard disk to make room for the new software. The system requirements on the outside of the software package will tell you how much free space you need on your hard disk to install the software.

What do I need to know when I buy a new hard disk? When you go shopping for a hard disk, there are two basic specifications to examine. The first is size. No matter how big a disk you get you will always run out of space. Over the years, I have gone from a 20 to 40 to 80 to 400 to 1,400 megabyte hard disk and have always run out of space within a year. It will probably take you and your family longer than a year to run out of space, but it will happen. The rule of thumb is, buy as big a drive as your budget will allow.

The second thing you need to look at when you buy a hard disk is access speed. The access speed of a hard disk is the amount of time it takes your computer to find information. The lower the access speed, the faster the hard disk can find the information. A good hard drive will have an access speed no longer than 15 ms (milliseconds).

Is a 3½-inch diskette a hard disk? No. Even though a 3½-inch diskette is not flexible or floppy like a 5¼-inch diskette, it is not a hard disk and should never be called a hard disk. Look up *access speed, accessory,* and *megabyte.*

hard drive *Hard drive* is another name for a "hard disk," a computer accessory that is used to hold lots of software programs and computer files. Look up *hard disk.*

hardware Your computer *hardware* is your computer equipment such as your CPU, hard disk, monitor, printer, CD-ROM drive, sound card, and so on. For the most part, anything that is not a diskette or software is considered hardware. Look up *software.*

Do you know your hardware from your software? Ten items are listed below. Which are **hardware** and which are **software**? *Answers appear in the Answer Section in the back of the book.*

1. Monitor.
2. Fonts.
3. Microsoft Windows.
4. Printer.
5. Disk First Aid.
6. Operating System.
7. CD-ROM.
8. Hard disk.
9. Modem.
10. Diskette.

header A *header* is a line of text that appears at the top of each page in a book, magazine, manual, or other document. The header may show the name of a book, the name of a chapter, the date of a magazine issue, the version of your software, and/or a page number. Sometimes the same header appears at the top of every page. Sometimes different headers appear on the even pages than on the odd pages.

Look up *footer*.

HELP command The *HELP command* is a DOS command that you can use when you need information about how to use the other DOS commands. Since DOS version 5.0 was the first version of DOS to have the HELP command, your computer needs to have DOS 5.0 or higher in order to use the HELP command. You can check which version of DOS is on your computer by using the VER command.

When you use HELP to get help on a DOS command, you are shown one or more screens of information about the command, such as what it's used for, how to use it, what options can be used with the command, and examples. HELP is really handy when you want to get quick information while you are sitting at your computer.

How do I use the HELP command? To get help about a specific DOS command, type the word HELP, a space, and the command that you want help with.

```
HELP CD [Enter]
```

If you want HELP, but are not sure what command to ask about, just type *HELP*.

```
HELP [Enter]
```

Look up *CD command, DOS command, DOS prompt, online help,* and *VER command.*

hidden file When you use the DOS command DIR, you will see all the files in a directory except the ones that are hidden. A programmer can hide certain files so that you cannot see them. Sometimes files are hidden so that you cannot accidentally erase them and cause great problems on your hard disk. Other times the *hidden files* are used to prevent you from making illegal copies of a software program and giving it to your friends.

Some utility programs like PC tools, Norton Utilities, and Microsoft Windows have features that allow you to view the hidden files on your hard disk. The DOS command named ATTRIBUTE can also be used to hide and unhide a file. See your DOS manual for detailed instructions on how use the ATTRIBUTE command to hide and unhide files. Look up *DIR command* and *DOS command*.

Can you find the hidden files? Several diskettes are hidden in the picture below. Can you find them all? *The answer appears in the Answer Section in the back of the book.*

high-density Diskettes come in two densities: double-density and *high-density*. The density indicates how close together information is placed on the diskette. High-density diskettes let you pack more information into the same amount of space as double-density diskettes.

The 5¼-inch double-density and high-density diskettes look exactly like each other. Sometimes the company that makes the diskette will put a label on the diskette to let you know whether it is a high-density diskette. But unless there is a label on the diskette, you cannot tell the difference.

The 3½-inch high-density diskette has two special markings so you can tell it from a double-density diskette. The high-density diskette

- Has the letters HD (for high density) in the upper, right-hand corner of the diskette.
- Has a hole in the bottom right-hand corner of the diskette.

How much information can fit on a high-density diskette? Even though the 5¼-inch diskette is bigger than a 3½-inch diskette, the 3½-inch can hold more information. The chart below shows you how much information each diskette size can hold. (Note: K = kilobytes, M = megabytes.)

Diskette Size		High-Density
3½	PC	1.44M (1440K)
	Mac	1.2M (1200K)
5¼ (PC only)		1.2M (1200K)

Look up *3½-inch diskette, 5¼-inch diskette, double-density, diskette, diskette drive, kilobyte,* and *megabyte.*

home computer Unlike most of the other computer terms in this book, *home computer* is not a technical term. Home computer is a term that was made up to sell computers to you and your family. There is no difference between a home computer and a personal computer or microcomputer. They are all different names for the same thing. Look up *microcomputer.*

Home key The Home *key* is a cursor movement key because many programs let you use it to move your cursor to the beginning of a line of text or to the top of your screen. Some game programs have special uses for the Home key. Check the instruction manual that came with your game program to see whether or not the Home key has a special purpose. Look up *cursor, cursor movement key,* and *text.*

horizontal scrolling When you have a page of text or a picture that does not all fit on your screen at one time, you can move the image from side to side so that you can see more of the picture or more of the text. Moving the picture from side to side is called *horizontal scrolling.*

To move the picture or text from side to side, you can use the ← and → keys or the horizontal scroll bar. The horizontal scroll bar is located at the bottom of your screen or window. Look up *scroll bar* and *vertical scrolling.*

host Have you ever been the host or hostess at a party? When you host a party, everyone comes to your house and you

need to make sure that each person gets something to eat and drink and is having a nice time. A *host* computer doesn't throw any parties, but it does have other computers come over to its place—at least by telephone.

Basically, a host computer is a computer that other computers call, either by telephone or through a network. If you call a bulletin board or an online service (such as America Online, CompuServe, GEnie, or Prodigy) the computer you are calling is the host computer.

If you have communications software and set up your computer to answer calls from other computers, then your computer is the host computer. Look up *bulletin board, communications software, network,* and *online service.*

hypertext *Hypertext* is a way of quickly moving from one place to another within a document. Hypertext is most often used in online help and computer versions of large reference manuals such as encyclopedias. For a document to have hypertext it must have been created that way—you cannot add hypertext to the help file or encyclopedia yourself.

How do I use hypertext? Hypertext is a way of jumping around from one place to another. Suppose for example you are reading about the Chesapeake Bay and the topic turns to fishing in the bay. Suppose the word "salmon" is colored and underlined to let you know it is a hypertext word. If you click on the word "salmon," you will be taken to another place in the encyclopedia that talks about salmon. Under the information about salmon, there may be other hypertext words that can take you to other places. Just like hyperspace in a video game, hypertext lets you go to a completely different area very quickly.

Look up *document* and *online help.*

I/O *I/O* is a symbol that represents input and output. It is pronounced by saying the two letters: I—O. Input is information that you put into the computer, such as a selection you make with the mouse or the keyboard. Output is something the computer sends back to you, such as a printout or a picture on your screen.

IBM *IBM* is an abbreviation for International Business Machines, Inc. one of the oldest and largest computer manufacturers. IBM was one of the first companies to make large, mainframe computers and continues to be the leader in mainframe computer technology.

In 1981, IBM introduced the IBM PC. Although it was not the first PC, it was very successful and helped to create the entire personal computer industry. The success and technical advancement of the personal computer is due in large part to IBM.

IBM still manufactures personal computers and continues to be very influential in the personal computer industry. However, they are no longer the main leader in personal computers that they were in the 1980s. Look up *mainframe.*

IBM-compatible A computer that was not made by IBM Corporation but will run all the software that will run on a personal computer made by IBM is called an *IBM-compatible* computer. An IBM-compatible computer is sometimes called a clone.

IBM-compatible computers are the most popular personal computers. More families own IBM and IBM-compatible computers than all other computers put together. Look up *clone* and *IBM.*

icon An *icon* is a small picture that stands for a diskette drive, file, directory, or software program. When you click on the icon with your mouse, you can begin the program or perform a special job (like copying files).

Icons are very small. Most are less than ½-inch tall and less than ½-inch wide. Microsoft Windows, OS/2, and the Macintosh all use icons to start software programs. When a computer or software program uses icons it is said to have a graphical user interface (GUI). Look below for some samples. Look up *GUI, Macintosh, Microsoft Windows,* and *OS/2.*

ID *ID* is an abbreviation for <u>id</u>entification. Your user ID is the name or number that a computer network, online service, or bulletin board system uses to identify you.

Look up *acronym* and *user ID.*

---

image *Image* is another word for the picture or screen of information that appears on your monitor.

---

inactive When a menu item in a software program is active, it may be selected. When a menu item is *inactive,* it may not be selected. When a menu item is inactive, it is displayed in a different color than the active menu items so that you know right away that it cannot be selected. Inactive menu items are usually displayed in gray, or are dimmer in color than active ones.

Why are menu items inactive? The programmer may make some menu items inactive at times when it doesn't make sense to use those menu items. For example, suppose you are using a new game for the first time. The "Save" option may be inactive until you actually start the game because it doesn't make sense to save a game you haven't played.

Look up *active, menu,* and *menu bar.*

---

information superhighway A superhighway is a very large road with many traffic lanes. It has faster speed limits than the local roads, does not have many (if any) traffic lights, and has several ramps to get cars, trucks, and buses on and off the road

quickly, easily, and safely. The *information superhighway* is also a high-speed road, but rather than being traveled by cars, trucks, and buses, what travels on the information superhighway is information.

"Information superhighway" is a fairly new buzzword. It means that many people are sending information and receiving information by modem or cable television all at the same time—creating a superhighway of information.

The information superhighway is not a single place that you can see or connect to with your computer. It is tens of thousands of places such as businesses, colleges, governments, homes, schools, and more—located all over the world. The information superhighway is a collection of computers, networks, online services, telephone lines, satellites, fiber optic cables, and all the equipment and programs that these computers use to communicate with each other—and with you!

Have you ever sent or received electronic mail on America Online, CompuServe, Delphi, GEnie, Internet, Prodigy, or another online service? If you have, then you've traveled on the information superhighway! Look up *buzzword, Internet, modem, network,* and *online service.*

information surfing When you go looking around cyberspace with no particular goal in mind, you are said to be *information surfing.* When you go information surfing on the Internet, you are said to be "surfing the net." Another name for information surfing is cybersurfing. Look up *cyberspace* and *Internet.*

initial caps *Initial caps* is a special way of capitalizing letters. Initial means first. Caps is short for capital letters. Initial caps means that the first letter of each word is capitalized. Initial caps are often used for headings in school reports, titles of books, names, and places. If you look through this book, you will see that initial caps are used for the headings in each section (such as the Answer Section).

inkjet printer An *inkjet printer* puts characters on your paper by spraying the paper with tiny dots of liquid ink. Because the inkjet printer does not strike the paper (or press against it) to make an image, it is called a nonimpact printer.

Inkjet printers can produce very high-quality printouts. Newer inkjet printers can produce printouts that are as high quality as the printouts from some laser printers. Inkjet printers are quickly becoming the choice for color printing since they can produce good-quality color printouts at a price that is less than a laser printer that only prints in black and white. Look up *laser printer* and *printout.*

input device An *input device* is a piece of computer equipment that lets you scan, select, or type information into your computer.

Which of these are input devices? Can you figure out which of these computer terms listed below are input devices? *Answers appear in the Answer Section in the back of the book.*

Monitor	Keyboard
Printer	Mouse
Joystick	Scanner
Sound Card	Game Software
Word-Processing Program	

install When you get a new game, you need to copy the game files from the diskettes that came in the package to your computer's hard disk. Copying the files to your hard disk is called *installing* the software.

When you get a new computer accessory, like a sound card, the accessory needs to be added to your computer setup. When your mom or dad connects the accessory to your computer, he or she is installing the accessory.

Some accessories need to be installed inside your computer. Be sure to remind your mom or dad to unplug all the computer equipment (computer, monitor, CD-ROM, and so on.) before opening the computer.

Never open a computer without your parent's permission. You and your computer can both get hurt when you don't know what you're doing and you go poking inside electronic equipment.

installation program An *installation program* is a program that automatically installs your new game or software on your computer's hard disk. Almost every software product includes an installation program.

An installation program from one software product cannot be used to install another software product. So you must use the installation program that comes with the new software to install that new software on your hard disk.

The installation program makes a directory for the new software, automatically changes your computer files as needed, and creates a new group or folder for the software (if necessary). Another name for an installation program is a setup program.

Look up *directory.*

"I can't wait to try out this new game on my PC. Want to play?" Dov asked Yaakov.

"Don't you need to wait for your dad to install it?" asked Yaakov.

"Nope, he's showed me how to install software before. It's easy. Most of the time you just put disk #1 in drive A and type INSTALL A: to run the **installation program**. *The game installs automatically," explained Dov.*

"That's it?" asked Yaakov.

"Almost. My dad said I should always read the instruction booklet that comes with the software—just in case," responded Dov.

instruction manual An *instruction manual* is a book that explains how to set up your computer or how to install and use your new software (such as how to play the game). An instruction manual comes with every new software program, computer, and computer accessory. The instruction manual is also called the manual, user manual, or documentation. Look up *accessory.*

integrated circuit A circuit is a collection of special parts and wires that connect to each other. For example, the circuit in a lamp includes the switch (to turn the lamp on and off), the socket (to hold the light bulb), and the wires that connect the switch and socket together. Integrate means to make something by bringing parts together. An *integrated circuit* is a lot of tiny parts and wires that are connected together to make one, very complicated, circuit.

An integrated circuit is made in layers, like an Oreo cookie. The bottom layer is a wafer. But rather than being a thick chocolate cookie wafer, it is a very thin wafer of a semiconductor material, such as silicon.

Then, instead of vanilla creme, a grid of tiny metal lines is carved into the top of the wafer. On top of that layer goes another layer of semiconductor material and another grid of metal lines. Several more layers of semiconductor material, each with metal lines, may be added.

When all the layers are finished, you have a small, flat integrated circuit in the shape of a square or rectangle. Inside the integrated circuit are transistors and other parts that were created by the wafer layers and connecting metal lines. An integrated circuit does not make a good snack, but it is much more useful to your computer equipment than an Oreo cookie. Look up *semiconductor* and *silicon chip.*

Intel Corporation *Intel Corporation* is the company that invented the first microprocessor chip—the brains of a personal computer. Intel manufactures the 80386, 80486, and Pentium microprocessors that are used in many personal computers. Look up *microprocessor.*

interface The *interface* or user interface is the part of a software program that allows you (the user) to interact with the software. In every software program there are selections that you make (like menu selections) or actions that you take (like shooting at space aliens). When you click the mouse or press a key on the keyboard, you are using the interface to communicate with your software program.

internal clock All computers today come with a built-in clock that keeps track of the date and time—even when your computer is turned off or unplugged. This built-in clock is called an *internal clock* because the clock is located inside your computer. Another name for the internal clock is the system clock.

Unlike a clock on the wall, your computer's internal clock does not have a face you can look at to get the time. However, many software programs have a feature that checks the computer's internal clock and displays the date and time for you on your screen. Look up *date, DATE command,* and *TIME command.*

internal font When something is internal it is located inside something else. Your internal organs (your heart, lungs, and kidneys) are located inside your body. *Internal fonts* (also called resident fonts) are located inside your printer. Look up *font* and *resident font.*

International Business Machines, Inc. *International Business Machines, Inc.* is the full name of the company that most people know as IBM, a leader in the computer industry. Look up *IBM.*

Internet A computer network is where many computers are connected to each other by wire and cables, or by telephone. The *Internet* is a network of networks. Many computer networks are all connected to

each other in what has become the world's largest network. The Internet is sometimes referred to as an information superhighway, although the term "information superhighway" does not only apply to the Internet.

The Internet began in the early 1970s and was called ARPAnet (Advanced Research Projects Agency Network). ARPAnet was controlled by the U.S. Department of Defense. It connected the computers in government agencies to the computers that were located in colleges and universities and was used primarily for military and computer science research.

As local area networks (LANs) began to develop, universities connected their LANs to ARPAnet, thus increasing the number of people and computers that could communicate with each other.

In the late 1980s, the National Science Foundation (NSF), another government agency, developed five supercomputer centers. NSF established high-speed networks (called NSFNET) so that colleges and universities could communicate with the supercomputer centers and with each other. The National Science Foundation encouraged the colleges and universities to allow anyone at the school to use the NSFNET. NSFNET made it possible for almost every college student and faculty member to communicate with computers at colleges and universities all over the country.

Over time, more and more networks connected to the collection of networks. Goverment agencies connected; high schools, junior highs, and elementary schools connected; businesses connected; and foreign governments, schools, and businesses connected. Collectively all these networks came to be known as the Internet.

As you can now see, the Internet is not a single place or computer network, but a connection of computers and networks all over the world!

What can I do on the Internet? You can use the Internet to send electronic mail to other kids around the world. You can find reference material to use in your school reports or get information about your hobbies, favorite musical groups, video games, pets, TV shows...practically anything. Some rock bands even use the Internet to communicate with their fans!

How can I "surf the net"? The Internet is like a huge wave of information. When you use the Internet to connect to other computers or to look for information, you are said to be "information surfing," or "surfing the net."

Does your family belong to America Online, CompuServe, Delphi, or another popular online service? If so then you are already connected to the Internet. All you need to do to check it out is to get your parents' permission and catch a wave. Look up *computer science, local area network, information superhighway,* and *network.*

italic *Italic* is a type of font characteristic. Unlike a normal font where the letters are straight up and down, the letters of an italic font are slanted. Look up *font* and *font weight.*

This is an example of a normal font
This is an example of an italic font

jargon *Jargon* is a collection of special words that are used to discuss a specific subject. Computer jargon is the collection of technical words that are used to discuss computers. Once you learn a few of the terms in this book, you too will be speaking computer jargon.

jewel case When you buy a software or music CD, it usually comes in a clear, plastic, square-shaped container. That container is called a *jewel case*. The jewel case has a raised, circular center that fits into the hole in the middle of your CD to keep the CD from moving around when you carry the CD from place to place. The jewel case helps to protect your CD from getting scratched or damaged. Look up *CD*.

joystick A *joystick* can be used to control the action in some computer games. The joystick has a lever that you move left, right, back, and forth, to move or point at various objects on the screen. The joystick also has one or more buttons that trigger actions such as firing a missile or dropping a bomb. Joysticks are very popular for air combat and flight simulator-type games. Look up *flight simulator* and *input device*.

justification *Justification* is a word that describes how a paragraph is formatted. When the paragraph has edges that form a straight line, the paragraph is said to be flush or fully justified. When the edges of the paragraph do not form a straight line, the paragraph is said to be ragged. Look up *flush left*, *flush right*, *ragged left*, and *ragged right*.

K The letter *"K"* is an abbreviation for kilobyte, the amount of space that it takes to store approximately 1,000 (one thousand) letters, numbers, and symbols on your hard disk, diskette, or in memory.

Unlike "M" for megabyte and "Gb" for gigabyte, "K" is a term that can be spoken or written. You can say, "The file is ten K." You can also write that the file is 10K.

Look up *byte* and *storage.*

keyboard The *keyboard* is the portion of your computer that looks like a typewriter. It has all the letters from A to Z, all the numbers from 0 to 9, and a variety of other special keys and symbols. The keyboard is used to make selections in your software programs, to navigate from place to place inside your computer, and to enter text. (A picture of the PC and Mac keyboards can be found on page 2.)

keyboard buffer Do you (or someone you know) type so fast that it takes a moment or two for the computer to catch up to what has been typed on the keyboard? The *keyboard buffer* is an area inside your computer that holds your extra keystrokes while the computer catches up to your selections. If you type too much at one time, the keyboard buffer gets full, and your computer will beep to let you know that you have to wait for it to catch up.

"Wow, your mom can type really fast!" Norma told her friend Beth.

"She works at a law firm and types on the computer all day," replied Beth.

"Why does your computer keep making that beeping sound?" asked Norma.

"My mom types so fast that the **keyboard buffer** *gets full. My mom says that the beep reminds her to slow down," replied Beth.*

keyboard cursor The *keyboard cursor* is a blinking horizonal line (_), blinking vertical line (|), or blinking box (▮) that shows you the place on your screen where your next keypress will appear. You can move the keyboard cursor by pressing an arrow key or one of the other cursor movement keys that are located on your keyboard. The keyboard cursor is particularly useful in keeping track of your place in a word-processing program. Without it, you would never know where your next keypress is going to appear.

Look up *blink rate, cursor movement keys*, and *keypress.*

keypress When you push a key on your keyboard, you have pressed the key. Pressing a key or a combination of keys (such as Alt–F3) is called a *keypress.* Another name for keypress is keystroke.

keystroke *Keystroke* is another name for keypress. Look up *keypress.*

kill To *kill* a file is to toss it into the trash (Macintosh) or delete it from your hard disk (PC). To kill a software program is to stop running it.

> *"Mom, I want to use the computer to finish my history report," called Blair to her mother, who was busy making dinner. "Do you want me to save your file?"*
>
> *"No," responded her mom, "just* **kill** *it."*

kilobyte A *kilobyte* is a way of measuring space—both the space on your diskette or hard disk, and the space in your computer's memory. A kilobyte is the amount of space that it takes to store about 1,000 characters of information. Kilobyte is abbreviated "K."

A lot of people confuse computer memory (how much information your computer can remember at one time) with computer storage (the space on your hard disk or diskette) since both are measured in K. Look up *byte, character, memory,* and *storage space.*

LAN *LAN* is an acronym for Local Area Network, a special type of network that is designed to connect a small number of users, all of whom are located near each other. Look up *acronym* and *local area network.*

landscape orientation When you take a piece of paper and turn it so it faces sideways, rather than up and down, you have *landscape orientation*. This is the direction that an artist turns the canvas when painting a landscape (an outdoors picture of an area—like mountains, valleys, and trees). Look up *orientation.*

When Shandel pressed a key to print the map to her house that she was including with her birthday party invitations, the computer displayed a message box that asked her whether she wanted the map printed in portrait or **landscape orientation**.

laptop computer A *laptop computer* is a very small computer system (screen, keyboard, and CPU) that can fit on your lap. The entire computer folds in half like a notebook. As a matter of fact, laptop computers are also called notebook computers.

Laptop computers are good for traveling since they come with a rechargeable battery that will run the computer for two or more hours without electricity. Some laptops also have a docking station that includes a sound card, speakers, and CD-ROM drive. Look up *CD-ROM drive, docking station,* and *sound card.*

laser printer A *laser printer* is a very fast printer that uses a laser beam to make printouts that look like they were printed at the print shop. The quality of printouts you get from a laser printer is measured in dots per inch (called dpi). Most laser printers print at 300 dpi or higher. The higher the dpi, the better the quality of your printout. Most laser printers come with several fonts that you can use in your documents and reports.

The speed of a laser printer is measured in pages per minute (called ppm). Slow laser printers—called personal laser printers—print at about 4 pages per minute. Medium speed laser printers print at 8 to 10 pages per minute. High speed laser printers print at 15 pages per minute and faster.

Laser printer ink is called toner. Toner comes in a long cartridge that slides into a bracket inside your laser printer. Depending on your printer, you can print

from 3,000–7,000 pages before having to change your toner cartridge.

Just like your computer, a laser printer also has memory. The more memory in your printer, the more graphics you can print on a single page and the more font changes you can make on a single page. Using graphics and fonts on the same page takes the most memory. If you only have one megabyte (or less) of memory in your printer, you may not be able to print a full page of charts and graphics from your drawing or paint program. Look up *dots-per-inch, font, megabyte, memory,* and *toner cartridge.*

launch To *launch* a software program is to start it. When you launch a spaceship, you send it off into space. When you launch a software program, you send it off to carry out a bunch of instructions.

Mark's grandfather teaches math at the high school. Mark likes to **launch** *the software program that his grandfather uses to figure out the students' final grades. When the software has finished running, it shows all the students grades on the screen. When a student fails the class, his or her name appears in red flashing letters—and then blows up with a loud "BOOM!"*

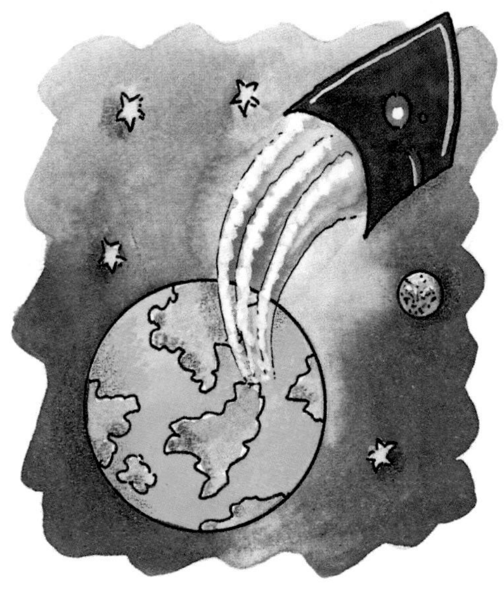

left arrow key The *left arrow key* (←) moves the keyboard cursor one space to the left. Look up *cursor movement keys* and *keyboard cursor.*

left justified *Left justified* is a phrase that describes how the left-hand side of a paragraph is formatted. Another term for left justified is flush left. When the text is left justified, the left-hand side of the paragraph forms a straight line. Every line in the paragraph begins at the same place on the page. Look up *ragged left.*

This is an example of text that is left justified. The left-hand side of the text forms a straight line while the right-hand side of the text is uneven.

line surge A *line surge* is a sudden jump in voltage on the electrical line coming into your house. Look up *surge.*

load When you run a software program, the program places one or more of its files into your computer's memory. This process is called *loading* the software. Each time you tell your computer you want to run a game or other program, you are actually instructing your computer to load a software program.

local area network When something is in the local area it is nearby. Your local library is the library that is nearest your home. Friends that are in the local area are friends that live in your neighborhood or are walking distance from your house. When computers are connected in a *local area network,* all the computers on the network are located near each other—such as the same classroom, hallway, or school building. The acronym for local area network is LAN.

The host computer is the computer that runs the network. The host computer on most LANs is just a personal computer that runs very fast and has one or more very large hard disks inside it. The hard disk in the host computer holds lots of different software programs. People who connect to the LAN can use the software that is located on the host computer in addition to the software on their own PCs. Look up *network.*

"Class, next week our classroom computer is getting connected to the school's **LAN**, *" announced Mr. Lawrence.*

"What will we be able to do with the **LAN** *that we can't do now?" asked Janie.*

"For one, you will each be given a **LAN** *login that includes a unique ID and password. Each of you will have access to the e-mail system where you can send messages to each other."*

"You mean we can send notes back and forth?" asked Nolan.

"Yes," replied Mr. Lawrence, "but the idea is to keep it class related. We will also be able to get announcements, communicate with other students and

teachers in other classrooms, and be able to use many more software programs than we have on the hard disk of our class PC. The **LAN** *offers some exciting possibilities."*

LocalTalk To hook your Mac to an AppleTalk network, it must have a special connector. The *LocalTalk* connector, made by Apple Computers, is one type of connector you can use. Look up *AppleTalk* and *local area network.*

lock up When you are using a software program and your keyboard stops responding to your keypresses, your mouse no longer makes selections in your software program, or your whole computer system freezes, your computer has *locked up.* When your computer locks up, the only thing you can do is reboot it. Look up *crash.*

log off When you are using your computer to talk to a network or online service, you will eventually need to let the online service or network know that you are ready to disconnect. The process of signing off a computer network or service is called *log off.*

Different computer services use different commands to log off. Popular commands for ending an online session include "bye," "exit," and "logoff." Although you can end the connection to another computer by turning off your computer, you have only logged off when you use a command to end your online session.

Logging off is the recommended way to end an online session. If you turn off your computer to end the session, the host computer (the one that your computer is connected to) may not realize that you have disconnected for a half hour or longer. If you have just ended a session with an online service that has an hourly fee (such as America Online, CompuServe, GEnie, Prodigy, or any other popular service), you can end up paying for the time it takes the host computer to realize you disconnected. Look up *host, log on, network,* and *online service.*

"Grace, are you still connected to Prodigy?" asked Dad.

"Yes, Dad," replied Grace.

"Well it's time to **log off**,*" said Dad.*

log on When you connect to a network or computer service, the host computer checks to see whether or not you are someone who is allowed to use the network or service. The host computer first checks to see if your ID is on the list of IDs that are allowed to use the network or service. Next the host computer checks to see whether the password you entered is the correct password for the ID.

You *log on* when you enter your user ID and password so that the host computer can check whether or not you are allowed to use the network or service. Look up *host, login, network, online service, password,* and *user ID.*

> *"Dad, please don't use the phone, I'm calling the network at school," said Kelsey as her father was about to make a phone call.*
>
> *"Did you* **log on** *yet?" asked Dad.*
>
> *"I just connected. I'm going to* **log on** *right now," replied Kelsey.*
>
> *"Alright, let me know when you're done. And don't stay on too long," warned Dad. "I need to make my call before 7:00."*

---

login **(1)** One meaning of *login* is the same as log on—to enter your user ID and password so that a host computer can check whether or not you are allowed to use a computer network or online service. Look up *log on.*
(2) *Login* is also the user ID and password that you use when you log on to a network or online service. Look up *ID, network, online service,* and *password.*

> *"I'm trying to log on to CompuServe and it won't let me in," complained Pete.*
>
> *"Maybe you made a mistake when you typed your user ID or password," replied Bob. "Do you want me to try for you?"*
>
> *"Sure," replied Pete.*
>
> *"What's your* **login***?" asked Bob.*
>
> *"My user ID is 74377,64," said Pete.*
>
> *"Okay, just type your password and you should get in," said Bob.*
>
> *"Thanks!" said Pete.*

---

lower case A *lower case* letter is a letter of the alphabet that is not capitalized. The lower case letters include a, b, c, d, e, f, g, h, i, j, k, l, m, n, o, p, q, r, s, t, u, v, w, x, y, and z. Look up *upper case.*

LPT A port on a computer is a place where data can go into the computer (from the mouse, modem, and keyboard) or out of the computer (to the printer). *LPT* is the name that is given to your computer's parallel ports. LPT is an abbreviation for line printer.

Parallel ports let several bits of data come into or go out of the computer at the same time. The first parallel port on your computer is called LPT1. If your computer has more than one parallel port, the others are called LPT2, LPT3, and so on. The LPT port is usually used to connect your computer to a printer. Look up *port.*

M *M* is an abbreviation for megabyte, the amount of space that it takes to store approximately 1,000,000 (one million) letters, numbers, and symbols on your hard disk, diskette, or in memory.

M is not a term that is spoken out loud. It is a term that is used when writing about megabytes. For example, the computer has 4M of RAM. Megabyte can also be abbreviated as "Mb." Look up *byte* and *megabyte.*

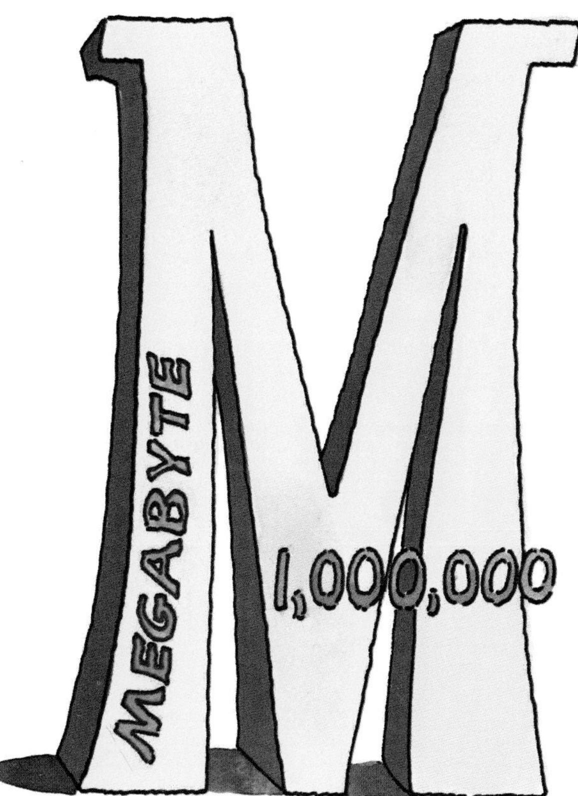

Mac *Mac* is short for Macintosh, a type of computer made by Apple Computers, Inc. Look up *Macintosh.*

Mac clone A *Mac clone* is a computer that runs all the software that will run on a Macintosh, but was not manufactured by Apple Computers (the company that makes the Macintosh). Look up *clone.*

Mac OS *Mac OS* is short for Macintosh Operating System. Introduced in 1984, Mac OS is the operating system used on all Macintosh computers and some Mac clones. Mac OS is the software that controls your computer's basic functions such as how information is stored on your hard disk.

Mac OS has a graphical user interface (GUI). That means that all the commands you need to give your computer and many of the activities you want to do can be done by clicking the mouse, making menu selections, and dragging icons from one place to another.

Mac OS always shows you how information is organized on your hard disk. For example, the icons and windows on your desktop are a picture of how directories and files are organized on your hard disk. When an icon is moved from one window to another, one or more files on your hard disk are moved from one directory to another. Look up *directory, directory structure, Macintosh,* and *operating system.*

Macintosh A *Macintosh* is any computer made by Apple Computers, Inc. that uses Mac OS, the Macintosh operating system. Since 1984, when the first Mac was sold, there have been over ninety different types of Macintosh computers. The Macintosh is often called "Mac" for short.

Macs have built-in sound and network abilities. They also have a feature called "plug and play." Plug and play means that when you buy a new accessory for your computer, you can easily connect it to your computer and use it. You do not need to spend time figuring out how to get your new accessory to correctly work with the other accessories on your computer.

Although Macintosh computers are not used by as many people as IBM and IBM-compatible computers, they are very popular in schools, homes, and many businesses. Look up *accessory, Mac OS,* and *network.*

mailbox Can you send and receive e-mail? If you can, then you already have an electronic *mailbox*! A mailbox is the place where you send and receive e-mail. You must have a modem or be connected to a network to use e-mail.

If you have e-mail, it is a good idea to check it at least once a week. The reason is that most networks and online services have a limit to how much mail you can store in your mailbox—and for how long—before it is automatically deleted. So like the mailbox at your home, your electronic mailbox can get full! When your mailbox gets full (preferably before it gets full), you should read all

the messages, print out the most important messages, and then delete all the messages you no longer need. Look up *electronic mail, modem, network,* and *online service.*

mainframe Did you ever have to wait for a program to finish (or a report to print) before you could start a new program? Imagine what it would be like if your computer could run many programs all at the same time, even while printing or sending e-mail to another computer.

A *mainframe* computer can run many programs all at the same time, and be used by hundreds of people all at the same time! Mainframes are used by government agencies, big companies, and colleges to process large amounts of information very quickly.

For example, the mainframe computer in a bank might process thousands of checks every night, store information about each check (who wrote it, how much it was for, etc.), and send this information to other banks.

Mainframe computers are very expensive (they cost over $100,000), very fast, and very large (the size of a refrigerator or bigger). Look up *microcomputer* and *minicomputer.*

make directory command Files on your computer are stored in directories. You can make a new directory by using a DOS command that tells your computer you want to make a directory. The *make directory command* is a DOS command called MD (or MKDIR). Look up *MD command.*

malfunction When you turn on your computer and it doesn't work, it has a *malfunction.* If your computer has a malfunction when you turn it on, try rebooting it. If the malfunction continues, tell your parents about it. Look up *reboot.*

Mb *Mb* is an abbreviation for megabyte, the amount of space that it takes to store approximately 1,000,000 (one million) letters, numbers, and symbols on your hard disk, diskette, or in memory.

Mb is not a term that is spoken out loud. It is a term that is used when writing about megabytes. For example, the computer has 4Mb of RAM. Megabyte can also be abbreviated as "M." Look up *byte* and *megabyte.*

MD command The *MD command* is a DOS command that means make directory. Files on your computer are stored in directories. You can create a new directory by using the MD command.

How do I use the MD command? You must tell your computer the name of the new directory and where you want the new directory to be located. The easiest way to make a directory is to go to the directory where you want the new directory to be added.

1. Use the CD command to move to the directory where you want to add the new directory.

   Suppose you wanted to move to your GAMES directory. As you can see from the diagram below, the GAMES directory already has one subdirectory called SPACE.

   To go to the directory called GAMES, you would type the following command at your DOS prompt.

   ```
   CD C:\GAMES Enter
   ```

2. Type the MD command followed by the name of the new directory you want to create. Suppose you wanted to make a directory for your Yahtzee game. To make a directory called YAHTZEE, you would type the following command at your DOS prompt.

   MD YAHTZEE Enter

   Once you created the YAHTZEE directory, your games directory structure would look like the diagram below. Look up *CD, directory, directory structure, DOS command,* and *DOS prompt.*

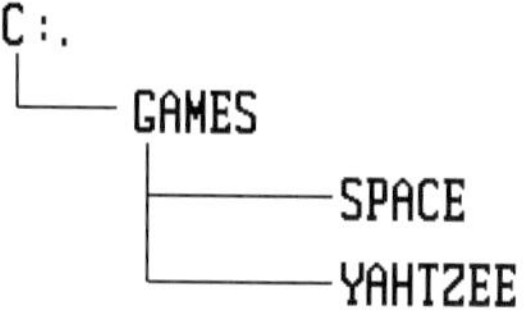

meg *Meg* is short for megabyte, the amount of space that it takes to store approximately 1,000,000 (one million) letters, numbers, and symbols on your hard disk, diskette, or in memory.

Meg is a term that is spoken out loud. It is not usually used when writing about megabytes. For example, you might say, "The computer at school has four megs of RAM." Look up *byte* and *megabyte.*

megabyte A *megabyte* is a way of measuring space—both the space on your diskette or hard disk, and the space in your computer's memory. A megabyte is the amount of space that it takes to store about 1,000,000 (one million) letters, numbers, and symbols.

When you write about megabyte it is abbreviated "M" or "Mb." When you talk about megabytes, you can call them megs, for short. Look up *byte, memory,* and *storage.*

megahertz The speed of a car is measured in miles per hour (mph). The speed of a computer is measured in *megahertz.* Megahertz is abbreviated "MHz." The speed of your computer is called its clock speed. When you play a strategy game (like chess) against the computer, a computer with a fast clock speed (such at 66 MHz) makes its next move much faster than a computer with a slow clock speed (such as 8 MHz). Look up *microprocessor.*

memory How good is your *memory*? Can you remember a lot of things at one time? If so, you have a good memory. The amount of information that your computer can remember at one time is called computer memory.

There are two basic types of computer memory: ROM and RAM. ROM (read-only memory) is memory that is permanently stored in your computer. ROM can only be used by your computer. RAM (random access memory) is what most people are referring to when they talk about computer memory. RAM is the memory in your computer that you use to run programs. RAM is temporary because all the information in the RAM is erased when you turn off your computer.

Computer memory is measured in kilobytes (K) or megabytes (Mb) depending on how much memory your computer has. Some computer programs, such as Windows or OS/2, let you use more than one program at a time. The more RAM memory your computer has, the more programs you can use at the same time.

Look up *kilobyte, megabyte,* and *storage.*

Test your memory. Do you think that you have a good **memory**? Look at the picture below for two minutes, then close the book. Write down as many **items** in the picture as you can remember. Then check the picture again. How did you do?

menu When you go to a restaurant with your parents, you get to select your meal from a list of choices on the *menu*. A menu in a software program is also a list of choices. When you select an item from the menu, the feature that you select is activated, or put into effect.

Just as the menu in a restaurant has different sections (such as Appetizers, Salads, Entrées, and Desserts) the menu in a software program also has various sections, such as File, Edit, Window, and Help.

The menu bar lists all the submenus that are available. Similar activities are placed in the same submenu. For example, your program may have a menu called "View" with options such as "Zoom In" and "Zoom Out" that let you make the view on your screen bigger and smaller.

There are basically two types of menus: drop-down menus and pull-down menus. To see what's on a drop-down menu you click the menu. To see what's on a pull-down menu you click and hold down the mouse button. Most programs on your PC use drop-down menus. Most programs on your Mac use pull-down menus. Look up *active, drop-down menu, menu bar, menu item*, and *pull-down menu*.

menu bar Many software programs display a wide, horizontal label across the top of the screen. The label is called the *menu bar* because it lists all the different menus that are available. When you select a menu, a list appears on your screen that shows

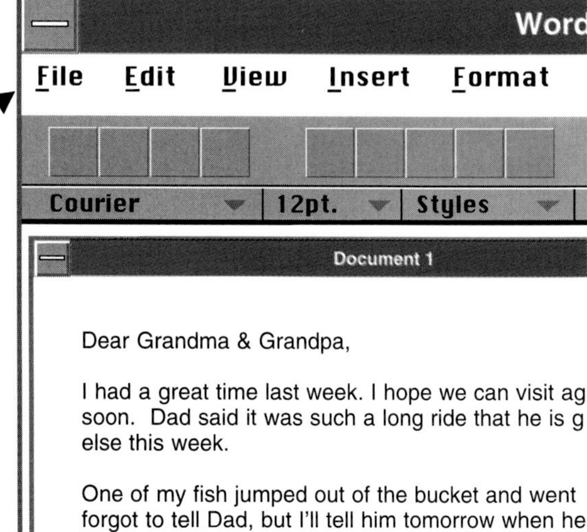

you all the options and features that are available in that menu. When you select an item from the menu, the feature or option that you select is activated, or put into effect. 👁 Look up *menu* and *menu item.*

menu item When you select a menu in a software program, you are shown a list of features and options. Each individual feature and option on the menu is called a *menu item.*

Sometimes the software will not let you select an item that you see on the menu. When you cannot select a menu item, the item is said to be inactive. 👁 Look up *active, inactive, menu,* and *menu bar.*

message A *message* is an electronic note, announcement, or warning. You and your friends can send each other messages on a bulletin board system or online service. You can also get messages from the software program on your computer. Your computer displays a message from your software program to let you know what it is doing or that there is something wrong. 👁 Look up *bulletin board system, error message,* and *online service.*

MHz *MHz* is an abbreviation for megahertz. 👁 Look up *megahertz* and *microprocessor.*

microcomputer *Microcomputer* is the more technical name for a personal computer, PC, or home computer.

When computers were first invented in the 1940s, a single computer took up an entire room. Today, the microcomputer you have at home has more computing power than the most powerful business computers of just a few years ago.

Like many computer terms, the meaning of microcomputer has changed over the years. In the 1970s and early 1980s, the term microcomputer meant any computer that had a microprocessor chip as its brain. Since only the small computers (like a personal computer) used microprocessors, there was no confusion. But today, microprocessors are used in computers of all kinds and sizes, so the term microcomputer now means personal computer. See page 9 for a brief history of the computer.

microprocessor The brain inside your computer is called a *microprocessor.* Micro means very small. A processor is something—or someone—that figures things out. Put the two words together: micro + processor = a small brain that figures things out.

What does a microprocessor look like? A microprocessor is a thin, square piece of plastic with a complex metal pattern running through it. The metal pattern determines how fast the brain works and how much information it can think about at one time. Microprocessors vary in size. Small ones are the size of a pencil eraser. Large ones are the size of a peanut butter cup.

Has anyone asked you what kind of computer you have? When you own a Mac and you are asked that question, you usually respond with "I own a Mac." The most popular microprocessors found in Macintosh computers are shown in the chart below.

Popular Macintosh Microprocessors (made by Motorola)	
PowerPC 601	One of the fastest and most powerful microprocessors for Macs. (Developed by Apple, IBM, and Motorola.)
68040	More powerful than the 68030, but less powerful than the PowerPC 601. One of the most popular microprocessors. A Mac with a 68040 is often called an 040 machine.
68030	More powerful than the 68020 but less powerful than the 68040. A Mac with a 68030 is often called an 030 machine.
68020	More powerful than the 68000 but less powerful than the 68030. The 68020 was only used in Macs for a short period of time. A Mac with a 68020 is often called an 020 machine.
68000	Used in the first Macintosh computers, the 68000 processes information very slowly and is now considered outdated.

When you own an IBM or IBM-compatible computer you are usually being asked, "Which microprocessor is inside your computer?" The most popular microprocessors for IBM and IBM-compatible computers are shown in the chart below.

Popular PC Microprocessors (made by Intel Corp.)	
Pentium	One of the fastest and most powerful microprocessors available for IBM-compatible computers.
486	More powerful than a 386 but less powerful then a Pentium, the 486 is short for 80486 microprocessor.
386	More powerful than a 286 but less powerful then a 486, the 386 is short for 80386 microprocessor. Many software programs (including many games) will not run on a computer less powerful than a 386.
286	The 286 is short for the 80286 microprocessor. A computer with a 286 is also called an AT compatible computer because the 286 was used in a computer made by IBM called PC/AT.
8088	The 8088 processes information very slowly (it has a slow clock speed) and is now considered outdated. A computer with an 8088 is also called an XT compatible computer because the 8088 was used in a computer made by IBM called PC/XT.

Microprocessors vary in how fast they process information. Their processing speed is called clock speed. The speed of a car is measured in miles per hour—the clock speed of a computer is measured in megahertz. Megahertz is abbreviated as MHz.

How well can you process information? Copy the following puzzle onto a sheet of paper. Write down as many words as you can find. *Our list of words appears in the Answer Section in the back of the book.*

T	I	G	R
N	A	E	S
L	O	P	K
S	H	U	N

Rules:

- All the letters in your word must connect. For example, S-L-A-P.
- The first letter must touch the second letter, the second letter must touch the third letter...and so on.
- The letters do not need to be in a straight line. (Look at S-L-A-P).
- Do not use the same letter twice (unless the letter appears twice in the puzzle).
- Words must be three or more letters.
- Words with capital letters such as names and places are not allowed.

Microsoft Corporation *Microsoft Corporation* is one of the largest and most influential computer software companies in the world. Microsoft was founded in 1975 by Bill Gates and Paul Allen. Microsoft is the company that makes MS-DOS, the most popular operating system for IBM and compatible personal computers. Many Microsoft products begin with the letters "MS" for Microsoft.

Microsoft Corporation also makes Windows and Bob (programs with a graphical user interface), Excel (a spreadsheet program), Word (a word-processing program), and Visual BASIC (a popular programming language). Microsoft also makes several games and educational programs such as Dinosaurs, Golf, Flight Simulator, Magic Schoolbus, Space Simulator, and others. Look up *DOS, GUI, Microsoft Windows, programming language, spreadsheet,* and *word processing.*

Microsoft Windows *Microsoft Windows* is an operating system with a graphical user interface (GUI). It was developed by Microsoft Corporation for use on IBM and IBM-compatible computers. Windows lets you use menus, buttons, and pictures to communicate with your computer. Windows lets you run many programs all at the same time—as long as you have enough memory in your computer to do so.

Most companies that make IBM-compatible computers now include Windows on every computer they sell. Because of this, there are now tens of millions of people that have Microsoft Windows on their PC. To find out if Windows is installed on your computer, type the following command at the DOS prompt. If Windows is installed on your computer, the program will start

```
WIN [Enter]
```

Is Microsoft Windows an operating system? The newer versions of Windows are operating systems but some of the older versions are not. When a version of Windows is an operating system it does not need DOS installed on the computer in order to run.

Windows version 3.1 (the version of Windows on many IBM-compatible computers) is not an operating system because it will only run on a computer that already has DOS installed. But Windows NT and Windows 95 have an operating system built into them. With NT or 95 installed on your computer, you do not need DOS. Look up *GUI* and *operating system.*

millimeter A *millimeter* is one thousandth (1/1000) of a meter. You can also think of a millimeter as one twenty-fifth (1/25) of an inch. If you were to take an inch and break it into 25 parts, a millimeter would be just one of those parts. Millimeters are often used to measure the dot pitch of your computer screen. Look up *dot pitch.*

millisecond A *millisecond* is one thousandth (1/1000) of a second. If you were to take a second and break it into a thousand parts, a millisecond would be just one of those parts. Milliseconds are often used to measure how fast a hard disk or CD-ROM drive can find information.

minicomputer A *minicomputer* is smaller than a mainframe computer, but bigger than a personal computer. A minicomputer can run many programs at the same time, and be used by many users at the same time—but cannot run as many programs or have as many users as a mainframe.

Minicomputers were very popular in colleges and businesses in the 1970s and 1980s. But today, personal computers and networks of personal computers have become more popular than minicomputers. Look up *mainframe* and *network*.

MIPS *MIPS* (rhymes with "flips") is an acronym that stands for million instructions per second. Computers process information so quickly that a computer's performance is often measured in how many millions of instructions it can process in one second. The more MIPS the computer can process, the faster and more powerful the computer. For example, a computer that runs at 5 MIPS is faster than a computer that processes information at 3 MIPS. Look up *acronym*.

MKDIR command The *MKDIR command* is a DOS command that means make directory. A shorter (and more popular) DOS command for making a directory is the MD command. Look up *MD command.*

mm *Mm* is an abbreviation for millimeter. Look up *millimeter.*

modem A *modem* is a computer accessory that lets your computer talk to other computers over the phone lines. In order to use a modem you must have communications software and someone—actually, a computer—to call. The term modem is an acronym for modulator/demodulator.

Many online services such as America Online and Prodigy provide you with special communications software to use with your modem. The communications software provided by the online service is used to call the specific online service, but cannot be used to call any other computer. Look up *acronym*, *communications software*, and *online.*

"Gayle, does your family belong to America Online?" asked Kip. "We just joined and it's a lot of fun."

"No, we don't have a **modem** *yet.*

My mom says we can buy one as soon as we finish paying for our new printer," replied Gayle.

"We don't have a printer yet. My dad says we have to build our computer system one accessory at a time," said Kip.

"Yeah, my mom said something like that too," replied Gayle.

monitor The *monitor* is the part of your computer system that looks like a television set. The picture on your monitor is made of many tiny little dots called pixels. A monitor is an essential part of any computer system. Look up *pixel* and *screen.*

monitor resolution *Monitor resolution* is how sharp and clear the picture is on your computer screen. Look up *dot pitch, resolution,* and *screen.*

monochrome Mono means one. Chroma means color. A *monochrome* monitor is a monitor that only displays text and pictures in one color. A black-and-white TV is monochrome since the only color it can display is white.

Doesn't black count as a color? When you use paint or crayons, you think of black as a color. When you color with light, as is done on a TV set or monitor, black is not considered a color—it is considered no color (the absence of color).

Why not call monochrome monitors black-and-white monitors? Monochrome monitors are not called black-and-white monitors because the one color on a monochrome monitor is not typically white. It is usually green or amber (orange-like). Rather than call the monitor a black-and-green or a black-and-amber monitor, it is called a monochrome monitor.

Even though a monochrome monitor has a green or amber color, it is not considered a color monitor. To be considered a color monitor, the monitor must be able to display many colors. Look up *monitor.*

mono-spaced font A *mono-spaced font* is a font whose letters each take up the same amount of space on the line. Another term for mono-spaced font is fixed-space font. Look up *fixed-space font* and *font.*

MORE command The *MORE command* is a DOS command that tells your computer, "Don't show me more information than can fit on my screen at one time."

MORE is used with other DOS commands like DIR (which shows you a directory) and TREE (which shows you a directory structure). DIR and TREE often have more than one screen of information to show you. When you do not use MORE, the information passes by on your screen so quickly that you don't have time to read it.

When you use the MORE command, your computer shows you one screen full of information and the word "MORE" at the bottom of your screen. When you want to see the next screen of information, just press Enter.

How do I use the MORE command? You use MORE by adding it to the end of your DIR or TREE command. You must separate MORE from the other command with the pipe (¦) symbol. Be sure to use the pipe (¦) symbol and not a colon (:) symbol or the command won't work. The pipe symbol is usually located above the backslash (\) character on your keyboard. Two examples using the MORE command are shown below. Look up *DOS command, DIR, directory structure, pipe,* and *TREE command.*

```
DIR ¦ MORE

TREE ¦ MORE
```

morph *Morph* is a special technique in which one thing is turned into another thing right before your eyes—like magic.

The term morph comes from the word metamorphosis—which means to change shape. You may have seen morphing used in movies, music videos, television commericals, and television shows. There are several software programs for personal computers that include a feature that lets you create your own morphs.

motherboard If you look inside a personal computer, you will see a circuit board that sits on the bottom of the case. This is the *motherboard*. The motherboard holds the microprocessor, the memory chips, and has the expansion slots that the expansion cards plug into. Look up *expansion card* and *expansion slot*.

mount Each time you insert a diskette into your diskette drive, your Mac *mounts* the diskette. To mount the diskette means that your computer automatically reads the diskette and displays an icon for it on your desktop.

When you are finished using the diskette, simply drag its icon to the trash can. Your diskette will eject automatically.

mouse A *mouse* is a small plastic box that is used to move the cursor around the screen. It is used to highlight text, draw pictures, and make selections from the menus in your software programs.

A mouse usually has one, two, or three flat buttons on its top, and is connected to the computer with a long cord. A plastic ball on the underside of the mouse lets it glide smoothly across your desk, although some mice glide more smoothly when used on a mouse pad.

Not all software programs are designed to work with a mouse. Those that are designed to work with a mouse are called mouse-driven programs. Some mouse-driven programs require that you use a mouse with the program. Other mouse-driven programs let you use the mouse or the keyboard.

Is the mouse easier to use than a keyboard? It depends on the type of software program you are using. If you are drawing a picture or selecting items from a menu, it is usually easier to use the mouse. But when you are using a word-processing program and already have your hands on the keyboard (which you need to do to type), making selections from the keyboard is usually easier—and definitely faster—than using the mouse.

Look up *mouse button* and *mouse pad.*

mouse button The one, two, or three flat buttons on the top of a mouse are called *mouse buttons*. Depending on which software program you are using, you can draw, make menu selections, and fire at the enemy by pressing one or more mouse buttons. There are three basis ways to use the mouse buttons.

- **Click.** A single press of a mouse button is called a click. You usually click the mouse when you want to select an item on your screen.
- **Double-click.** Pressing a mouse button two times is called a double-click. Double-clicking must be done quickly or the computer may think that you made two single clicks instead. You double-click the mouse when want to use a command or start a software program.
- **Drag.** Pressing a mouse button and holding it down while you move the mouse is called a drag. You drag the mouse when you want to move an item on your screen from one place to another.

Look up *mouse.*

mouse cursor The *mouse cursor* shows you where the mouse on your computer screen is pointing. Most programs use a pointer (↗) or cross hair (+) for the mouse cursor, although the programmers who make the software can give it any shape at all. For example, in the game 7th Guest, the mouse cursor is a skeleton hand! As you move your mouse on your desk, the mouse cursor on your screen moves in the same direction.

mouse pad A *mouse pad* is a small mat (usually made of plastic or foam rubber) that is designed to let your mouse glide smoothly so you can move your game char-

acter faster or solve a puzzle more quickly. Over time, the ball underneath the mouse will wear down and cause the mouse to move slower. A mouse pad can often be used to improve the speed of an old or worn out mouse.

mouse pointer *Mouse pointer* is another name for the mouse cursor. The mouse cursor is sometimes called a "pointer" because it is sometimes shown as a pointing arrow(↗). Look up *mouse cursor.*

mouse support When a software program has *mouse support,* a mouse (rather than a keyboard) can be used to play the game or make selections in the software. Look up *mouse.*

mouse-driven Games and other software programs that are designed to work with a mouse are called *mouse-driven* programs. Some games require that you use a mouse, but most mouse-driven games also allow you to use the keyboard—although the game play is not usually as good with the keyboard as it is with a mouse. Look up *mouse.*

MS When *MS* is in capital letters it is an abbreviation for Microsoft Corporation. Look up *Microsoft Corporation.*

ms When *ms* is in small letters it is an abbreviation for millisecond. Look up *millisecond.*

MS-DOS *MS-DOS* (DOS rhymes with "boss") is an acronym for Microsoft disk operating system. MS-DOS is the operating system used on most IBM-compatible computers. Look up *operating system.*

multi-user Multi means many (as in the words multiple, multiply, and multigrain). A user is someone like you who uses the computer. When a computer game is *multi-user,* more than one person can play the game at the same time. Some multi-user games must be played with more than one person—in other words, one person cannot play the game alone or against the computer; two or more real people are needed. Other multi-user games can be played with one person or more than one person.

Bruce was playing a new computer game that he got for his birthday. When his sister Debbie saw it, she watched for a while and then wanted to play.

"Can more than one person at a time play that game?" asked Debbie.

"Yeah, it's a **multi-user** *game," said Bruce. "Just wait 'til I get killed then I'll restart it so we both can play."*

multimedia *Multimedia* is any software program that uses a combination of text, pictures, sounds, video, and animation. Multi means more than one. Media is an artistic way of communicating—such as through writing, sound, and pictures. Multimedia is an acronym for multiple media.

Many game programs are examples of multimedia because they combine the use of sound, graphics, video, and animation. Look up *acronym*.

multiprocessing Imagine how fast you could do your homework if you had more than one brain! One brain could study for your big history test, another could practice your lines for a play, and a third could solve math problems. In a computer, *multiprocessing* is like having more than one brain at your command. Multiprocessing means that the computer has more than one microprocessor (or other processing unit). Each of the processing units can run different programs at the same time. Look up *multitasking*.

multitasking Can you rub your stomach and pat your head at the same time? If you can, then people may say you are coordinated because you can do two things at once. Doing two things at one time also means you are *multitasking.*

Computers such as the 386, 486, and Pentium are multitasking because they can run more than one program at a time and perform more than one task at a time—such as playing a game with you while printing out the homework you just finished.

In order for your computer to perform more than one task at a time, you must have special software (such as IBM's OS/2) that can use your computer's multitasking features. Look up *microprocessor, multiprocessing,* and *OS/2.*

nanosecond A *nanosecond* is a very short amount of time. It is precisely one billionth (1/1,000,000,000) of one second. If you were to take a second and break it into a billion parts, a nanosecond would be just one of those parts. Nanoseconds are often used to measure how fast a computer can use information. Nanosecond is abbreviated "ns."

natural language A *natural language* is a language that is spoken by people. The languages that are spoken by people are called natural languages because they evolved naturally, over time. Examples of natural languages include English, French, German, Spanish, and Russian. Computer languages are not natural languages because they were made up by scientists to talk to computers. Look up *artificial language.*

nested subdirectory All the games and software programs on your computer's hard disk are organized into groups called directories. A directory that is located inside another directory is called a subdirectory. When a subdirectory is located inside another subdirectory, it is called a *nested subdirectory.* Look up *directory.*

network In a computer *network*, many computers are connected to each other by wire and cables, or by telephone. Most networks also have one or more computers that host all the computing activity. These computers are called host computers or servers.

When your computer is connected to a network, your computer can use the software, hard disks, printers, CD-ROM drives, and other equipment that is connected to the network. For example, suppose you want to play a game that you don't have on your computer but you know is on the network computer. If you login to the network with your computer, you can play the game without ever leaving your computer or copying it to your hard disk.

Most networks have a type of software program called electronic mail (or e-mail) that lets you send messages, letters, pictures, stories, sounds, and video clips to other people on the network. Each person on the network has an electronic mailbox that can receive mail. When you log on to the network, you can check your mailbox and read your mail. The biggest difference between electronic mail and post office mail (sometimes called snail mail) is that e-mail doesn't require any postage, and is delivered much, much faster—instantaneously, in most cases. Look up *electronic mail, host, local area network, log off, log on, snail mail,* and *wide area network.*

non-system disk error Sometimes when you turn on your computer, it may display the *non-system disk error* message shown below.

```
Non-system disk or disk error
Replace and press any key when ready
```

There are two basic problems that can cause this error to appear.

- Someone left a diskette in drive A. Remove the diskette from drive A and press Enter.
- There is a serious problem with your hard disk (or you do not have a hard disk). Try turning your computer off and then on again. If you continue to get this message, tell your parents about it. Your computer may need to be repaired.

Look up *error message.*

not ready reading error Sometimes your computer will display the *not ready reading error* shown below.

```
Not ready reading drive A (or B)
Abort, Retry, Fail?
```

There are two basic problems that can cause this error to appear.

- You did not put a diskette in the disk drive. Put a diskette in the drive and press R to retry.
- You put a diskette in one drive but typed the letter for a different drive. Follow the steps below to escape from the error message and try again.

1. Press F for fail. Your computer may respond with the following message.

```
Current drive is no longer valid=
```

2. If you get the message above, press C : Enter to return to your C drive.
3. Try your command again, using the correct drive letter.

Look up *error message.*

notebook computer A *notebook computer* is a very small computer system (screen, keyboard, and CPU) that folds in half like a notebook. A notebook computer is also called a laptop computer. Look up *laptop computer.*

NS *NS* is an abbreviation for nanosecond. Look up *nanosecond.*

NuBus A computer card is an accessory that plugs into one of the slots inside your computer. *NuBus* (pronounced "new bus") is a type of connection that is found on some computer boards. To use a NuBus card, you must have a computer that has a NuBus expansion slot—not all Macs have NuBus expansion slots. If you do not know whether or not your Mac has a NuBus slot, check your manual. Look up *computer board* and *expansion slot.*

Num Lock key On most keyboards, the keys on the numeric keypad can be used for:

- Entering numbers.
- Moving your cursor.

The *Num Lock key* is the key on your keyboard that controls whether the keys on the numeric keypad work as numbers or cursor keys. Num Lock is short for "numbers locked."

When Num Lock is pressed (turned on), the numeric keypad may be used to type numbers. When Num Lock is pressed again (turned off), the numeric keypad may be used to move the cursor. Many keyboards have an indicator light that lets you know that Num Lock is on.

Can I move the cursor when Num Lock is on? Beside arrow keys on the numeric keypad, most keyboards have a separate set of arrow keys to move the cursor. When Num Lock is on, you can use the separate set of arrow keys.

PC If you hold down Shift before pressing a key on the numeric keypad, you can use the keypad to move your cursor instead of typing a number.

Can I type a number when Num Lock is off? Whether Num Lock is on or off, you can always use the number keys that are located above the rows of letter keys.

PC If you hold down Shift before pressing a key on the numeric keypad, you can use the keypad to type a number instead of moving your cursor.

numeric keypad The *numeric keypad* is the group of number keys on the right-hand side of your computer keyboard. Unlike the number keys that are located above the letters, the keys on the numeric keypad are laid out like a calculator.

Once you get used to the calculator layout, you'll find that you can enter numbers much faster from the keypad than you can from above the letter keys—particularly if you need to create a table or chart of numbers for a report or other project.

On many keyboards, the keys on the numeric keypad are also used to move the cursor from place to place. To use the numeric keypad to enter numbers (rather than to move the cursor) press Num Lock to turn on Num Lock (numbers locked). Look up *cursor* and *Num Lock key.*

numerical order *Numerical order* means in order by number. When you put a list of words in alphabetical order, you place them in order based on the letters of the alphabet, starting with "A." When you place a list of numbers in numerical order, you place them in order beginning with the lowest number. The smaller the number, the closer it is to the top of the list. The larger the number, the closer it is to the bottom of the list. Look up *ascending order, chronological order, descending order,* and *sort.*

Can you find the mistakes? Ms. Cassidy, Brian's math teacher, told all the students to make a list of all the prime numbers they could find and place those numbers in **numerical order**. (Prime numbers can only be evenly divided by themselves and the number one.) Brian wrote the following list of numbers. Brian made **four mistakes** in his list. Can you find them all? Can you think of other prime numbers? *Answers appear in the Answer Section in the back of the book.*

1, 3, 5, 7, 9, 11, 13, 19, 17, 23, 25, 27

obsolete Something that is *obsolete* is outdated. Have you ever used a dial telephone, an eight-track tape cartridge, a record player, or an outhouse? These items are all obsolete.

When an item is obsolete, it does not mean that no one uses it anymore, it just means that most people have replaced the item with a more modern one. For example, the dial phone has been replaced by the push button phone. Record players and eight-track tape cartridges have been replaced by CD players. Outhouses have been replaced by bathrooms and indoor plumbing.

OCR *OCR* is an abbreviation for optical character recognition, a combination of software and computer equipment that helps your computer read. Look up *optical character recognition.*

off line When your printer is *off line* it is not ready to print. Your printer may be off line because it is not turned on, not connected to your computer, or out of paper.

You can take your printer off line, on purpose, by pressing the ON LINE button. The ON LINE button is a toggle switch that takes your printer on line and off line. You may want to take your printer off line when you are adding paper or at other times when you want to temporarily stop your printer from printing. Look up *on line.*

off-line *Off-line* indicates that your computer has the ability to talk to another computer, but you are not talking to another computer right now. You are off-line when:

- Your computer can talk to another computer by modem, but you are not connected to another computer at the moment.
- Your computer is connected to a network, but you are not currently logged on to the network. Look up *log off, log on, network,* and *online.*

"Toby, are you and that computer on the phone again?" asked Mom, "I need to make a call."

"No, I'm **off-line** *Mom. Go ahead and use the phone."*

on line You are *on line* when your printer is turned on, connected to your computer, and ready to print. Look up *off line.*

"Jack, I need to print a report for work," said Dad. "Is your printer **on line***?"*

"No, it's off line," replied Jack, "but I'll turn it on for you."

online You are *online* when your computer is connected to another computer by modem or you are logged onto a network. Look up *log off, log on, network,* and *off-line.*

online help Some software programs have instructions that you can look at while you are using the software. These instructions are inside the software program itself. They are called *online help.*

You can get to the online help area of most software programs by selecting the Help menu. Most software programs on the PC also give you online help when you press F1.

online service An *online service* is a computer system that you can connect to with your computer by modem. You must be a member of the online service in order to use it. There is usually a monthly or hourly fee that you are charged to use the service. Some popular online services include America Online, CompuServe, Delphi, GEnie, and Prodigy.

If your family belongs to an online service, make sure you have your parents' permission before you use it.

Online services have lots of information, features, and files. For example, most online services have the following features.

- E-mail so that you can send messages to other people who use the service.
- News areas where you can read headlines, news stories, and sports information.
- Games that you can play against other people who use the service (some with prizes).
- Special interest groups (SIGS) where you can get and share information about your hobbies and interests.
- Shareware programs that you can download and use on your computer.

Many online services also let you send and receive e-mail on the Internet—which means that you can send e-mail to any other person in the entire world who has an Internet address! Look up *download, e-mail, Internet, modem, shareware,* and *SIG.*

operating system An *operating system* is the software program that controls what a computer does—it is the big boss of all the programs, much like the captain of a ship. Just as a ship's captain controls all the activities aboard ship, the operating system controls all the activities on the computer. The captain is responsible for keeping the ship's cargo organized and safe. The operating system manages disk storage; some operating systems even include virus protection software to help keep your files safe. Just like the captain follows the orders of the ship's owner; the operating system follows the orders of the computer's owner (namely you).

And, just as the captain of a ship does not run everything alone, an operating system is not a single controlling program, but a collection of programs (a crew) that work together to make things run smoothly. Examples of operating systems include MS-DOS from Microsoft, OS/2 from IBM, and Mac OS from Apple. Look up *Mac OS*, *MS-DOS*, and *OS/2*.

Operating System/2 The full name of the IBM operating system is known as *Operating System/2* or OS/2. Look up *OS/2*.

optical character reader An *optical character reader* is a piece of computer equipment that helps your computer read. The optical character reader (like a scanner or barcode reader) takes printed text (like the text in a book) and codes (like the bar codes on candy) and changes them into letters and numbers your computer can understand. Look up *barcode*, *barcode reader*, and *scanner*.

optical character recognition *Optical character recognition* is a combination of software and computer equipment that helps your computer read. Optical character recognition is usually just called by its abbreviation: OCR. OCR helps your computer read by letting it recognize each of the letters in the alphabet.

How can a computer read? A computer can read by looking at printed text (like the pages in a book) with a scanner. Just like a camera takes a picture of you, a scanner takes a picture of your text. The scanner is controlled by a software program that converts the picture of your printed text into letters that your computer can understand.

The OCR software looks at the text one character at a time and tries to match the character to a letter of the alphabet. The software does this for every character. When the software has matched all the letters in the text, it checks the words against an electronic dictionary, and makes a list of the words it can't find. Look up *character*, *scanner*, and *spell checker*.

optical scanner *Optical scanner* is the more technical word for scanner, a computer accessory that can photograph artwork, pictures, and text in a form that your computer can use for your reports, desktop publishing, multimedia, and other applications. Look up *scanner*.

optimizer An *optimizer* is a computer program that organizes the files on your hard disk so your computer can find programs and other information more quickly. When your hard disk is optimized, your computer seems to run faster, because it does not need to look all over your hard disk for information.

"Mark, is this the same computer you always had?" asked June.

"Yeah, why?" responded Mark.

"It seems like it's running faster than it used to."

"That's 'cause my mom optimized the hard disk last night," said Mark.

"What does that do?"

"My mom said the computer stores information all over the place on your hard disk—sort of like a junk drawer. The **optimizer** *program finds all the pieces that go together and puts them all in the same place on the hard disk," explained Mark.*

"Doesn't the computer lose the information if it's scattered all over the hard disk?" asked June.

"That's funny, I asked my mom the same question."

"What did she say?"

"She said the computer has some kind of map that shows it where everything is kept."

option key There are many more symbols that you can use in addition to the ones that are located above the number keys. The *option key* is used to create some of these symbols.

How do I use the option key? Do you know how to use the Shift key? You hold down Shift while you press another key. Option is used the same way. You hold down Option while you press another key.

What symbols can I create with Option? Symbols vary depending on which font you are using. However, the Mac has a tool that lets you see all the symbols you can create with any of the fonts that are installed on your computer.

1. Pull down the menu.
2. Select the Key Caps tool. A picture of your keyboard is shown on your screen.
3. Press Option and hold it.
4. All the letters in the picture of your keyboard change to characters. Press Option with another key to choose any of the symbols that you see on your screen.
5. To see more symbols that you can use, press Shift and Option at the same time. To use any of those symbols, hold down Shift and Option, then press the key you want.

Below are just a few of the symbols you can create with the option key.

£ ¥ ¢ ® Δ ß ¶ © Ω ∑ ™

orientation *Orientation* is a fancy word that describes which way your paper is facing. Since your paper is a rectangle, you can turn the paper two ways: up and down, or sideways. When you turn your paper up and down, you have portrait orientation. When you turn your paper sideways, you have landscape orientation.

orphan When you are using a word-processing program, sometimes part of a paragraph appears at the bottom of one page, and part of the paragraph appears at the top of the next page. When only one line from the paragraph can fit on the page, and the rest of the lines go to the next page, you have an *orphan.*

In society, an orphan is a child whose parents have died or gone on without the child. The orphan is left behind. In computers, the orphaned line is left behind while the other lines in the paragraph have gone on to the next page.

Many word-processing programs have a feature that allows you to turn off orphans. When you turn off orphans, the program makes the orphaned line go to the next page with the rest of the paragraph so the orphan line is not alone. Look up *widow.*

OS/2 *OS/2* stands for Operating System 2, an operating system for IBM and compatible computers. It was jointly developed by IBM and Microsoft, but is now sold by IBM. OS/2 is a multitasking operating system, which means that a computer that uses OS/2 can run two or more programs at the same time. This is different than DOS, which allows you to run only one program at a time.

Similar to Microsoft Windows and the Mac OS, OS/2 has a graphical user interface (GUI) that lets you interact with the software by selecting and moving pictures (little graphics or icons) rather than by typing words. OS/2 also has a feature that allows you to communicate with the computer by typing commands (if you prefer to work that way). Look up *GUI, Microsoft Windows, multitasking,* and *operating system.*

output **(1)** One meaning of *output* is result. Sometimes you may want to use the computer to solve a problem or give you an answer to a question. When you search for information on a computer, or run a program to get a solution to a problem, your answer is called the output.

(2) Another meaning of *output* is the printed paper that comes out of your printer. Other terms for this type of output are printout and hard copy.

output device An *output device* is a piece of computer equipment that can display information or print it out. Printers and monitors are output devices.

page down key The *page down key* moves your cursor to the bottom of the current screen, the top of the next screen, or the top of the next page. The page down key performs a different job depending on which software program you are using. Look up *cursor movement keys* and *keyboard cursor.*

page up key The *page up key* moves your cursor to the top of the current screen, the top of the previous screen, or the top of the previous page. The page up key performs a different job depending on which software program you are using. Look up *cursor movement keys* and *keyboard cursor.*

pages per minute *Pages per minute* is a measurement that indicates how many pages an inkjet or laser printer can print in one minute of time. If the printer can print eight pages of text in one minute, the printer is called an eight-page-per-minute printer. The abbreviation for pages per minute is "ppm."

Slow laser printers—sometimes called personal laser printers—can print about four pages per minute. Medium speed laser printers print about 8 to 10 pages per minute. High speed laser printers print at 15 pages per minute and faster.

It is important to know that when laser or inkjet printers are being measured for speed, they are being measured while printing text—not charts, pictures, or other graphics. It takes longer to print graphics than text. Look up *inkjet printer* and *laser printer.*

paint program A *paint program* is a software program that is designed for drawing pictures, greeting cards, advertisements, invitations, notices, illustrations for your school reports, and any other artistic type printout. Most paint programs come with lots of clip-art that you can use in your artwork.

What is the difference between a paint program and a draw program? Paint programs and draw programs can both make the same types of pictures. However, the pictures that you make in a paint program are bitmaps; the pictures that you make in a draw program are not bitmaps. Look up *bitmap* and *clip-art.*

park When your dad drives to the store, he parks his car as soon as he gets there. Why? So it won't roll around the parking lot and get damaged while he's not using it.

Hard disks should also be parked when they are not in use. The hard disk on your computer has a part called the read/write head that moves back and forth across the hard disk when you use it. When the hard disk is not being used, most computers automatically *park* the hard disk by moving the read/write head away from the hard disk.

Moving the read/write head away from the hard disk prevents the read/write head from accidentally hitting (crashing into) the hard disk when the computer gets moved or bumped.

PC Some older PCs have read/write heads that only park when you run a special program. The only way to know if you need a special program to park your computer is to look in the manual that came with your computer.

password A *password* is a secret word. Many computer games ask you to enter a secret word before you can use the game. For example, Where in the USA is Carmen San Diego? asks you for a secret word at various times during the game before it lets you chase the bad guys across the country. The secret word is called a password because it lets you pass by the software security guards and get into the program.

password protection When a computer or software program has *password protection*, it can only be used by people who know the correct password. The computer or software is protected from people who are not allowed to use the computer. Password protecting your computer or software is like locking your bedroom door. It keeps out unwanted visitors. Look up *password*.

PATH *PATH* is a DOS command that tells your computer where to look for a software program. When you want to run a software program from DOS, you type the name of the program at the DOS prompt. Your computer then goes on a treasure hunt to find the program. The path is a type of treasure map. It tells your computer where to look when you ask it to run a software program. The path is usually located in a file on your computer called AUTOEXEC.BAT.

What if I don't have a path? If you do not have a path, your computer will only look for a software program in the current directory. This can be a problem. Suppose you are using Microsoft Windows and want to go to DOS to play a game. When you exit Windows, you are in the C:\WIN directory. This is not the directory that contains your games. Without a path, your computer may have trouble finding the game program you want to play.

Does the PATH ever need to change? Your computer can only run a program when it knows where to find it. When you install a new software program, the path needs to change so your computer knows where to find the new software. The installation program that comes with your software usually changes the path for you.

How do I use the PATH command? There are two main ways to use the PATH command. First, you can use the PATH command to see what's already on your path. The path lists all the directories and subdirectories that your computer looks in when you tell it to start a software program. To look at your path, type the following command at the DOS prompt.

PATH [Enter]

Second, you can use the PATH command to change the path that you want your computer to follow. To make a path,

1. Type the word PATH.
2. Type a directory that you want your computer to look in when you tell it to run a program. (Use the complete directory name, such as C:\GAMES\CARMEN.)
3. Type a semicolon (;).
4. Type the complete directory name for another directory you want your computer to look in when you tell it to run a program.
5. Repeat steps #3 and #4 until you have listed all the directories you want your computer to look in when you tell it to run a program.
6. Press [Enter].

For example, if you want your computer to search the C:\DOS directory, the C:\WIN directory, and the C:\GAMES\YAHTZEE directory, you would type the following command at the DOS prompt.

```
PATH C:\DOS;C:\WIN;C:\GAMES\YAHTZEE [Enter]
```

Always include the DOS and Windows directories in your path so that the computer can find your DOS and Windows files.

Can I make a temporary change to my path? Yes. When you type PATH at the DOS prompt, you are temporarily changing the path on your computer. The new path you make is used by your computer until you turn off your computer—or make a different path.

How can I make a permanent change to my path? To make a permanent change to your path, you need to change the list of directories that follow the PATH command that is located in your AUTOEXEC.BAT file. The AUTOEXEC.BAT file is located in the root directory of your computer. It can be changed with the EDIT command.

- DO NOT change the AUTOEXEC.BAT file on someone else's computer (such as the one in your class or library at school).
- DO NOT change the AUTOEXEC.BAT file on your computer at home unless you have your parent's permission.
- DO NOT change the AUTOEXEC.BAT file on any computer unless you are absolutely sure that you know what you're doing!

Look up *AUTOEXEC.BAT, current directory, directory, DOS prompt, EDIT command, install, installation program,* and *root directory.*

PC *PC* is an abbreviation for personal computer. PC is a popular name for the computers you use at home or at school. The more technical name for a personal computer is a microcomputer. Although a Macintosh is both a personal computer and a microcomputer, PC is a term that is usually used to refer to IBM and IBM-compatible computers. Look up *microcomputer.*

PC-DOS *PC-DOS* (DOS rhymes with "boss") is an acronym for personal computer disk operating system. PC-DOS is the operating system used on most personal computers made by IBM Corporation. Look up *acronym* and *operating system.*

Pentium computer A *Pentium computer* is a computer that has a Pentium microprocessor as its brain. Look up *microprocessor.*

perfs Continuous paper has small holes punched along its edges. The holes are used by a tractor feed that keeps each page straight as it goes through a dot-matrix printer. The edges of continuous paper are perforated so that the part with the holes can be easily removed after you print. *Perfs* are the perforated edges that you pull off the continuous paper. Look up *continuous paper, dot-matrix printer,* and *tractor feed.*

> *"Here," said Newt, handing Jack a printout. "I printed out my portion of our report."*
>
> *"At least pull off the* **perfs** *and separate the pages," said Jack.*
>
> *"Sheeesh," replied Newt.*

personal computer A *personal computer*, or PC, is a popular name for the computers you use at home or at school. The more technical name for a personal computer is microcomputer. Look up *microcomputer* and *PC.*

personal message A *personal message* is a semiprivate message that you post in the message area of a bulletin board system or online service. The personal message is only supposed to be read by the person to whom you are sending the message, rather than by everyone who reads messages in the message area.

When you write a personal message you may think that only the other person you send it to can see the message. Although it is true that the message cannot be read by just anyone who uses the message area, the people who run the bulletin board system or online service can read all the messages that are posted in the message area.

You might feel that it is an invasion of your privacy or that it may be illegal for them to read your messages. But part of their job is to keep rude, nasty, and offensive messages from being posted in the message area—a task that would be impossible to do without reading the messages. As a matter of fact, some online services make a point of having someone read each and every message before it is allowed to be posted. Look up *bulletin board system, online service,* and *sysop.*

PgDn key PgDn is short for Page Down. The Page Down *key* moves your cursor to the bottom of the current screen, the top of the next screen, or the top of the next page. The page down key performs a different job depending on which software program you are using. Look up *cursor movement keys* and *keyboard cursor.*

PgUp key PgUp is short for Page Up. The Page Up *key* moves your cursor to the top of the current screen, the top of the previous screen, or the top of the previous page. The page up key performs a different job depending on which software program you are using. Look up *cursor movement keys* and *keyboard cursor.*

Photo CD A *Photo CD* is a special type of CD-ROM. A Photo CD contains a collection of photographs that have been changed to a format that can be used by your computer. Not all CD-ROM drives can read Photo CDs. If you want to use Photo CDs, make sure that the CD-ROM drive that your family purchases is able to read Photo CDs. Look up *CD-ROM* and *CD-ROM drive.*

pie chart A *pie chart* is a graph in the shape of a pie. A whole pie represents the total number, such as the number of students in a class. Each wedge of the pie represents a portion of the class, such as those students with blond hair, red hair, brown hair, or black hair. Look up *bar graph.*

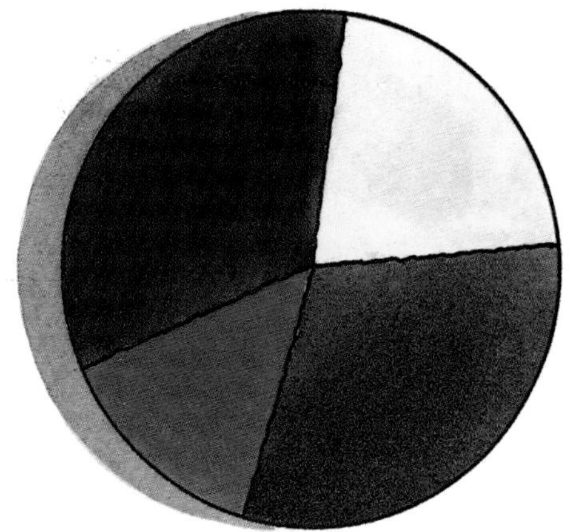

pipe (¦) The ¦ symbol is called a *pipe.* The *pipe* is used to separate two DOS commands. You can usually locate the pipe symbol on your keyboard by looking for the backslash (\) character. The pipe and the backslash usually share the same key.

The pipe character can be difficult to find because it looks different when printed (and when displayed on your screen) than it looks on the keyboard. On your screen and when printed, the pipe looks like a straight line |. But on your keyboard, the pipe character looks like a vertical dashed line. Look up *DOS command, DIR command, MORE command,* and *TREE command.*

piracy *Piracy* is when you make a copy of a software program owned by someone else instead of buying your own copy of the software. Look up *software piracy.*

pixel All the pictures, text, and colors on your computer screen are made up of tiny dots called *pixels*. Pixel is an acronym for pi̲cture e̲lement.

The terms CGA, EGA, VGA, and Super VGA each refer to a type of computer monitor. What separates one type of monitor from another is the number of colors the monitor can display and its screen resolution. Screen resolution is the number of pixels that the monitor can display. The more pixels the monitor can display, the sharper the picture on the screen.

Today, most people buy a VGA or Super VGA monitor for their computer. A VGA monitor can display at least 256 colors, 640 pixels from left to right across the screen, and 480 pixels from the top to the bottom of the screen. The screen resolution is shown as a multiplication formula. For example, the minimum resolution of a VGA monitor is 640 × 480. Look up *acronym, bitmap,* and *resolution.*

point The height of a font is measured in *points*. A single point is about 1/72 of an inch. That means that a 72-point font is about one inch tall. The text in most reading books is 10 to12 points in size. Look up *font* and *font size.*

pointer Your mouse cursor is sometimes called a *pointer*, because it is used to point at the items on your screen that you want to move or select. Look up *mouse cursor.*

pointing device A device is a gadget or tool. A *pointing device* is an accessory you connect to your computer to move the cursor (which is also called a pointer) on your screen. Many of the pointing devices that are attached to games at an arcade are the same type of pointing devices that can be attached to your computer.

Can you name the pointing devices shown below? *Answers appear in the Answer Section in the back of the book.*

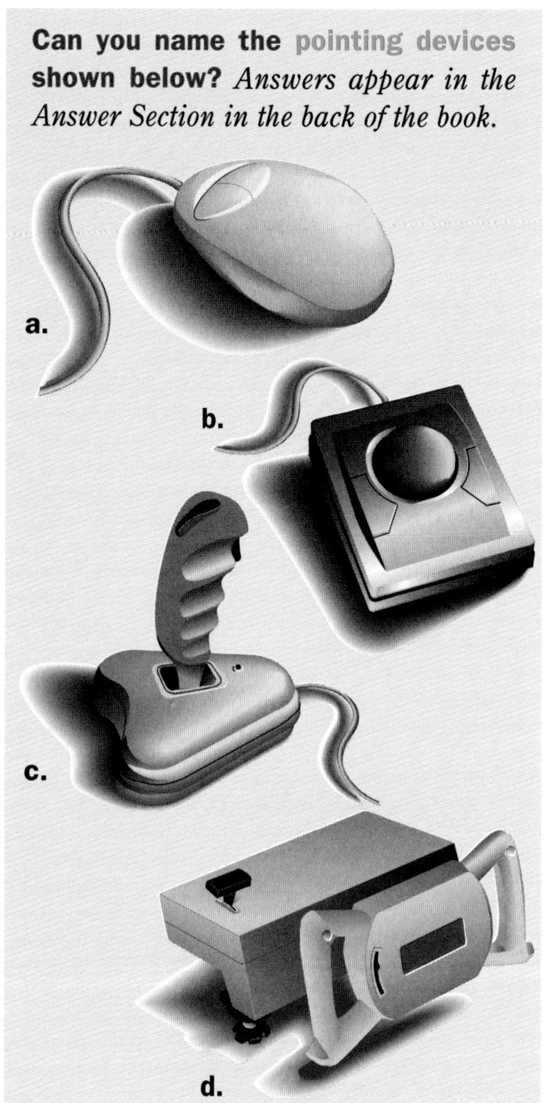

port Have you ever visited a city that has a *port*? When a city is located on a body of water, like a river or ocean, the city often has an area where ships can dock to load or unload goods and passengers. This area is called a port. If the waterway that leads to the port is wide, it may be possible for many ships to enter the port at the same time, moving side-by-side. If the waterway leading into the port is narrow, the ships may have to travel in single file.

On the computer, a port is a place where data can come into the computer and go out of the computer. Personal computers often have two or three ports. Usually a computer has one parallel port and two serial ports.

Parallel ports let several bits of data come into or go out of the computer at the same time. This is like the wide waterway, where many ships can move along side-by-side. Most computers use the parallel port to send data to the printer. The parallel port is called LPT1. If a computer has more than one parallel port, the others are called LPT2, LPT3, and so on.

Serial ports only let the data bits come into or go out of the computer one by one. This is like the narrow waterway, where ships have to move in single file. Serial ports are usually used to send data from the mouse to the computer, and from a modem in your computer to a modem in another computer. The first serial port is called COM1. If a computer has more than one serial port, then the others are known as COM2, COM3, COM4, and so on.

Since parallel ports can handle many bits of data at the same time, parallel ports handle data more quickly than serial ports.

---

portable computer A *portable computer* is a small, light-weight computer system that you can carry from place to place. Many have color screens, can use a CD-ROM, have sound, a modem, lots of memory, and hard disks that are as big as the hard disk in a desktop computer. Today's portable computers also come with rechargeable batteries so that they can be used where there is no electricity.

When were the first portable computers made? Portable computers were first made in the early 1980s. They were the size of a small suitcase and did not have a battery, so they had to be plugged in. They were heavy to carry but were easier to move than a desktop computer.

What is a laptop computer? By the mid-1980s, laptop computers had been created. A laptop is a portable computer that is small enough to fit on your lap—but the early laptops weighed several pounds, so you couldn't keep them on your lap for very long or your legs would fall asleep. Laptops ran on electricity or a rechargeable battery, and folded in half for traveling. The top half of a laptop held the screen, while the bottom half held the keyboard and CPU. All laptops had monochrome screens, a small hard disk (or none at all) and a limited amount of memory.

What is a notebook computer? Around 1990, the notebook computer was developed. A notebook computer is smaller than a laptop—about the size of a spiral-bound notebook. Today, the terms "notebook computer," "laptop computer," and "portable computer" are used to mean "notebook computer." Today, you can buy a notebook computer that is as powerful (or more powerful) than the computer you have on your desk at home.

What are subnotebook and palmtop computers? The subnotebook computer is a portable computer that is smaller than a notebook computer. A palmtop computer is so small that you can hold it in the palm of your hand. Subnotebooks and palmtops have fewer features than notebook computers.

What is a personal digital assistant? The personal digital assistant, PDA for short, is a very different type of personal computer. A PDA, which is about the size of a paperback book, doesn't have a keyboard! Instead it has a screen that you can write on with a pointed stick called a stylus. Special software in the PDA understands your handwriting. The PDA lets you save notes, drawings, and anything else you can write.

portrait orientation When you take a piece of paper and turn it so it faces up and down, rather than sideways, you have *portrait orientation.* This is the direction that an artist turns the canvas when painting a portrait (a picture of a person). Look up *orientation.*

post To *post* a message is to put a message in the message area of a bulletin board service (BBS) or online service. Look up *bulletin board service* and *online service.*

"My mom said I can invite all the kids on the school BBS to my pool party," said Shannon.

"How are you going to let everyone know?" asked Toni.

"I'll **post** *a message," replied Shannon.*

PostScript *PostScript* is a programming language that was developed by Adobe Systems, Inc. Programmers use PostScript to create high-quality fonts and graphics that can be printed on a laser printer. Some drawing programs (such as Corel Draw and Adobe Illustrator) let you save your pictures in a PostScript format. You can also buy PostScript fonts and graphics at the computer store.

Can all printers print PostScript? No. To use PostScript fonts and graphics you must have a printer that can print PostScript. Some printers have PostScript built into them. Other printers can use a PostScript cartridge that you buy and plug into your printer. But not every laser printer can use PostScript fonts and graphics.

What happens if I try to print PostScript on a non-PostScript printer? If you try to print a PostScript graphic on a printer that can't read PostScript, your printer will print dozens of pages with nothing but numbers and symbols.

Look up *font* and *true type.*

Power Mac Any Macintosh that uses a PowerPC microprocessor is called a *Power Mac.* Look up *microprocessor* and *PowerPC.*

power strip A *power strip* is a long box with several electrical outlets on it. The power strip plugs into the wall outlet, and each piece of your computer equipment plugs into the power strip. Besides being a convenient way to plug in all of your equipment, most power strips also include a circuit called a surge protector that protects your computer equipment from a sudden charge of electricity. Look up *surge* and *surge protector.*

power user When a person is very experienced in using a particular software program, that person is called a *power user* of that program. A power user is also someone who is very experienced with computers and software.

Janice's dad was helping her create some charts in Lotus Freelance for her history homework.

"Dad, you're a computer expert when it comes to Freelance aren't you?" Janice asked.

"Well," replied her dad, "you could say I'm a Freelance **power user**.*"*

power-down To *power-down* is to turn off all of your computer equipment and accessories.

power-up To *power-up* is to turn on all of your computer equipment and accessories.

PowerPC A *PowerPC* is a desktop computer that has a PowerPC 601, PowerPC 603, or PowerPC 604 microprocessor for its brain. Although you may think of a PC as an IBM-compatible machine, PowerPC microprocessors are used in a variety of different computers including PCs, Macs, and minicomputers. Look up *microprocessor* and *minicomputer.*

PowerPC 601 The *PowerPC 601* is the microprocessor that is used in many Power Mac computers. Look up *microprocessor.*

ppm The abbreviation *ppm* stands for *p*ages *p*er *m*inute, the number of pages that an inkjet or laser printer can print out in one minute of time. Look up *pages per minute.*

preformatted Before you can use a new diskette for the first time, it must go through a process called formatting. Rather than format the diskettes yourself, you can buy *preformatted* diskettes that have already been formatted by the manufacturer. Preformatted diskettes are more convenient to use, but are more expensive to purchase. Look up *FORMAT command.*

PRINT command The *PRINT command* is a DOS command that you can use to print simple files that contain text. The PRINT command will not print files that contain sound, video, graphics, or text that was created with a word-processing program such as Ami Pro, WordPerfect, or Microsoft Word.

How do I use the PRINT command? To use the PRINT command to print a file, type PRINT and the name of the file that you want to print. For cxample, if you want to print a file called README.TXT, you would type the following command at the DOS prompt.

```
PRINT README.TXT [Enter]
```

print job When you tell a software program to print something, you have created a *print job*. If you create another print job before the first job is finished printing, your computer puts the second print job on a waiting list. Most software programs can handle many print jobs at one time. Your computer just puts the jobs on a list and prints them in the order in which you asked for them.

Print Manager *Print Manager* is a program in Microsoft Windows that keeps track of all your print jobs, the things you have selected to print. The Print Manager is responsible for every print job in every program that you use with Microsoft

Windows. For example, if you ask to print a report from Ami Pro (a word-processing program), Print Manger keeps track of that print job. Look up *print job.*

print monitor *Print monitor* is the program that keeps track of all your print jobs, the things you have selected to print. The print monitor is responsible for every print job in every program that you use on your Macintosh. For example, if you ask to print a report from Microsoft Word, the print monitor keeps track of that print job. Look up *print job.*

printer A *printer* is a machine that can make a paper copy of what you see on your computer screen—and even some things you can't see on your screen. The printer connects to a port on your computer with a cable. The paper that comes out of your printer is called the output, a printout, or a hard copy.

Most printers can only print in one color (usually black) but full-color printers are becoming both more popular and more affordable. Look up *cable, dot-matrix printer, ink jet printer, laser printer* and *port.*

printer driver A *printer driver* is a program that tells your computer how to send information to a specific printer. Before any printer can be used with your computer, you must install a printer driver. There are hundreds of different printer drivers. Most printer drivers are built-in to your software programs. All you need to do is select the right one for your printer.

PC When you install Microsoft Windows you need to tell Windows which printer you have. The installation program then selects the correct printer driver for you. If you ever get a new printer, you need to change the printer driver by selecting Control Panel, then Printer, then the name of your printer.

If you are using programs in DOS, you must select a separate printer driver for each program. Of course you only need to select a printer driver if the program has a print feature—some games, for example, do not have a print feature.

Mac All printer drivers are kept in the Extensions folder. (The Extensions folder is located inside the System Folder.) To change your printer driver, pull down the Apple menu, select Chooser, and select your printer. Look up *Apple menu.*

printer stand A *printer stand* is a shelf or piece of furniture that is designed to hold a printer that is connected to a computer. The printer typically sits on top of the stand. Paper and accessories can usually be stored on the shelves below or inside the stand.

Some printer stands are designed for printers such as dot-matrix printers, which use continuous paper. When a printer uses continuous paper, the stack of paper sits on a shelf below the printer. The paper comes out through a slot that has been cut in the top of the stand. From there the paper is fed into the printer. Look up *dot-matrix printer* and *continuous paper.*

printer resolution *Printer resolution* is a measurement of how sharp your printer can print text and pictures. Printer resolution for laser and ink jet printers is measured in dots-per-inch. The more dots-per-inch, the sharper your printouts. Look up *dots-per-inch* and *resolution.*

printout The printed paper that comes out of your printer is called a *printout.* Other terms for printout are hard copy and output.

program **(1)** *Program* is the short name for a software program. A program gives your computer instructions that make it play a game, display a graphic, run an animation, edit text, send e-mail, and all the other activities that make your computer useful and fun. Look up *software program.*
(2) To *program* is to use a programming language (such as BASIC, C, COBOL, or PASCAL) to create a software program that plays a game or does a job. Look up *programming language* and *software program.*

programmer A *programmer* is a person who writes instructions to make a software program do what it is supposed to do. The programmer uses a programming language—a language that the computer can understand—to tell the computer what it should do when you make a selection within the software program.

Most software programs are not written by one programmer but a team of programmers. Each programmer on the team is responsible for making part of the software program work. Look up *software program.*

programming language Unlike English, French, Spanish, Japanese, and other languages that are spoken by people, a *programming language* is a language that is used to talk to computers. The languages that are used by people can be spoken or written down. Programming languages are not spoken, they are just written down. Programming languages are called artificial languages because they are made up by scientists so that programmers can talk to computers more easily.

Why are there different programming languages? One reason that there are different programming languages is that each programming language is good for creating certain types of software programs (such as a game program) and not as good for creating other types of software programs (such as a word-processing program). So the different languages are used to create different types of programs.

Another reason that there are different programming languages is that just like other people, different programmers like to work in different ways. Some programmers find it easier to use one programming language and some find it easier to use another. Look up *software program.*

"My dad said that when we get a computer, he's going to teach me a language," said Morgan.

"You mean like German or Chinese?" asked Leslie.

"No," laughed Morgan. "A **programming language**—*like BASIC."*

prompt A *prompt* is a signal from your computer that it is ready for your next command or instruction. Since most computers can't talk, your computer usually signals you by typing words or symbols on your screen.

PROMPT command The *PROMPT command* is a DOS command that you can use to change how the DOS prompt appears on your screen. The PROMPT command is usually used in the AUTOEXEC.BAT file so that your prompt looks the same each time you start your computer.

How do I use the PROMPT command? You can make a special prompt for your computer by typing PROMPT, a dollar sign, and a letter that has a special meaning. Some of the letters and their meanings are shown below. For a complete list of letters and meanings, check the DOS manual that came with your computer.

```
t    current time
d    current date
p    current drive and directory
v    DOS version number
```

For example, to use a DOS prompt that displays the word BASEBALL and the time, you would type the following command at the DOS prompt.

```
PROMPT BASEBALL $t  [Enter]
```

To use a DOS prompt that displays the time and date at the DOS prompt, type the following command.

```
PROMPT $t $d  [Enter]
```

Although it is fun to play around with different prompts, over time you will find that the most useful prompt is a simple one that displays the current drive and directory (so you always know in which directory your cursor is located). To create a simple prompt, type the following command. (The $q places an equal sign after the directory name.)

```
PROMPT $p$q
```

Look up *AUTOEXEC.BAT*, *DOS command*, and *DOS prompt*.

propeller key The *propeller key* is the key on your keyboard with the ⌘ symbol. The technical name for this key is command key. The command key is sometimes called the propeller key, butterfly key, or flower key because many people think that the symbol on the key looks like a propeller, butterfly, or flower.

The command key can be used in many programs to give an alternate (or different) meaning to another key. To use the command key, you hold it down while you press another key. Look up *command key*.

proportionally spaced font If you look at the text in some of your books (including this one) you will see that different letters take up different amounts of space on a line. An "i" for example, takes up less space on the line than an "m." When some letters in a font take up more space than other letters, the font is called a *proportionally spaced font*. Look up *font*.

Here are some samples of proportionally spaced fonts.

Avant Garde

Chicago

Clarendon

Marriage

Square Serif

Univers

pt. *Pt.* is an abbreviation for point. The height of a font is measured in points. A single point is about 1/72 of an inch. That means that a 72-point font is one inch tall. The text in most reading books is 10 to 12 points in size. Look up *font* and *font size.*

pull-down menu When you use a software program that has a menu bar across the top of the screen, the menu bar will have drop-down or *pull-down menus.*

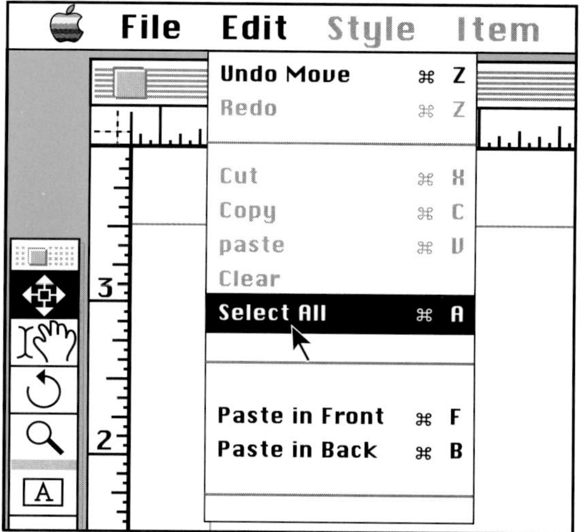

A pull-down menu works like a stretched rubber band. While you are holding the rubber band it stays in place, but as soon as you let go, the rubber band goes flying. To open a pull-down menu, click and hold the mouse button so you can see the menu you want to read.

To make a selection, drag the mouse to the selection and then let go of the mouse button. Be careful that you do not let go of the mouse button before you make a selection, or you will either make a selection that you don't want or make no selection at all.

Pull-down menus snap closed when you let go of the mouse button. If you decide not to make a selection from the menu, move the mouse pointer away from the menu and then let go of the mouse button. Look up ***menu, menu bar,*** and ***pull-down menu.***

question mark (?) A wildcard is a symbol that is used to take the place of some or all of the letters in a filename or the filename extension. The *question mark* is used to take the place of a single letter in a filename or extension. You might use the question mark when you can't remember one or more of the letters in a filename. Look up *wildcard*.

QuickDraw *QuickDraw* is the set of instructions inside every Macintosh that controls how icons, graphics, windows, and text look on your screen. Some printers are called "QuickDraw printers" because they use the same instructions to print on paper as your Mac uses to display things on your screen.

ragged right *Ragged right* is a phrase that describes how the right-hand side of a paragraph is formatted. When the text is ragged, the lines in the paragraph have different lengths so the right-hand side of the paragraph does not form a straight line. Ragged right is another term for flush left. Look up *flush left* and *flush right.*

ragged left *Ragged left* is a phrase that describes how the left-hand side of a paragraph is formatted. When the text is ragged, the lines in the paragraph have different lengths so the left-hand side of the paragraph does not form a straight line. Ragged left is another term for flush right. Look up *flush left* and *flush right.*

RAM *RAM* (rhymes with "ham") is an acronym for random access memory. Your computer's RAM is the amount of information that your computer can remember at one time. All the information in your RAM is erased each time you turn off your computer. Look up *acronym* and *memory.*

random access memory *Random access memory* is the amount of information that your computer can remember at one time. The acronym for random access memory is RAM. All the information in your RAM is erased each time you turn off your computer. RAM is measured in kilobytes (K) or megabytes (M), depending on how much RAM you have inside your computer. Look up *acronym, kilobyte, megabyte,* and *memory.*

random number Pick a number from 1 to 1,000. Ask your mom, dad, and some other people to pick a number from 1 to 1,000. Did you get the same answer? Probably not. The answer that you got was a *random number.* The people you asked could have picked any number (within the boundaries of 1 to 1,000). Their answer was left to chance.

What are random numbers used for? Can you think of a time when you use random numbers? If you said that you use random numbers when you roll the dice in the computer version of popular board games such as Risk, Clue, Monopoly, or Trivial Pursuit, you are correct. Games wouldn't be any fun if you always rolled the same number. Look up *random number generator.*

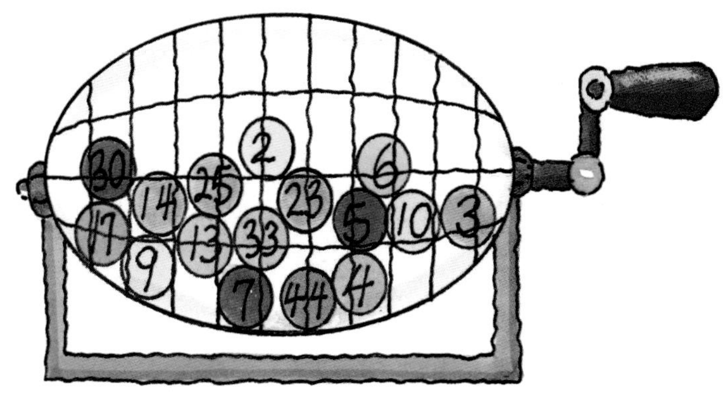

random number generator A *random number generator* is a software program or feature of a programming language that is designed to select random numbers. Random numbers are often needed in game programs so the game is different every time you play. Look up *programming language* and *random number.*

range A *range* is a way of describing a group of numbers. When you describe a range, you give the lowest number in the group and the highest number in the group. The range includes the low number, the high number, and all the numbers in between. For example, the range 1—10 includes the numbers 1, 2, 3, 4, 5, 6, 7, 8, 9, and 10.

> *Karlie was concerned about how well she did on the spelling test she took yesterday. She was very relieved when her teacher announced that all the grades for the test were in the 80 percent to 100 percent* **range**.

RD command The *RD command* is a DOS command that means remove directory. When you have deleted all the files from a directory and want to delete the empty directory from your hard disk or diskette, you can use the RD command. All the files and subdirectories must be deleted before you can delete the directory itself.

How do I use the RD command? To remove a directory, type RD followed by the name of the directory that you want to remove. For example, to remove the directory C:\SCHOOL\HOMEWORK\OLD, type the following command at the DOS prompt. (Hint: You cannot remove a directory if your cursor is located in that directory.)

```
RD C:\SCHOOL\HOMEWORK\OLD [Enter]
```

Look up *CD command, delete, directory, DOS command, DOS prompt,* and *subdirectory.*

read-only A *read-only* file is a special kind of information file. The file is called read-only because you can use it, read it, and copy it. But unlike most files, which you can change and delete, a read-only file is protected. If you try to change or delete a read-only file you will get an error message (such as "access denied"). Look up *access, error message,* and *file.*

> *Mark was using his encyclopedia on CD-ROM.*
>
> *"I don't like this part," he thought, "I'll just delete it so I don't have to read it again next time."*

But when Mark pushed the delete key he got a message that said "access denied."

"That's right," said Mark, "I can't delete anything from a CD! CDs are **read-only**.*"*

---

read-only memory *Read-only memory* is a special area of computer memory. Unlike random access memory (RAM) which you can use to store computer programs and information, read-only memory can only be used by your computer.

The information in your computer's read-only memory is permanent. Read-only memory is not erased when you turn off your computer. The acronym for read-only memory is ROM. Look up *acronym, memory,* and *RAM.*

ream A *ream* of paper is 500 sheets of paper. A case of paper contains 10 reams (5000 sheets). Although most office supply stores will sell you less than 500 sheets of paper, you can usually get a better buy if you purchase paper for your laser or ink-jet printer by the ream.

---

reboot To *reboot* is to restart your computer after you have already turned it on. On occasion, you may be using your computer and it will suddenly freeze or stop working. When this happens you need to reboot your computer. You can always reboot by turning off your computer and turning it on again.

PC You can also reboot by pressing Ctrl-Alt-Del or your computer's reset button.

Mac If you can still make any menu selections, the best way to reboot your computer is to select Restart from the Special menu.

Look up *boot, Ctrl-Alt-Del,* and *reset button.*

---

recover To *recover* a file is to get back a file that was deleted or erased. Recover also means to fix a file that has been damaged in some way. Look up *DELETE command,* and *UNDELETE command.*

---

registration card The *registration card* is a form that comes with a new computer, computer accessory, or software program. Another name for registration card is warranty card.

It's a good idea to fill out and send in the registration card so that you can get on the company's user list. When the company is going to upgrade the software or release a new product, some of the first people to get information about the new product are the people on the user list. Also, many companies will not answer your technical questions about their software unless you have returned the registration card.

remove directory command Files on your computer are stored in directories. You can remove an empty directory by using a DOS command that tells your computer that you want to delete (remove) a directory. The DOS *remove directory command* is RD (or RMDIR). Look up *directory* and *RD command.*

RENAME command The *RENAME command* is a DOS command that you can use to change the name of a file. Each file in a directory must have a unique name—a name that is unlike any other filename. However you can use the same filename again when the files are in different directories.

How do I use the RENAME command? The easiest way to rename a file is to go to the directory that contains the file you want to rename. Just follow these instructions:

1. Use the CD command to change to the directory that contains the file you want to rename. Suppose the file you want to rename is in a directory called HOMEWORK.

   ```
   CD C:\HOMEWORK [Enter]
   ```

2. Type the RENAME command, the name of file you want to change, and the new filename. Suppose you had started writing a report on dogs and you changed it to a report on cats. To change the name of your report from DOG.RPT to CAT.RPT type the following command.

   ```
   RENAME DOG.RPT CAT.RPT [Enter]
   ```

Can the RENAME command be used with wildcards? Yes. The RENAME command can be used with the DOS wildcards so that you can rename many files at the same time. Suppose you wanted to change all files in a directory that had the extension .DOG to the extension .CAT, so that you would know that the file is part of your cat report. By using the asterisk (*) wildcard shown below, you could rename the files all at once—instead of renaming them one at a time.

```
RENAME *.DOG *.CAT [Enter]
```

If your directory contained the files HOUND.DOG, HOT.DOG, and BARKING.DOG, the files would be renamed HOUND.CAT, HOT.CAT, and BARKING.CAT. You must be careful when you use the RENAME command with wildcards, or you could end up renaming files you didn't mean to change. Look up *directory, DOS command, DOS prompt,* and *wildcard.*

reset button Many PCs have a *reset button* that can reboot your computer. The reset button is usually located on the front of your computer. Pressing the reset button is similar to pressing Ctrl-Alt-Del from your keyboard. Look up *Ctrl-Alt-Del* and *reboot.*

resident font A resident of an apartment building is someone who lives in the apartment building. A *resident font* is a font that lives inside a printer. Resident fonts (also called internal fonts) are permanently built-in to your printer and cannot be easily removed or erased.

Every printer has at least one resident font. Many printers—such as laser printers—come with several resident fonts. In addition to resident fonts, many printers also accept external fonts that can be added to your printer and removed from your printer as needed. Look up *external font* and *font.*

resolution *Resolution* refers to how clearly text and pictures are displayed on your computer screen or how clear pictures and text are printed out on paper from your printer.

- Low resolution text is difficult to read and the pictures may be difficult to make out.
- Medium resolution text is readable and the pictures can be seen but are not very sharp.
- High resolution text is very sharp and easy to read and the pictures are equally sharp. Obviously, high resolution is better than medium and low resolutions.

Unfortunately, the monitors and printers that provide high resolution are more expensive than the monitors and printers that provide low and medium resolution.

restart To *restart* your computer is to start it again after you have already turned it on. Another name for restart is reboot. Look up *reboot.*

Return key The *Return key* is another name for Enter. Look up *carriage return* and *Enter key.*

right-click To *right-click* the mouse is to press the right mouse button one time. Right-click is different than click, which means to click the left mouse button.

Why is right-click a PC term? Since most Macs only have one mouse button, you cannot right-click the mouse that comes with a Mac. Look up *mouse button.*

right arrow key The *right arrow key* → moves the keyboard cursor one space to the right. Look up *cursor movement keys* and *keyboard cursor.*

right justified *Right justified* is a phrase that describes how the right-hand side of a paragraph is formatted. Another term for right justified is flush right. When the text is right justified, the right-hand side of the paragraph forms a straight line. Look up *flush right* and *ragged right.*

RMDIR command The *RMDIR command* is a DOS command that means remove directory. A shorter and more popular DOS command for removing a directory is RD. Look up *RD command.*

ROM *ROM* (rhymes with "Tom") is an acronym for read-only memory. ROM is a special area of computer memory. Unlike RAM (random access memory), which you can use to store computer programs and

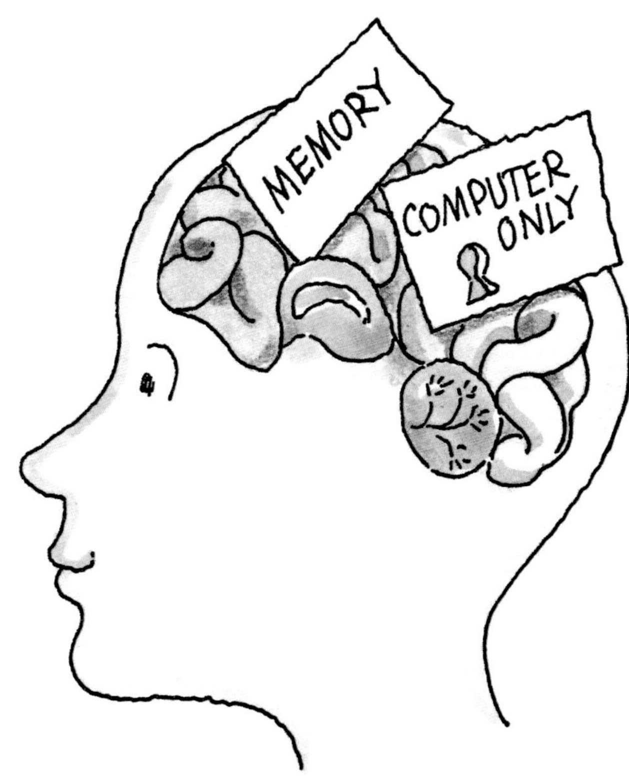

information, ROM can only be used by your computer. The information in your computer's ROM is permanent. ROM is not erased when you turn off your computer.

What is ROM used for? Since all the information in your computer's memory is erased each time your turn off your computer, your computer needs to know how to find your disk drive and files in your operating system. The ROM provides your computer with this basic information so your computer can boot. Look up *acronym*, *boot*, *memory*, *operating system*, and *RAM*.

root directory All the games and software programs on your computer's hard disk are organized into groups called directories. The *root directory* is the top directory on your hard disk. Since the root directory is the top directory, it is never inside another directory. However, a root directory usually has many subdirectories. Look up *directory*.

Galit gave Kimi a copy of a picture she created in Adobe Illustrator. "Should I put the picture in the root directory?" Kimi asked her dad.

"No, make a separate directory for your pictures. Only special computer files should go in the **root directory**,*" said Dad.*

row A *row* is a line of information that is formatted horizontally. Most tables (like your multiplication tables) are made up of rows and columns. The rows are made up of information you read from left to right across the line. A column is the vertical line of information you read up and down. Look up *column*.

2	4	6	8	10	12
3	6	9	12	15	18
4	8	12	16	20	24
5	10	15	20	25	30
6	12	18	24	30	36
7	14	21	28	35	42
8	16	24	32	40	48
9	18	27	36	45	54

run To *run* a software program is to start it up. You don't have to be using a software program to be running it; you just have to have it turned on.

Sad Mac Uh oh. Usually when you turn on your Mac you see the Happy Mac that lets you know that your computer has found the files it needs to start your computer. The *Sad Mac* is a sad face that means you have trouble . When you get a Sad Mac, you either have a problem with your computer, or your Mac can't find the files it needs to start your computer. In either case, when you see a Sad Mac, turn off your computer and tell your parents about it.

sans serif If you look very closely at the letters in a book or magazine you will see that some of them have little feet or edges on the ends of the letters. These little feet are called serifs. Sans is a French word that means "without." *Sans serif* means without serifs—or without the little feet. Below are some samples of sans serif letters.

Avant Garde
Franklin Gothic
Futura
Univers

Look up *font, font style*, and *serif.*

save If you are playing a software game and select the *save* feature, your computer records where you are in the game—your score, settings, players, opponents, and so on. The computer puts this information into a file on your hard disk so that you can come back and continue the game where you left off.

The save feature is very useful in games where your character can get killed. With the save option you can replay a particular portion of your game until you find a solution that works or are able to overcome the enemy.

The save option is available in many other software programs besides games. Many programs, such as a word-processing program, have save options so that you can write a letter, report, or other document and come back and work on it later or use it again.

"Crystal, did you finish your report on satellites?" asked Mom.

"I'm planning on working on it after Girl Scouts," replied Crystal.

"Did you remember to **save** *the work you did yesterday?" asked Mom.*

"I sure did. I don't want to lose all my hard work," replied Crystal.

---

scan **(1)** When you *scan* a diskette or your hard disk for a computer virus, you are using an anti-virus program to make sure that no computer virus exists in your files. Look up *anti-virus program* and *virus*. **(2)** When you *scan* text or a picture, you use a scanner to convert something printed (like a magazine or a photograph) to a file you can use on your computer. Look up *scanner*.

---

scanner A *scanner* (also called an optical scanner) can look at a document, drawing, or photograph, and store a picture of that item to a file on your computer's hard disk. The scanner, along with software on the computer, makes a picture of the item that you scan. The picture is then stored in a special format (called a digital format) so you can use the picture in any of your software programs that can work with graphics.

Most scanners are flatbed scanners. A flatbed scanner looks like a copy machine without all the paper trays. It has a flat, glass surface that you lay the document on, and a thick plastic cover that comes down to hold the document in place (just like a copy machine). Another type of scanner is so small that you can hold it in your hand. This type of scanner is called a hand scanner. With a hand scanner, you move the scanner over the picture you want to copy.

Scanners can be used to scan photos, artwork, newspapers, handwriting, and any flat printed item that you want to use on your computer.

---

screen Your *screen* (or computer screen) is the part of your monitor that looks like the picture portion of a television set. It is here that your computer displays text and graphics, and other information. Look up *monitor*.

---

screen dump A *screen dump* is a quick print out of what's on your screen. Screen dumps can only be made from the DOS prompt, or while running some DOS programs.

How do I do a screen dump? First, make sure your printer is on. Then hold down Shift while you press Print Screen.

"Peter, I think I accidentally deleted a file from my computer," said Dad. "Please give me a printout of your C:\WINDOWS\SYSTEM directory."

"How do I do that?" asked Peter.

"Just go to the directory, type D-I-R to see the files on your screen, and then do a **screen dump***," replied Dad.*

"Okay," said Peter.

---

screen resolution *Screen resolution* is how sharp and clear the picture is on your computer screen (monitor). All the pictures, text, and colors on your computer screen are made up of tiny dots called pixels. The more pixels you have, the better your screen resolution.

The terms CGA, EGA, VGA, and Super VGA each refer to a type of computer monitor. What separates one type of monitor from another is the number of colors the monitor can display and its screen resolution.

Today, most people buy a VGA or Super VGA monitor for their computer. A VGA monitor can display at least 256 colors, 640 pixels from left to right across the screen, and 480 pixels from the top to bottom of the screen. The screen resolution is shown as a multiplication formula. For example, the minimum resolution of a VGA monitor is 640 × 480. Look up *bitmap* and *resolution.*

---

screen saver A *screen saver* is a program that is designed to protect your computer screen. When you walk away from your computer and leave the same text or picture on the screen for hours at a time, you may see a ghostly image of that picture or text when you finally turn off your monitor. The ghostly image is called burn-in. Many monitors today are made in a way that protects them from burn-in, but it is still not a good idea to leave the same image on your screen for hours at a time.

A screen saver prevents burn-in by displaying changing designs or pictures on your computer screen. Since the picture changes over and over again, no single picture has the time to burn-in to your monitor. You can set the screen saver to turn on automatically after a certain period of time (five minutes for example). The screen saver only turns on if you do not touch your mouse or keyboard for the period of time you set (the five minutes). The screen saver turns off as soon as you move your mouse or press a key on your keyboard.

There are many screen saver programs from which to choose. The different programs include cartoons, outer space scenes, geometric designs, and scenes from television shows and movies. Some screen savers even make sounds.

---

scroll When you have a page of text or a picture that does not all fit on your screen at one time, you can *scroll* the image up and down or from side to side so that you can see more of the picture or more of the text.

Moving the picture up and down is called vertical scrolling. To move the picture or text up and down, you can use ↑ and ↓ or the vertical scroll bar.

Moving the picture from side to side is called horizontal scrolling. To move the picture or text from side to side, you can use ← and → or the horizonal scroll bar. Look up *scroll bar.*

---

scroll bar When you have text or a picture that does not fit in a window, you can move the image up and down or from side to side so that you can see more of the picture or more of the text. To move the image, you can use your mouse on a long, narrow rectangle called a *scroll bar.*

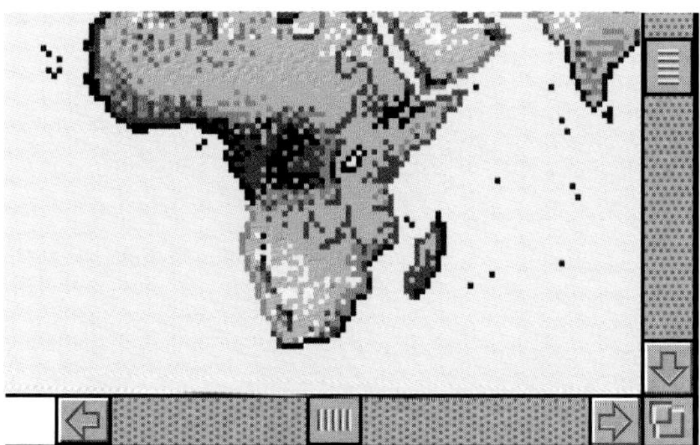

When you need to move the image up and down, a vertical (up and down) scroll bar appears on the right-hand side of your screen. When you need to move the image from side to side, a horizontal (side to side) scroll bar appears at the bottom of your window. When you need to move both up and down, and side to side, both scroll bars appear in your window.

Each end of the scroll bar has a button with an arrow. If you click on the arrow, the image moves in the direction that the arrow is pointing. For example, if you click on the up arrow on the vertical scroll bar, your text or picture moves up the screen.

Inside the scroll bar is another button called a slider. To move the image up and down, you drag the slider in the vertical scroll bar. To move the image from side to side, you drag the slider in the horizontal scroll bar. Look up *drag.*

SCSI *SCSI* (pronounced "scuzzy") is a special type of connection that is used to hook some CD-ROM drives, scanners, and hard disks to your computer. SCSI is an acronym for small computer systems interface.

Usually computer equipment must be plugged directly into a port on your computer. That means that if you have two ports, you can only connect two pieces of computer equipment to your computer. The advantage of a SCSI port is that only one piece of computer equipment needs to be plugged into your computer; the others can be daisy-chained together.

All Macs have a SCSI port. Many PCs also have a SCSI port; some PC manufacturers offer a SCSI port as an option. But not all CD-ROM drives, scanners, and hard disks can use SCSI connections. If your computer has a SCSI port, and your family wants to add a new piece of computer equipment to the SCSI chain, make sure that the new computer equipment has a SCSI connection. Look up *daisy-chain* and *port.*

---

seek time *Seek time* is the amount of time it takes your computer to find a file on your computer's hard disk or CD-ROM. When you play hide-and-seek you look for a person who is hiding. When your computer seeks a file, it looks for the file.

semiconductor A *semiconductor* is a crystal-like material that is used when making electronic parts such as transistors and integrated circuits. Silicon and germanium are the two semiconductors that are used most often when making electronic parts for computers.

Why are semiconductors useful? Semiconductors are not good conductors of electricity, but when other materials are added to the semiconductor, their ability to carry electricity can be changed and controlled. So semiconductors are used in electronic circuits to control the flow of electricity. Look up *integrated circuit.*

serif If you look very closely at some of the letters in a book or magazine you will see that some of them have little feet or edges on the ends of the letters. These little feet are called *serifs*. Below are some samples of serif letters.

Century Old Style
Courier
Garamond
Times Bold

Look up *font, font style*, and *sans serif.*

server When you serve someone, you do something for them that is useful. Here are some of the ways you can serve people. You can

- Do something for them.
- Get something for them.
- Tell them that something has happened.
- Let them use something that is yours.
- Find the answer to a question.

A software program can be a *server.* When a program is a server, it does something for another program. For example, a program that controls the files at the printer is called a print server. When you tell your software program to print something, it sends your drawing or text to the print server. The print server then takes over the printing so that your software program can continue with whatever you want to do next.

A computer can also be a server. When a computer is a server, other computers are connected to it to form a network. The server usually has several hard disks with programs and data that can be used by other computers on the network. Look up *client server* and *network.*

session Your *session* is the length of time you were logged onto (or are allowed to stay logged onto) an online service or network.

👁 Look up *network* and *online service.*

> *"Did you get to spend much time on the network at school?" asked Mom.*
>
> *"Not really. Since everyone's report is due next week, they are limiting our* **sessions** *to twenty minutes each," replied Cyd.*
>
> *"That's not much time at all."*

---

setup program A *setup program* is a special program that you use to install new software on your computer's hard disk. A setup program comes with most software that you buy.

The setup program makes a directory for the new software, creates a new group for the software (if necessary), and copies the files from the diskette to your hard disk. Another name for a setup program is an installation program.

---

shareware Not all software programs are sold in stores. Some programmers (particularly programmers who design computer games) prefer to sell their software as *shareware,* a policy that lets you try the software before you buy it. The rules of shareware are very simple and rely on you to be an honest person.

When you get a shareware program you can install it on your computer and use it for a couple of weeks. After you try the software, you are supposed to pay for it or stop using it and erase it from your hard disk. If you choose to buy the software—which is usually less expensive than buying a software program in a store—you send your money directly to the programmer who made the software.

As a bonus (and as an additional reason to send in your money) the programmer usually sends you the latest copy of the game or a copy that has some features that are not included in the shareware program that you used.

---

showstopper In the theater, a *showstopper* is a performance that is so fantastic that the show is temporarily interrupted—stopped—by the applause and cheers of the audience. In the theater, a showstopper is a sign that the show is a hit. Unfortunately, the same is not true for computers.

In computers, a showstopper is a very bad bug in a new software program. The bug is so serious that the software company must stop the show—delay the software from being sold—until the bug is fixed.

shut down When you *shut down,* you turn off all your computer equipment including your computer, monitor, CD-ROM drive, printer, and any other piece of computer equipment that runs on electricity.
Mac Shut Down is a command on your Special menu. When you are ready to turn off your computer, select Shut Down. Your Mac will take care of some housekeeping chores and then turn itself off in a few seconds (or prompt you to turn it off).

SIG *SIG* is an acronym for Special Interest Group. A SIG is a computer club whose members are interested in a specific software program (like Corel Draw), type of computing (like adventure gaming), or technology (like virtual reality). Look up *acronym, special interest group, user group*, and *virtual reality.*

silicon chip A *silicon chip* is a small, flat integrated circuit. Your microprocessor is a silicon chip. So is your computer memory. Silicon chips are usually in the shape of a square or a rectangle. Many are smaller than an inch on each side and contain over a million transistors. Look up *integrated circuit, memory,* and *microprocessor.*

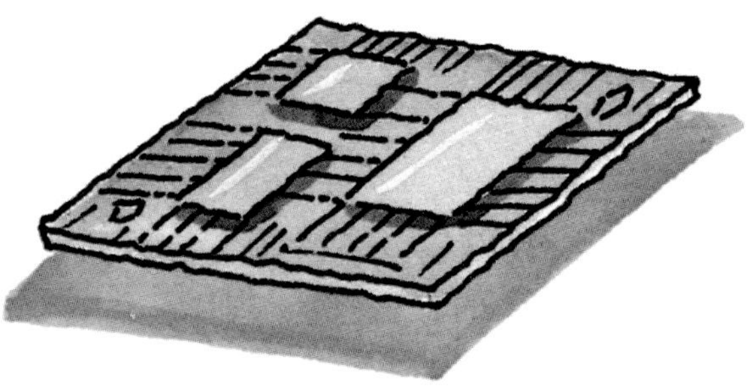

single click To *single click* the mouse is to press a mouse button, one time. Single click is usually just called click. Look up *mouse button.*

> *Jason was showing his dad how to play a Dungeons & Dragons game.*
> *"How do I select which warrior I want?" asked Dad.*
> *"Just move the cursor to the one you want and* **single click** *the left mouse button," replied Jason.*
> *"Hey, this is fun," said Dad.*
> *"Told you."*

slash A *slash* is a slanted line. There are two slashes on your keyboard and many people get them confused.

\ Backslash
/ Forward slash

You can remember which slash is which by looking to see which direction the slash is pointing. The slash that points forward toward the rest of the sentence is the forward slash. The slash that points back to the beginning of the sentence is the backslash. Backslashes are used in directory names (C:\DOS). Forward slashes are used in dates (10/31/96).

slider A *slider* is the button inside a scroll bar or another graphic (such as a volume control) that can be moved up and down or from side to side by dragging the mouse. A slider in a scroll bar can be used to view another part of the text or picture that you do not see on your screen. A slider in a sound or music program can be used to change the balance of different musical instruments or adjust the sound volume of the speakers that are connected to your sound card. Look up *drag* and *scroll bar.*

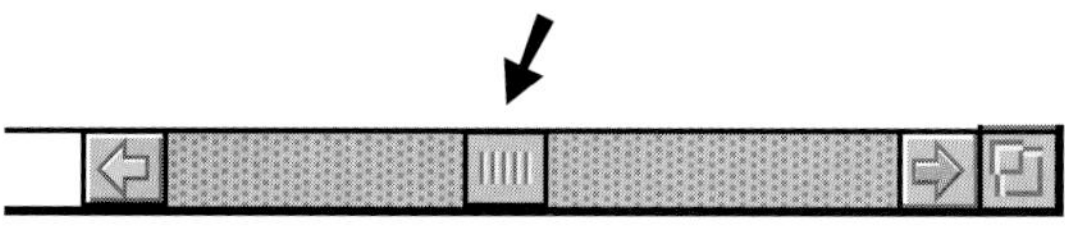

slot *Slot* is short for expansion slot, a place inside your computer's CPU where you can add computer boards. Look up *CPU, computer board,* and *expansion slot.*

small caps *Small caps* is a special type of font appearance. When a font is in small caps, all the upper case letters are shown as normal size capital letters while all the lower case letters are shown as smaller size capital letters.

There are no lower case letters in small caps. In the example below, the words *The, Pennsylvania,* and *Harrisburg* are capitalized. See how the first letter of each of those words is larger than the capital letter that is used for the other letters? Look up *font.*

THE CAPITAL OF PENNSYLVANIA IS HARRISBURG.

snail mail A snail is an animal that moves very slowly. Some people who use electronic mail like to call the mail that is delivered by the Postal Service—the type of mail you get at your home every day—*snail mail.* Even though the Postal Service can get a letter across the country in a few days, electronic mail can get a message across the country in a few seconds. Look up *electronic mail.*

sneaker net *Sneaker net* is a funny phrase that computer people use when the computer network is not working. On a computer network, you can send letters, pictures, stories, and sounds to your friends on other computers without leaving your desk. When the computer network breaks down, everyone has to walk their letters, stories, pictures, and diskettes from one place to another. Sneaker net is when you walk information from place to place instead of sending it over the network. Look up *network.*

Oh, no! What a mess! Al, Tommy, Maria, Joseph, and Simon were e-mailing letters to Lauren, Mary, Charlie, Billy, and Jamal when the computer network went down. Now Randal, the system administrator, has to **sneaker net** all the letters. The only problem is that Randal does not know who gets which letter. Using the clues below, can you help Randal deliver the **correct letter** to the **correct person**?

Use the chart below to help Randal figure who should get which letter. When you are able to eliminate a combination (a **sender** and **receiver**) put an "X" in the corresponding box. For example, since Maria sent her letter to a girl, an"**X**" has been placed in the boxes for Charlie, Billy, and Jamal. *Answers appear in the Answer Section in the back of the book.*

1. Maria sent her letter to a girl.
2. Al doesn't know Jamal or Lauren.
3. Tommy only knows Charlie and one of the two girls.
4. Joseph did not send a letter to a girl.
5. Lauren received her letter from a girl.
6. Charlie got his letter from Joseph or Simon.
7. Mary got her letter from a boy.
8. One sender and receiver have names that begin with the same letter.

		Receivers				
		Billy	Charlie	Jamal	Lauren	Mary
Senders	Al					
	Joseph					
	Maria	**X**	**X**	**X**		
	Simon					
	Tommy					

soft copy When you have a *soft copy* of your report or homework, you have a copy of your work on a diskette or your computer's hard disk. When you have a hard copy you have a printed copy of your report or homework.

"Dad, I'm going over to the park to play softball...OK?" asked Ryan.

"Is your report finished?" asked Dad.

"Yup, I have a **soft copy** *on diskette and a hard copy for Mrs. Peterson," replied Ryan.*

"Have a good time," said Dad.

soft font A font that can be used in a software program or that can be downloaded for use by your printer is called a *soft font*. A soft font is a font that is software. Look up *download* and *font*.

software *Software* is another name for a program. Software gives your computer instructions that make it play a game, display a graphic, run an animation, edit text, send e-mail, and all the other activities that make your computer useful and fun. Look up *software program*.

software company A *software company* is a business where people design, make, and sell computer programs. Software companies are sometimes called software houses.

software house *Software house* is another name for software company. It is a business where people design, make, and sell computer programs.

software license Did you know that when you buy computer software, you don't actually own it? What you do own is the right to use the software. The right to use the software is called a *software license*.

When your family buys a piece of software, a software license comes with it. You can usually find the software license on the envelope that contains the diskettes, on a separate card in the software box, or in the user's manual. The software license tells you what you can—and what you can't—do with the software.

For example, you can usually make one copy of the diskettes to keep as a backup. You are always allowed to install the software on a hard disk on one computer—but you are not supposed to install it on more than one computer at a time. And you're definitely not supposed to make copies for your friends.

Computer software is protected by United States copyright laws. A software license is a legal document. Take a look at one sometime. If you don't understand all the legal terms, ask your parents to explain them to you. Look up *software piracy.*

software package A *software package* is another name for a computer program that can be purchased at a computer store. Look up *software program.*

software piracy A pirate is a thief. *Software piracy* is when you make or use an unofficial copy of a software program. The software that you can buy in a computer store is protected under the United States copyright laws. What that means is that it is against the law to copy a software game or other program so that it can be used on more than one computer at a time.

For example, if your friend owns a copy of a software game, you can play the game on his or her computer, but it is against the law for you to make a copy of the software to put on your computer. It is also against the law for you to make a copy of a game that you own for one of your friends to put on his or her computer.

Pearl's mom is a programmer. One day she gave Pearl a computer puzzle game she created.

"Here Pearl, take a look. I finally finished the puzzle game I've been promising you," said Mom.

"Wow, that's really neat. Can I give a copy to Sarah?" asked Pearl.

"Sure. You can give a copy to whomever you like," replied Mom.

"If I give a copy to my friends, am I a **software pirate***?" asked Pearl.*

"No," laughed her mom, "but it's a good question. It is illegal to copy software that is protected by the copyright laws, such as the software we buy at the computer store. But if you make a program yourself—like I did—you can give it to whomever you want."

software program A *software program* gives your computer instructions that make it play a game, display a graphic, run an animation, edit text, send e-mail, and all the other activities that make your computer useful and fun. There are two basic types of software programs: application programs and operating system software.

It is the job of your software to act as a translator between you and the computer. When you play or work on a computer, you see animations, graphics, and text on your screen. You respond to the game or other program with mouse clicks and keypresses.

At its very basic level, all your computer can understand is a complex combinations of zeros (0) and ones (1). It is the job of your software program to translate the mouse clicks and keypresses that are meaningful to you into the zeros and ones that are meaningful to your computer. Look up *application program, binary numbers,* and *operating system.*

software publisher *Software publisher* is another name for a software company that makes software programs that are sold to computer stores. Look up *software company.*

sort When you *sort* a list of words, the files on your computer, or your clean socks from the laundry, you put those things in a particular order. You can sort them by alphabet, size, color, type, or any other order.

Many computer programs (such as word-processing and database programs) can create many different types of sorts. The sorts that are used most often in computer programs include:

- Alphabetical sorts (in order by the letter of the alphabet)
- Numerical sorts (in order by number)
- Chronological sorts (in order by date).

Look up *ascending order, chronological order, descending order,* and *numerical order.*

The Spirit Club at Lincoln Elementary School has the following seven members.

Lincoln Elementary School Spirit Club Members

Name	Grade	Birthday
Lizzy Cohen	6	10/16
Zarek Kaminski	6	4/19
Kira Kalan	5	8/21
Rose Mary O'Brien	4	12/5
George Beam	5	1/3
Bernice Fisher	4	9/7
Harry Rizzo	5	7/7

- Lizzy Cohen, the president of the club, wants an **alphabetical** list of all the members so she can take attendance at the club meetings.
- Zarek Kaminski, the club's vice president, wants a **chronological** list of all the club members by birthday so he can send each member a birthday card on his or her birthday.
- Kira Kalan, the club's secretary, wants a **numerical** list of all the members by grade so she can get their names in the correct section of the school yearbook.

Can you create the three **sorts** for Lizzy, Zarek, and Kira? *Answers appear in the Answer Section in the back of the book.*

sound card A *sound card* is an accessory that you can put inside your computer so that you can hear the music, voices, and sound effects that exist in many software programs. Once you have installed a sound card in your computer, you usually have to hook the card up to a speaker (not usually included with the sound card) in order to hear the sounds.

There are many different sound formats—such as Aria, Sound Blaster, and others. Ask your parents to be sure that the sound card that they purchase has a sound format that can be used with the different software programs you want to hear.

source disk When you copy files from one diskette to another diskette, the *source disk* is the diskette that contains the information you are going to use. It is the diskette from which you get the information. The target disk is the diskette that receives the information that you get from the source disk.

special interest group A *special interest group* is a computer club whose members are interested in a specific software program (like Flight Simulator), type of computing (like computer graphics), or computer technology (like virtual reality). The acronym for special interest group is SIG.

Special interest groups usually meet once a month. Often the club will have a guest speaker who demonstrates a new software program or discusses a new idea or topic having to do with the special interest. Look up *acronym, user group,* and *virtual reality.*

speech recognition Are you a good listener? Some computers with *speech recognition* software are beginning to listen to what their owners say. Speech recognition software is designed to let your computer understand spoken commands. Another term for speech recognition is voice recognition. Look up *voice recognition.*

speech synthesis Computers that have *speech synthesis* software can talk to you. The computer voice does not sound very natural—probably because it is just a combination of sounds that come from a file on your computer. You can type words for the speech synthesis program to say, or you can have it read you a story that is in a file on your computer. The speech synthesis program examines each word in the story and decides how to pronounce it according to a set of rules about grammar and pronunciation.

You usually need a sound card to use a speech synthesis program. Many sound card manufacturers even include a speech synthesis program when you buy their sound card. Look up *sound card.*

spell checker Have you ever written a report and wanted someone to check your spelling? Well, that's what a *spell checker* program does. A spell checker reads your entire report (of course the report has to be typed into the computer) and tells you which words it does not find in its dictionary. It can even suggest the correct spelling for the words it could not find in its dictionary.

If you know that a particular word is spelled correctly, then you can add it to the dictionary and the spell checker will not think that the word is misspelled the next time it sees the word. A spell checker is included with most word-processing programs.

spreadsheet A *spreadsheet* is a computer program that arranges data (usually numbers) in rows and columns. A spreadsheet is often used to perform calculations with math figures or money. Some popular spreadsheet programs are Lotus 1-2-3 and Microsoft Excel.

In most spreadsheets, the columns have letter names (A, B, C, and so on) and the rows are numbered (1, 2, 3, and so on). Where each row and column intersect, you have a little box where you can type data. This box is called a cell. Each cell is named by the intersection of the column and row number. For example, if the cell is located in the third column (called C) and the second row (called 2) then the cell is called C2.

	A	B	C	D
1	cell A1	cell B1		
2				cell D2
3			cell C3	

What can I put in a cell? There are three basic types of data that you can enter into a cell:
- Text.
- Numbers.
- Mathematical formulas. For example, A1 + B1 means to add the number in cell A1

to the number in cell B1.

What is a range of cells? A range of cells is a group of cells that are all connected. To describe the range, give the top left cell in the range and the bottom right cell in the range. For example, to describe the first three columns (but not column D) in the spreadsheet below, the range is A1-C3 since the top left cell is A1 and the bottom right cell is C3.

	A	B	C	D
1				
2				
3				

What does a spreadsheet look like? Let's take a look at a spreadsheet that Marcia uses to keep track of the extra money she earns doing small jobs for her neighbors.

	A	B
1	Job	Amount Received
2	Walked Kashi for 1 week	$10.00
3	Washed Mr. Ford's car	$11.00
4	Raked the front yard	$8.00
5	Sorted books for garage sale	$ 4.00
6	TOTAL	$33.00

Look at the total above in cell B6. Marcia added up the numbers herself and typed the dollar amount in the cell. But she could have entered a formula so that the spreadsheet would do the math for her! Below is the same spreadsheet, but showing the formula that Marcia could have used in cell B6.

	A	B
1	Job	Amount Received
2	Walked Kashi for 1 week	$ 10.00
3	Washed Mr. Ford'scar	$ 11.00
4	Raked the front yard	$ 8.00
5	Sorted books for garage sale	$ 4.00
6	TOTAL	(B2+B3+B4+B5)

---

star A wildcard is a symbol that is used to take the place of some or all of the letters in a filename or the filename extension. When an asterisk (*) is used to take the place of other letters, it is called a *star.*

If you want the star to take the place of both the filename and the extension, you must use the star twice, as in

.

The stars must be separated with a period—just like you separate the filename and extension with a period. Look up *extension*, *filename*, and *wildcard*.

"Dad, how can I copy all the files in my directory to a diskette in my drive?" asked Francis.

"Just type COPY A: **star** *dot* **star**,*" responded Dad.*

"Like this?"

Francis showed his dad the following command on his computer screen.

```
COPY A: *.*
```

"Yes, that's right," said Dad. "Now just press Enter."

Startup Items folder Inside the system folder is a folder called Startup Items. Any file or program that you place in Startup Items automatically opens each time you turn on your computer. An experienced computer user will put aliases of files in the *Startup Items folder* so the files themselves can be kept in their regular folders. Look up *alias* and *system folder.*

"How did you get that neat sound to play when your Mac started?" asked Bobbie.

"Nothing to it! I just dragged an alias of the sound file to the **Startup Items folder**,*" replied Tom.*

Startup window On your Microsoft Windows desktop is a window called Startup. If you want a program to begin automatically each time you start Windows, place its icon in the *Startup window.* Look up *desktop* and *Microsoft Windows.*

---

storage Do you know the difference between a closet and your memory? Both the closet and your memory store things until you need them. But your closet is permanent *storage.* Things will stay in the closet until you take them out. Your memory is temporary storage. There are many things that you don't remember anymore. For example, what color shirt did you wear this day last year? What day of the week was it when you learned how to tell time? What did you have for dinner ten days ago? There are lots of things that you can't remember. Memory and your closet space are very different.

Why all the discussion about memory and closets? Because the single most common bit of computer technology that people get confused about (kids and adults alike) is mixing up computer memory and computer storage. The main reason that people get these two confused is that both computer storage (the space on your hard disk) and computer memory (the amount of memory in your computer) are both measured in megabytes.

Computer storage is like closet space. The more computer storage you have the more software programs you can store on your hard disk. Your hard disk is your computer's closet space. Just as you can always use more closet space, you can always use more computer storage. When your family purchases a hard disk, buy the largest hard disk within your budget. No matter how big a disk you buy, you will eventually fill up the space.

When you go to buy software, it is important to know if you have enough storage space on your hard disk to store the new software program. If you don't have enough free space, you can choose not to buy the software (yeah, right), or you can remove enough files from your hard disk to make room for the new software (which is what most people do). The system requirements on the outside of the software package will almost always tell you how much free space you need on your hard disk to install the software. Look up *megabyte*, *memory*, and *storage device*.

storage device A *storage device* is a piece of computer equipment that holds your files and software programs. The storage devices on your computer are your hard disk and diskette drives. Your computer may also have other storage devices such as removable hard disk cartridges (like Bernoulli and Syquest) or a tape drive (for making backup copies of the information on your hard disk). Look up *hard disk* and *storage*.

subdirectory All the games and software programs on your computer's hard disk are organized into groups called directories. A directory that is located inside another directory is called a *subdirectory*.

Mac On a Mac, directories and subdirectories are called folders.

Look up *directory*, *folder*, and *nested subdirectory*.

suitcase A *suitcase* is a file that contains font information. The information in the suitcase varies, depending on whether you are using PostScript or TrueType fonts. Usually, a PostScript suitcase only contains fonts for your screen (your printer fonts are in separate files). A TrueType suitcase contains fonts for your printer and fonts for your screen. Look up *font, PostScript,* and *TrueType.*

Super VGA monitor Super means superior or better than. A *Super VGA monitor* is a monitor that is better than a VGA monitor. For a monitor to be Super VGA, it must be able to display more pixels (better resolution) and more colors than a VGA monitor. This means that a Super VGA monitor must be able to display more than 640 pixels across the screen (from left to right) and more than 480 pixels down the screen (from top to bottom). A Super VGA monitor must also be able to display more than 256 colors at the same time. Look up *pixel, resolution,* and *VGA monitor.*

supercomputer *Supercomputers* are extremely fast, mainframe computers. Supercomputers are the most powerful computers made—some can perform over a billion calculations every second! Supercomputers are used for applications that need to perform complicated calculations, such as designing new products, and scientific, medical, and military research.

The most popular supercomputers are made by a company called Cray Research, Inc. Because supercomputers are very expensive, they are usually only owned by governments, large companies, and big universities. Look up *mainframe.*

SuperDrive A *SuperDrive* is a diskette drive that can read double-density and high-density diskettes for both Macs and

PCs. SuperDrives now come with all Macintosh computers.

surf the net When you use the Internet to search for information, cruise the latest web/sites, or just look around, you are said to be "surfing" the Internet, or "*surfing the net.*" Look up *Internet* and *World Wide Web.*

surge In your house, do the lights dim when the refrigerator, air conditioner, heat pump, or other major appliance turns on? Things both inside and outside your home can cause the electricity coming into your home to vary. A sudden jump in electrical power is called a *surge.*

A surge can be caused by electrical transformers, appliances, lightning, or static electricity. If the power surge reaches your computer, it can damage the circuits and chips inside. You should protect all your computer equipment by plugging each component of your computer equipment into a surge protector rather than the outlet in the wall. Look up *component* and *surge protector.*

surge protector A surge in electrical power can damage your computer equipment. A *surge protector* is a special kind of power strip that protects your computer equipment from electrical surges. The surge protector contains a special circuit that can sense an increase in the voltage on the electrical line. It then prevents the surge from reaching your equipment.

How do I use a surge protector? Using a surge protector is very easy. First, you plug the surge protector into the wall outlet. Next, you plug each piece of computer equipment into the surge protector. Last, you turn the surge protector on. That's all there is to it.

Does a surge protector come with my computer? Not usually. You can buy a surge protector at a computer store or an electronics store. Look up *surge.*

sysop *Sysop* (pronounced "sis sop" or "sis op") is an acronym for system operator. A sysop is the person who operates a computer system that has many users, such as a BBS (bulletin board system).

The sysop sets up login IDs for users, keeps an eye on the electronic mail, and handles problems with the software and hardware. If the sysop has a particular hobby or interest—like rock music, sports, programming, or games—then the BBS usually has a lot of information about that subject. Look up *acronym, bulletin board system, electronic mail,* and *login.*

System 6 *System 6* is an earlier version of Mac OS, the Macintosh operating system. The current Mac OS is called System 7. Look up *Mac OS, operating system,* and *System 7.*

System 7 *System 7* is the current and most widely used version of Mac OS, the Macintosh operating system. Look up *Mac OS* and *operating system.*

system clock All computers today come with a built-in clock that keeps track of the date and time—even when your computer is turned off or unplugged. This built-in clock is called a *system clock* or internal clock because the clock is located inside your computer system. Look up *internal clock.*

system folder The *system folder* is the folder that contains the system software, the files that make up Mac OS. Look up *Mac OS, operating system,* and *System 7.*

system requirements When you buy a software program or computer accessory there is usually a section on the package marked *system requirements.* The system requirements describe the minimum computer system and software that you need to have in order to run a particular software program. You can always have a better computer, more memory, more storage, and a newer version of whatever software the company says you must have to run the software—you just can't have less and run the software.

system software All the files that together make up the operating system are called the *system software.* Look up *operating system.*

systems program A *systems program* is a software program that can only be used by your computer. For example, DOS, MAC OS, OS/2, and Windows all have systems programs that cannot be used by you. A systems program is different than an application program, which is used by people to do a job or produce a result. Look up *DOS, MAC OS, OS/2,* and *Windows.*

target disk When you copy files from one diskette to another diskette, the *target disk* is the diskette that receives the information. Another name for a target disk is destination disk. The source disk is the diskette that contains the information you are going to use.

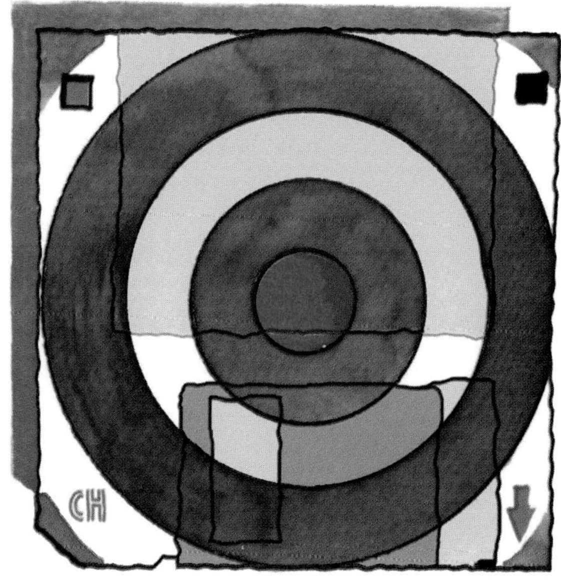

technical writer A *technical writer* is a person who writes instruction manuals for technical products like computers and software.

template **(1)** One meaning of *template* is a small chart that fits on or over the function keys on your keyboard. The template explains what all the function keys do in a specific software program. Since not all software programs use the same function keys to do the same thing, you need separate templates for each software program that uses the function keys. Many software companies provide a template free of charge when you purchase their software program. Templates for popular programs can also be purchased in computer stores. Look up *function key.*
(2) A second meaning of *template* is a stencil. Did you ever use a stencil to trace letters or pictures onto your paper? Computer professionals sometimes use a template to draw computer symbols on paper. Each symbol represents a different computer process or procedure.
(3) A third meaning of *template* is a sample design that comes with a word-processing, desktop publishing, or other program. For example, suppose you want to create an announcement for the school fair. You can look at the templates that come with your software programs and see if they have a design you can use. If you find a template that you like, you use it like any other document. You open the file, add your own text, and print it out.

text *Text* is information or data that consists only of letters, numbers, punctuation, and symbols that are found on your computer keyboard. The term text does not refer to graphics, lines, tables, charts, drawings, or pictures. Look up *graphic.*

text editor A *text editor* is a very simple word-processing program. Like a word processor, a text editor can be used to type and change text. But unlike any of the popular word processors, it cannot be used to add color, pictures, sound, fonts, tables, and charts. Text editors are useful for writing short notes or text that does not need any fancy formatting. Look up *word-processing program.*

> *"Ari, what word processor do you use?" asked Leah. "I like Ami Pro."*
>
> *"I just use a* **text editor.** *I don't need anything that fancy," replied Ari.*

TIME command All computers today come with a built-in clock that keeps track of the time—even when your computer is turned off or unplugged. The *TIME command* is a DOS command that you can use to display the time on your screen or set your computer's internal clock.

How do I use the TIME command? To show the time on the screen, type the following command at the DOS prompt.

```
TIME [Enter]
```

Your computer shows you what it thinks is the current time, and prompts you to change it. If you don't want to change the time, just press [Enter]. If you want to change the time, type the correct hours, minutes, seconds, and "a" for AM, or "p" for PM. You must place a colon (:) between the hours, minutes, and seconds. (Setting the seconds is optional.)

For example, if you wanted to set your computer's internal clock to 3:15 PM, you would type the following command at the DOS prompt.

```
TIME 3:15p [Enter]
```

If you wanted to set your computer's internal clock to 3:15 PM and 20 seconds, you would type the following command at the DOS prompt.

```
TIME 3:15:20p [Enter]
```

Look up *DATE command, DOS command, DOS prompt, internal clock,* and *prompt.*

---

title bar A *title bar* is a label that is located at the top of every window. It displays the name of a window, disk, or folder. To move a window from one place to another on your screen, click and drag the title bar. Look up *click, disk, drag, folder,* and *window.*

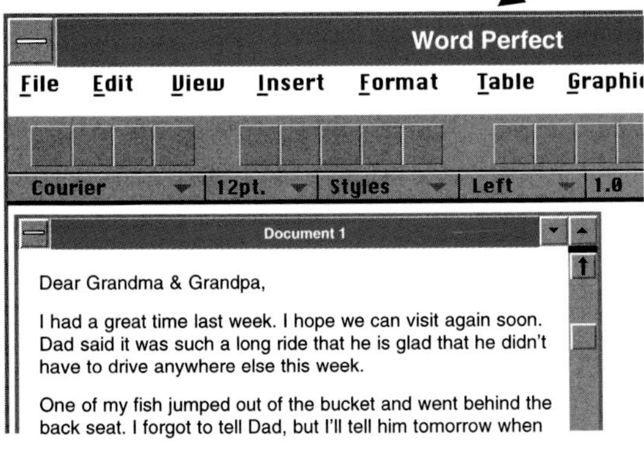

---

toggle A *toggle* is a switch that has two settings. Most light switches in your home are toggle switches because they have only two settings: on and off. Your keyboard has several toggle switches that turn on and off.

Try pushing Caps Lock, Scroll Lock, and Num Lock. Some keyboards have a light that comes on when a toggle switch is in the on position.

toner *Toner* is a fine, powdery ink that is used in the toner cartridges that you find in laser printers and copy machines. The toner ink forms the letters and pictures on each page that is printed by the laser printer. Look up *laser printer* and *toner cartridge.*

toner cartridge The *toner cartridge* is the part of the laser printer that holds the toner ink. The toner cartridge looks like a long drum. It slides into the laser printer much like the way a cassette tape slides into a tape recorder. When the toner is all gone, you can either buy a new toner cartridge, or have your empty cartridge refilled.

Don't throw away your old toner cartridge—it can be recycled! Because laser printers are so popular, many toner cartridges get used up every day. To reduce the environmental problems that all these empty cartridges can cause, many toner cartridge manufacturers will recycle your old cartridges. Some companies that sell refilled toner cartridges will even pay you a few dollars for your empty cartridges. Look up *laser printer* and *toner.*

touch screen A *touch screen* is a special type of monitor that knows where you are touching the screen. Some software programs are designed specifically for touch screens so you can make choices by touching the screen instead of using a mouse or keyboard. Touch screens are often used in zoos, museums, malls, automatic teller machines, and other public places where many people use the same computer.

How does a touch screen work? The touch screen bends a little when you touch it, and then pops back in place. Inside the screen are sensors that can tell where the screen was bent—so it also knows where you touched it. The software program that comes with the monitor tells the computer program where the screen was touched. The computer program then knows what selection you made.

tractor feed A *tractor feed* is the part of a dot-matrix printer that holds continuous paper in place as it goes through the printer. The tractor feed has small wheels with pegs that fit into the small holes on the edges of the continuous paper. As each line is printed, the pegs in the tractor feed move the paper to the next line so the dot-matrix printer can continue printing. Look up *continuous paper* and *dot-matrix printer.*

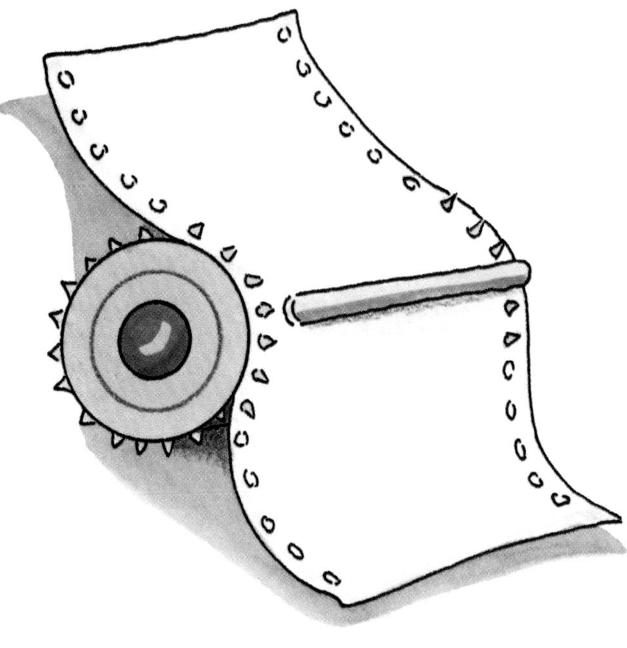

trash When you *trash* a file, you drag it to the trash can. Look up *trash can.*

"Tony, do you still need that file you were using?" asked Barbara.

"No, just **trash** *it," replied Tony.*

trash can The *trash can* icon is located in the bottom right-hand portion of your desktop. You delete a file by dragging it to the

trash can and then emptying the trash can. The trash can bulges when it contains trash.

Can I get back a file I have trashed? Just like a trash can at home, you can pull something out of the trash can as long as no one has emptied it. To take something out of your Mac trash can

1. Double-click on the trash can. A window opens and shows you the files you have trashed.
2. Drag the file from the trash can window to any other window or folder.

How do I empty the trash? To empty the trash can, pull down the Special window and select the Empty Trash command. Look up *desktop, double-click, drag, folder,* and *window.*

TREE command The *TREE command* is a DOS command that tells your computer to show you a picture of the directory structure on your hard disk or diskette. When you use the TREE command, your computer only shows you the current directory and its subdirectories; it does not show you any files that live in those directories.

How do I use the TREE command? To use the TREE command to see the directory structure on your hard disk, follow the instructions below.

1. Make sure you are using drive C. Type the following command.

   C: Enter

2. To see the entire directory structure, you need to be in the root directory (otherwise you will only see part of your hard disk's directory structure). To go to the root directory, type the following command.

   CD\ Enter

3. Since the directory structure of most computers cannot be shown on just one screen, you should use the DIR command with the MORE command. The MORE command pauses the screen so you can read the information. When you want to see the next part of your directory structure, just press Enter. To see the directory structure, type the following command.

   TREE ¦ MORE Enter

Note: Be sure to use the pipe (¦) symbol and not a colon (:) symbol before MORE or the command won't work. The pipe symbol is usually located above on the same key as the backslash (\) character. For fun, try typing the TREE command without ¦ MORE and see what happens.

Look up *CD command, directory structure, DOS command, DOS prompt, MORE command, pipe*, and *root directory*.

Trekker A *Trekker* is a fan of the popular TV series *Star Trek: Voyager, Star Trek: The Next Generation, Star Trek: Deep Space Nine*, and/or *Star Trek* (the original). All these TV shows are very popular among computer professionals. Many computer professionals comment that the various *Star Trek* series influenced their choosing computers as a career or influenced some part of their work in computers.

Although many non-fans call a *Star Trek* fan a "Trekkie," the official name for a *Star Trek* fan is "Trekker."

Trojan horse A *Trojan horse* is a computer virus that a programmer hides inside a game or other software program to trick people. Some Trojan horses are very destructive and will erase your entire hard disk! It is unlikely that you will find a Trojan horse in a software program you buy at a computer store. Most Trojan horses are hidden in shareware programs.

There are special software programs—called anti-virus programs—that can find a Trojan horse (or any other virus) on your computer. You can also use these programs to check if a diskette is infected with a virus, before copying any files from the diskette onto your computer. Always use an anti-virus program to check any new shareware programs you get. Look up *anti-virus program, clean, scan, shareware,* and *virus.*

Where does the term **Trojan horse** *come from? A Trojan horse is a trick that comes from the* Iliad, *a story written hundreds of years ago by a Greek writer named Homer. As the story goes, Helen, the Queen of Sparta, was the most beautiful woman in the world. One day she was kidnaped by Paris, the son of King Priam of Troy.*

King Menelaus sent an army of 1,000 ships and 100,000 men to Troy to bring her back. Because her husband sent 1,000 ships to Troy, it is said that Helen had the face that launched a thousand ships.

After the soldiers arrived in Troy, they fought the Trojans for nine years, but were unable to capture the city, which was surrounded by a great wall, or to get Helen back.

Finally, a Greek soldier named Ulysses, with the help of the goddess Athena, came up with a plan to build a huge wooden horse with enough room inside for 100 soldiers. The Greeks built the horse and put their best warriors inside.

Most of the soldiers pretended to leave Troy and offered the horse to King Priam as a parting gift. The Trojans opened the gates of their city to allow the wooden horse to be brought inside the city. As the Trojans slept that night, the soldiers climbed out of the horse and called back the soldiers who had pretended to leave. The Greeks killed the Trojans during the night, and Helen was finally brought back to her husband King Menelaus.

If you would like to read the entire story, the Iliad *can be checked out of your local or school library. Homer's other great work, the* Odyssey, *tells of Ulysses' adventures during his voyage back home to Ithaca.*

troubleshoot To *troubleshoot* is to look for the source of a problem. Suppose that every time you walked through the kitchen your mom told you to mop up a small puddle of water that had collected in front of the refrigerator. If you tried to find out where the water was coming from, you would be troubleshooting the problem.

When programmers or other computer professionals troubleshoot a problem, they look for a bug in a software program, or for a bad part or bad connection in a computer. Look up *bug* and *programmer.*

troubleshooter A *troubleshooter* is a person who looks for the source of a problem. Look up *troubleshoot.*

TrueType *TrueType* is the name of a font technology that was developed by the team efforts of Apple Corporation and Microsoft Corporation. When you use a TrueType font in a software program, you can make it whatever point size you want. The TrueType font automatically makes the font size you requested. Look up *font* and *point.*

TYPE command The *TYPE command* is a DOS command that you can use to tell your computer to print a file to your screen so you can read it on your monitor. TYPE can only be used to show you files that were written with a text editor (like the DOS EDIT command). TYPE will not display files that contain graphics or that were written with a word processor.

When you use the TYPE command to display a file, it looks like someone is typing lines of text on your screen, one line at a time. The TYPE command lets you read the information but does not let you change it.

How do I use the TYPE command? To use the TYPE command to display text on your screen, you type TYPE followed by the name of the text file you want to read. For example, to read the information in README.TXT, type the following command at the DOS prompt.

```
TYPE README.TXT ¦ MORE  [Enter]
```

Since most text files that come with your software programs contain more text than can fit on one screen, the example above shows the MORE command being used with the TYPE command. When you do not use MORE, the information passes by on your screen so quickly that you do not have time to read it. The MORE command lets you read one screen of information at a time.

What's all this garbage on my screen? If you use TYPE to display a file that is NOT a text file—such as a file that contains graphics or a program—you will see a lot of strange characters on the screen and your computer may beep a few times. While all this activity may look like you caused a big problem, DON'T WORRY! The TYPE command never changes what's in a file. Just wait for the computer to stop (this may take a few minutes depending on the size of the file) or press Ctrl-C to stop your computer from displaying the rest of the file.

Can I use the TYPE command to print a text file on my printer? Yes. To print the file on the printer (rather than your screen) just add ">LPT1" to the end of the TYPE command. Do not use the MORE command when you use ">LPT1."

```
TYPE README.TXT > LPT1 Enter
```

Warning: If you use the TYPE command to print a file that is not a text file, you may waste a lot of paper!

Look up *DOS command*, *DOS prompt*, *garbage*, *MORE*, *text*, and *text editor*.

typeface *Typeface* is another word for font style. It is the look and design of a font that makes the font unique. Look up *font* and *font style*.

UNDELETE command The *UNDELETE command* is a DOS command that lets you bring back a file that you accidentally deleted. UNDELETE can be used on computers that are using DOS 5.0 or higher. Use the VER command to find out what version of DOS you are using.

At one time or another, everyone accidentally erases a file that they did not mean to erase. When this happens to you—and it will happen some day—the UNDELETE command is a very good command to know.

Bringing back a file that has been deleted is called recovering the file. **The best time to UNDELETE a file is right after you delete it.** The more you use your computer after deleting a file, the smaller your chance of recovering the file.

How do I use the UNDELETE command? The easiest way to undelete a file is to first go to the directory where the file was deleted.

1. Use the CD command to change to the directory that used to contain the file you deleted. If the file you deleted was in a directory called HOMEWORK, you would type the following command at the DOS prompt.

   CD C:\HOMEWORK [Enter]

2. Type UNDELETE followed by the name of the file. Suppose you want to recover a story you wrote for English about a haunted house. If the file was named HAUNTED.DOC, you would type the following command at the DOS prompt.

   UNDELETE HAUNTED.DOC [Enter]

   If your computer can undelete the file, it displays a lot of technical information and tells you whether or not all the clusters are available. (If all the clusters are available you can undelete the entire file. If not all the clusters are available, only part of the file can be undeleted.) Your computer then responds with:

   Undelete (Y/N) ?

3. Press [Y].

What if I can't remember the name of my file? If you cannot remember the exact name of the file you deleted, follow the instructions below.

1. Type the following command at the DOS prompt.

   UNDELETE [Enter]

One at a time, your computer shows you the name of every deleted file it can find.

2. When you see the name of the file you want to undelete, press Y. Until then, just press N.

Since UNDELETE cannot always restore your file, you should get into the habit of copying your important files to diskette.

How does UNDELETE work? It will be easier to understand how UNDELETE works if we take a look at something else that works the same way—video tapes for your VCR.

Suppose your family has several videotapes for your VCR. Some are prerecorded tapes that you watch over and over again, and some are blank tapes that your mom and dad use to record TV shows or movies that your family doesn't want to miss. Suppose that once your family has watched the taped TV show, the tape is put in a pile of tapes to be used over again.

When the tape that has been watched is put in a pile to be used over again, has it been erased? No. It has just been set aside to be recorded over, when needed. If you take the tape out of the pile before it has been used again, can you watch the recording again? Yes, you can.

The UNDELETE command works a lot like the group of videotapes that has been set aside to be reused. Just as the video tape is not erased when you set it aside to be reused, *a file is not erased from your hard disk when you delete it!*

Your computer keeps track of where each file is located on your hard disk so that it does not reuse space on your hard disk that is already in use by another file. When you delete a file, your computer makes a note that it can reuse that space—it does not erase any information. As long as your computer has not reused the space, you can recover the deleted file. Look up *backup copy, DEL command, DOS command, DOS prompt, ERASE,* and *VER command.*

undo Many software programs have a feature called *undo* that undoes the last thing you did. For example, suppose you are drawing a picture with a paint program and accidentally draw a purple line through your drawing. Just select the undo command. Your picture will go back to the way it was before you made the change.

universal product code If you look on the back of a bag of potato chips, a box of cereal, or your favorite game or magazine, you will see a little box that contains a bunch of vertical (up and down) lines with some numbers underneath. These bunches of vertical lines (called bars) are a special type of bar code called a *universal product code.* Universal product code is abbreviated UPC. This is the UPC for this book:

When a company makes a product, it can't assign the product any bar code it wants since there may be another company using the same bar code. What would happen if two food companies used the same bar code? You might get to the checkout line in your supermarket and your Rice Krispies could get rung up as pickled beets!

Who assigns the bar code numbers? When a company wants to put a bar code on their products, the company contacts the Uniform Code Council. The council gives the company specific bar codes to use. These special bar codes are called universal product codes or UPCs. Once the council has given a company UPCs to use on their products, those bar codes are reserved and cannot be used for products that are made by other companies.

Why are there numbers underneath the bar codes? Each set of lines in the bar code represents a number from zero to nine. The number underneath each set of lines is there just in case the scanner that reads the codes has a problem. If the scanner stops working, the store checkout clerk can enter the numbers under the UPC into the cash register by hand. Can you imagine how long it would take to get through the checkout line if the person behind the counter had to figure out the number for each little group of lines in the UPC? Look up *bar code reader.*

---

unzip Many commercial software companies, and most shareware programmers, use a program called PKZIP, from PKWARE, Inc., to compress their files. Most software companies compress their files so that the software that they sell to you can be put on as few diskettes as possible—thus saving themselves some money. Files that have been compressed with PKZIP are said to be zipped, and have the file extension ".ZIP."

When you unzip a file, you expand it to its normal size. You must unzip a zipped file before you can use it. The installation program that comes with your store-bought software automatically unzips the files for you. Many shareware programmers assume that you already have a copy of the unzip software (PKUNZIP).

If you need a copy of PKUNZIP, you can get it from almost any BBS or online service, or from the company where you got the shareware. Look up *BBS, download, online service, shareware,* and *zip.*

up arrow key The *up arrow key* ↑ moves the keyboard cursor up one line. Look up *cursor movement keys* and *keyboard cursor.*

UPC *UPC* is an abbreviation for universal product code, the special barcode that appears on the back of most food products, magazines, toys, and other items. Look up *universal product code.*

update Changes are occurring all the time. Kids move, change schools, get new brothers and sisters, etc. When you *update* the information in a computer, you provide new information so that information in the computer is correct.

When Meredith's dad saw her report card he noticed that the address was wrong.

"This report card has our old address on it," said Dad.

"I guess we should **update** *our information in the school computer so they have our new address," replied Meredith.*

"You're right. Why don't you go to the school office tomorrow morning and ask the secretary for a change of address card," said Dad. "We'll fill it out together tomorrow night."

upgrade A new, improved version of a software program is called an *upgrade.* When a software company upgrades the software, it either changes the name of the software (for example Sim City to Sim City 2000) or it changes the version number of the software (for example version 2.0 becomes version 3.0).

If you already own a copy of the software, you can usually buy the upgrade for less money than you would pay if you were buying the software for the first time. The company that makes the software almost always has a special upgrade price. To get the upgrade price, you sometimes have to buy the software directly from the software company.

You can always find out which is the newest version of a software program and the upgrade price by calling the software company and asking them. **Be sure to get your parent's permission before making a long distance call.** Look up *version number.*

upload You *upload* a file when you send a file from your computer to another computer over the phone lines. Look up *download* and *modem.*

upper case An *upper case* letter is a letter of the alphabet that has been capitalized. The upper case letters include A, B, C, D, E, F, G, H, I, J, K, L, M, N, O, P, Q, R, S, T, U, V, W, X, Y, and Z. Look up *lower case.*

user *A user* is someone who uses a computer or software program—someone like you.

user friendly *User friendly* means that a computer or software program is easy to use. Many companies claim that their products are user friendly. It's up to you (the user) to decide whether or not the company's claim is correct. As a joke, some people who find a software program difficult to use will call the program "user hostile."

user group A *user group* is a computer club. The members of the user group have meetings (usually once a month) where a guest speaker demonstrates a new software program or discusses a new idea or topic having to do with computers.

In addition to a speaker, the meetings usually have a time for members to ask general questions about computers and software. If anyone at the meeting has a question or problem, he or she can ask the group if anyone knows the answer to the question or the solution to the problem. User groups are a great place to get good (and free) help and advice.

Most user groups discuss all kinds of computer topics. Other user groups are for people who are interested in specific topics (such as games, programming, virtual reality, desktop publishing, or other topics). User groups that only discuss special topics are called SIGs. SIG is an acronym for special interest group.

Before you attend a meeting at a user group or SIG, be sure to call and ask about their policy on kids. Many user groups are only for adults. They do not allow kids (or anyone under 18) to attend their meetings. If you can't find a user group you like (or one that will let you attend), start your own. You only need a computer and a few interested friends who want to share ideas and tips. Look up *acronym.*

user ID Your *user ID* is the name or number that a computer network, online service, or bulletin board system uses to identify you. ID is short for identification.

Do you know two people who have the same name? Maybe you have the same name as your dad, grandmother, or someone you know. Since many people across the country have the same name, large computer systems, and many small computer systems, do not use your name to identify you.

When you join a network, online service, or bulletin board system, you are given (or can select) a name or number to use as identification. If you select a name or number that is already being used, the host computer asks you to select a different name or number. Look up *bulletin board system, network,* and *online service.*

user interface The *user interface* is the part of a software program that allows you (the user) to work with the software. In every software program, there are selections that you make or actions that you take with the mouse or keyboard. The interface lets you communicate with the software program through keypresses and mouse clicks.

So the next time you are playing Sim Ant and a friend asks you what you are doing, just say, "I am interacting with the Sim Ant user interface."

user list The *user list* is a list of all of the people who own or use a specific software or computer product. The user list for your class computer is a list of all the people who use that computer. A user list for the game Outpost is a list of all the people who filled out and sent in the registration card that comes with the game.

It is a good idea to send in the registration card that comes with a new computer or software program so you can get on the company's user list. When the company is going to upgrade the software or release a new product, some of the first people to get information are the people on the user list.

user manual The *user manual* is the instruction book that comes with a piece of computer equipment or a software program. The user manual explains how to set-up the equipment, install the software, and use the product (such as how to play the game). The user manual is also called the instruction manual or documentation.

utility program Do you have chores you need to take care of around your home? You probably have to keep your room clean, put away your clothes, take out the trash, wash dishes, and other tasks. The chores that you do help things at home run smoothly.

A *utility program* is a software program that helps you take care of housekeeping chores on your computer. Some utility programs will let you edit text files, compress files so they take up less space on your hard disk, and undelete files that were erased by mistake. Look up *EDIT command* and *UNDELETE command.*

vaporware Vapor is like steam, fog, or a cloud—you can see it, but you can't seem to grasp it in your hands. *Vaporware* is a term that programmers use to describe a software program that a company keeps promising to release but doesn't. Sometimes the vaporware product is finally released (usually later than the date that the company had said the product would be available). Sometimes the software never gets released. The software is just like vapor; you can't seem to get your hands on it.

"Have you heard anymore about the SpaceWalk virtual reality game?" Cathi asked Helene. "I heard so much about it a few months ago and now, no one seems to know anything about it."

"SpaceWalk is **vaporware**,*" replied Helene. "I don't think it will ever be released."*

VER command The *VER command* is a DOS command that displays the version number of the DOS on your computer.

How do I use the VER command? To use VER, type the following at the DOS prompt.

```
VER [Enter]
```

Your computer displays the version of DOS it is using. For example, if your computer is using MS-DOS version 6.2, you will see the following message.

```
MS-DOS Version 6.2
```

Why would I want to know what version of DOS is on my computer? You should know which version of DOS is on your computer because some software programs cannot be used on computers that are using older versions of DOS. If you are thinking of buying a computer game or other program, you should look at the system requirements written on the software package to see if the software program will work with your version of DOS.

Also, there are many DOS commands described in this book that will only work with DOS version 5.0 and higher. You need to know what DOS version you are using to know whether or not the commands will work on your computer.

What does "or higher" mean? Many software programs say that you need DOS version 3.2 or higher, or Windows 3.1 or higher. The "or higher" means that the software program will work with the version listed (DOS 3.2, for example) or any number that is bigger than 3.2 (DOS 5.0, for example). Look up *DOS command, DOS prompt, system requirements,* and *version number.*

---

version number Many software companies make their software programs better and better each year. When a software program is successful (like Corel Draw, Microsoft Windows, and WordPerfect), the software company does not want to change the name of the software when they start selling the improved software, so they change the *version number* instead.

The version number is a numbering system that the software company, the programmer, and you can use to keep track of improvements to a software program. The version number usually consists of two numbers, separated by a decimal point. For example, 4.2, 5.0, or 6.1. When you read a version number out loud, you say each part of it, including the decimal point. For example, version 2.1 is pronounced "version two-dot-one" or "version two-point-one." The very first version number of a software program is usually (but not always) 1.0.

Why use the decimal point? Why not just count in whole numbers? The reason there are two numbers separated by a decimal is to indicate whether the software has had major changes or minor changes. Numbers before the decimal point indicate that the software has had some major changes. Numbers after the decimal point indicate that the software has had some minor changes. When the number before the decimal point increases, the number after the decimal point goes back to zero. For example, the next major release of a software program after version 1.3 is called version 2.0. (Software companies rarely get to version 1.9 before jumping to version 2.0.)

When major changes have been made to a software program that you use all the time, you will probably want to get the new version—which is called an upgrade. When minor changes have been made to the software program, you may or may not want to get the upgrade depending on what has been added and which features have changed.

How do I know which version is the most current version of the software program? Computer stores don't always have the most current version of a software program—particularly if the software program was recently upgraded. The way to make sure that you are buying the most recent version is to call the software company and ask them. (Do not rely on the advice from the salesperson at the computer store.) Most software companies have a toll-free 800 number, but **get your parent's permission before making a long distance call.** Look up *feature, upgrade,* and *VER command.*

"My mom said I could call Microsoft to find out what the newest version of Flight Simulator is, but I don't know what to ask them," said Tobias.

"When they answer the phone, just say 'Can you tell me the version number of the newest release of Flight Simulator?'" replied Omar.

"That's it?" asked Tobias.

"Sure. That's all you want to know, isn't it?" responded Omar.

"Yeah. Thanks," said Tobias.

---

vertical scrolling When you have a page of text or a picture that does not all fit on your screen at one time, you can move the image up and down so that you can see more of the picture or more of the text. Moving the picture up and down is called *vertical scrolling.* To move the picture or text up and down, you can use ↑ and ↓ or the vertical scroll bar. Look up *scroll bar.*

VGA monitor All the pictures, text, and colors on your monitor are made up of tiny dots called pixels. A *VGA monitor* is a computer screen that can display at least 256 separate colors at one time, and has a screen resolution of 640 × 480 pixels. Screen resolution is shown as a multiplication formula.

A screen resolution of 640 × 480 means that a VGA monitor can display 640 pixels from left to right across the screen, and 480 pixels from the top of the screen to bottom of the screen. Look up *bitmap, pixel, screen resolution,* and *Super VGA monitor.*

---

video clip Imagine presenting a report in school that you can show on a classroom computer using sound and video. Many word-processing, graphic, animation, and other software programs allow you to insert short movies into your projects. The short movie is called a *video clip*—or clip, for short.

Most video clips take lots of space on your hard disk. You must also have a special software program that lets you play the video clip on your computer. Most video clips have sound, but you can only hear the sound part of a video clip if you have a sound card and speakers connected to your computer.

Although you can enlarge a video clip to the size of your screen, video clips look best when you keep them small—about two inches by two inches. As you make the picture bigger, the clip tends to run at a slower speed and look choppy (like some of the frames of the clip have been chopped out).

"Why are you adding a **video clip** *to your report?" asked Brian, Fenella's big brother. "It'll never print out on the printer."*

"Mr. Grant said that if we want to add a **video clip** *to our report, we can turn in our report on diskette instead of paper," replied Fenella.*

"What's it of?" asked Brian.

"A polar bear in its natural habitat," replied Fenella.

---

virtual reality *Virtual reality* is a type of software program that goes beyond your normal software experience. With virtual reality software, you get more of a sense of being right there inside the program. Virtual reality is abbreviated VR.

Virtual reality uses 3-D graphics, sound, and touch to produce a very realistic effect. In many virtual reality systems, there is no computer screen or keyboard. You wear a special helmet that displays pic-

tures directly into your eyes so you feel like you are there looking at the scene, rather than just watching a scene on your computer screen. As you move your head from side to side, your view changes—just as it does when you move your head from side to side in real life.

The helmet usually has stereo sound built right in. The sound can be so real that you lose yourself into the experience and are unaware of other things that may be going on around you. Many virtual reality systems have some type of hand control—like a gun or trigger that lets you shoot an opponent (who is often times another live person who is connected to the virtual reality system).

---

virus Sometimes when you get sick, you get a really bad cold that is caused by a *virus.* When you go to school and cough on the other kids, they also get the virus—just as you probably got it from some other kid who coughed on you. Like you, your computer can get sick with a virus. But where your virus is caused by germs, a computer virus is caused by a naughty programmer's software program.

How does a computer get a virus? When one computer has a virus, and a second computer uses a diskette or a file from the infected computer, the second computer also gets the virus. Once the second computer has the virus, it, too can infect any other computer. That's how computer viruses spread.

What happens to the computer when it gets a virus? It depends on the virus. Some viruses are mischievous and just display a message or picture on your screen. Other viruses are destructive and erase every file on your hard disk. What makes viruses so dangerous is that you never know what will happen when your computer catches one.

Where does a computer virus come from? Unlike a virus caused by germs, a computer virus does not just exist or happen. Computer viruses are made on purpose by a programmer who wants to cause trouble. There are hundreds of known computer viruses. Creating and releasing a computer virus is a very serious crime that can be punished with a jail sentence.

How can I get rid of a virus on my computer? There are special software programs that can look for a virus on your computer and get rid of any virus found. These programs are called anti-virus programs. You can also use these programs to check if a diskette is infected with a virus before copying any files from the diskette onto your computer. Look up *anti-virus program.*

---

voice recognition **(1)** When we say that a computer is capable of *voice recognition,* it means that the computer can hear and process spoken information. Voice recognition is often used to enter commands or data by talking directly to your computer. You speak your command into a microphone that is connected to your computer. The voice recognition software converts your spoken command into a pattern that the computer can understand and act upon.

Since different people speak with different accents, the same words may be spoken different ways. Also, there are so many variations to the human voice that you may have to teach your voice recognition program how you say certain commands. This type of voice recognition is also known as speech recognition.

(2) Voice recognition is also used to mean the technology that allows a computer to recognize the voice of a specific person. This type of voice recognition is used in some security systems.

volatile memory Volatile (pronounced vol-ah-tile, "vol" rhymes with "ball") means unstable. *Volatile memory* is computer memory that is erased each time you turn off your computer. Your computer's RAM (random access memory) is considered volatile because all the information in RAM is erased each time you turn off your computer. Look up *memory.*

VR *VR* is an abbreviation for virtual reality. VR is a software experience that gives you a sense of being right inside a program. Look up *virtual reality.*

WAN *WAN* is an acronym for wide area network, a special type of network that is designed to connect a large number of users, some of whom are located far away from each other. Look up *acronym* and *wide area network.*

warm boot To boot your computer is to turn on your computer. If your computer is already on, and you start it up again due to a problem with a software program or some other reason, you are rebooting your computer.

Pressing the reset button or the Ctrl-Alt-Del keys to reboot your computer is called a *warm boot* because you are restarting your computer without first turning it off—while it is still warm. Look up *boot, cold boot,* and *Ctrl-Alt-Del.*

warranty When you buy any new product—for your computer or for any reason—the product's manufacturer often promises that if you treat the product correctly, it will not break for at least a certain amount of time (for example, two years). The manufacturer writes this promise down and includes it with the product. The promise is called a *warranty.*

If the product breaks before the time promised, called the warranty period, the manufacturer will fix or replace the product for free. Each warranty is different, so you or your parents need to read the warranty to see under what conditions the company will fix or replace a defective product.

wide area network Do you watch the weather report on the TV news? A meteorologist (the weather person) shows a map of the country and predicts the weather for the next two or three days. Sometimes thunderstorms or snowstorms will cover a wide area of the map. When a storm covers a wide area, many people in many different places are affected.

A *wide area network* is a network that connects computers that are all located in lots of different places that are not all near each other—such as different schools, towns, states, and countries. The acronym for wide area network is WAN.

The host computer on a WAN is one or more personal computers, minicomputers, or mainframe computers. If your school is connected to a WAN, you can write letters and pose questions to other kids who are connected to the same WAN. Depending on the WAN, some of those kids may be located in other parts of the country or even other parts of the world! Look up *acronym* and *network*.

widow When you are using a word-processing program, sometimes part of a paragraph is on the bottom of one page, and part of the paragraph is at the top of the next page. When only one line from the paragraph appears at the top of the next page, you have a *widow*.

In society, a widow is a woman whose husband has died. The widow is left to go on by herself, without her husband. In word processing, the widowed line goes on to the next page alone; the other lines of the paragraph stay behind.

Many word-processing programs have a feature that allows you to turn off widows. When you turn off widows, the program makes the second to last line in the paragraph go to the next page so the widow is not alone. Look up *orphan*.

wildcard Did you ever play a card game where one or more cards were wild? If so, then you know that the *wildcard* can be used to take the place of any other card. Although DOS is not a card game, it too has wildcards. The wildcards make it easy for you to work with more than one file at a time.

DOS has two types of wildcards. The most common wildcard is an asterisk (*). The other wildcard is a question mark (?).

When do I use the "?" wildcard? The question mark is used to take the place of a single letter in a filename or extension. You might use the question mark when you can remember part but not all of a filename. Suppose you want your computer to show you all the files that begin with "A," have two other letters, and then end with "NT." Use the question mark wildcard to ask your computer to show you all the files that match the above description by typing the following DOS command.

```
DIR A??NT  [Enter]
```

When do I use the "*" wildcard? The asterisk (*) wildcard is used much more often than the "?" wildcard. The "*" wildcard is called a star. The star can take the place of all the letters in a filename or all the letters in the filename extension.

What is *.* used for? The "*.*" means <u>any</u> file with <u>any</u> extension. Suppose a friend gave you a shareware game on a diskette and you wanted to copy the game to your hard disk (<u>after</u> you checked the diskette for viruses). Rather than copy each file one at a time from the diskette to your hard disk, you could use the star wildcard in the following DOS command to copy all the files at one time.

```
COPY A:*.*   Enter
```

The DOS command above copies all the files on the diskette in your drive A to your computer's hard disk. If you want the files to be copied to a particular directory, use the CD command to go to that directory before giving your computer the COPY command.

Should I always use *.* when copying files? Although there is no rule that says you cannot always use "*.*" when copying files, it does not always make sense. Suppose you and a partner were working on a report on Colombia, South America for school. Suppose you created a separate computer file for each topic. You might have one file on the Amazon area, one file on the Andes Mountain area, one file on great art and museums, and one file on local customs. Suppose that these files were in a directory that contained other school papers and reports. If you were to use "*.*" to copy the files, all your files from all your papers and reports would be copied onto the diskette (if there even was room on the diskette). How could you copy just the files that belong to the Colombia report?

One of the tricks to using wildcards is to make filenames that have something in common. Suppose you used the following filenames for your report. What do they have in common?

```
AMAZON.COL
ANDES.COL
ART.COL
CUSTOM.COL
```

All the files end in COL (for Colombia). Now you can use the star for the first part of the filename and COL for the second part of the filename (the extension) that identifies the files for the Colombian report. Look at the DOS command below.

```
COPY*.COL A:
```

The DOS command above means "copy all the files that have the extension COL from here to the diskette in the A drive." This use of the star wildcard lets you copy just the files you need—as long as you can find something in their names that they have in common.

Is DOS the only program that uses wildcards? No. Many programs allow you to use wildcards when referring to filenames. Check the user manual for the individual software program to see whether or not it allows you to use wildcards. Look up *CD command, COPY command, DIR command, DOS command, extension,* and *filename.*

window A *window* is a box on your computer screen that contains help, a message, a list of files, a question, a game, or an entire application program. In a graphical user interface (GUI) every program has its own window. The window can be moved from one place to another on the screen by clicking and dragging the window's title bar. The window can often be made larger and smaller by clicking different buttons on the screen.

When the window contains more information than can fit on the screen at one time, a scroll bar appears so that you can move the image up and down or from side to side to see more of the picture or more of the text. Look up *click, drag, GUI, scroll bar,* and *title bar.*

word processing A *word-processing* program is a software program that is used to type and format text. You can use a word-processing program to write letters, stories, poems, reports, articles for your school paper, and books. For example, I used a word-processing program called WordPerfect (version 6.2 for Windows) to write this book.

In addition to typing and formatting text, many word-processing programs let you make font changes, add pictures to your documents, and create tables and charts.

word wrap If you have ever typed on a typewriter, you know that you have to press the Return key to tell the typewriter that you are at the end of the line and you need to go to the beginning of the next line. When you use a word-processing program on your computer, you do not need to press Enter to move to the next line. The word-processing program wraps the remaining words to the next line for you. This feature is called *word wrap*. You only need to press Enter when you reach the end of a paragraph.

World Wide Web Some of the information on the Internet is part of the *World Wide Web.* The World Wide Web is sometimes called "WWW" or just the "Web." The Web is a collection of hypertext and hypermedia documents. These documents are located on many computers around the world.

Hypertext is a way of jumping from a place in one document to text that is located somewhere else. Hypermedia is similar to hypertext except that you jump to a sound, picture, or video rather than to text. When you jump from one place to another, you can jump to another place in

- The same document.
- A different document on the same computer.
- A different document on another computer, located anywhere in the world.

To get on the Web, you must have a special software program called a browser and be able to connect to the Internet. Many online services like America Online, CompuServe, and Prodigy have an area that gets you onto the Internet. Many of these services also have a built-in browser that lets you use the World Wide Web.

What is a Web site? A Web site is a location on the Internet that has hypertext or hypermedia documents.

What is a home page? The home page is the first screen you see when you enter the Web.

Look up *hypertext* and *Internet.*

---

write protect When you *write protect* a diskette, no one can save information to the diskette or erase information from the diskette—including you—although you (and other people) are able to read the information on the diskette.

Why write protect a diskette? You may want to write protect a disk when you have important information on the disk (like a report for school) that you do not want anyone to accidentally change or erase.

How do I write protect a 3½-inch diskette? To write protect a 3½-inch diskette, look for the slider button on the corner of the diskette.

To write protect the diskette, slide the button so you cannot see through the hole, located underneath the slider button.
To remove the write protection, slide the button until you can see through the hole.

NOT WRITE PROTECTED

WRITE PROTECTED

How do I write protect a 5¼-inch diskette? To write protect a 5¼-inch diskette, take one of the sticky rectangular strips that came with your diskettes (these black or silver strips are usually on the same sheet as the diskette labels), and fold it over the small square cutout on the edge of your diskette. Try to completely cover the square cutout with the strip. To remove the write protection, remove the strip.

NOT WRITE PROTECTED

WRITE PROTECTED

How do I write protect a CD-ROM? A CD is read-only. That means that you cannot write to the CD. Since you cannot write to the CD, there is no need to write protect it.

WYSIWYG *WYSIWYG* (pronounced "wizzy wig") is an acronym for "what you see is what you get." WYSIWYG means that what you see on the screen is what you will see when you print your file. WYSIWYG is a term that some software companies use to describe the formatting features of their word-processing or desktop publishing program. Look up *desktop publishing.*

zip To *zip* a file is to compress the file by making it smaller. Zipping files is like stuffing a suitcase. You make the files as small as possible so you can fit more files in to the same amount of space. Many commercial software companies, and most shareware programmers, use a program called PKZIP, from PKWARE, Inc., to compress their files. When the files are compressed, the software can be put on fewer diskettes (thus saving the software company some money). Files that have been compressed with PKZIP are said to be zipped, and have the file extension ".ZIP."

Unzipping a file is like taking things out of your suitcase—only without the wrinkles. Just as you must unpack your bathrobe and slippers before you can wear them, you must unzip a file before you can use it.

The installation program that comes with your store-bought software automatically unzips the files for you. Many shareware programmers assume that you already have a copy of the unzip software (PKUNZIP). If you need a copy of PKUNZIP, you can download it from almost any BBS, or online service, or get it from the company where you got the shareware. Look up *compress, download, extension, shareware,* and *unzip.*

zoom in When you *zoom in* on an area of your computer screen, you make that one section of your screen bigger so that it is easier to see. Many drawing programs have a zoom feature that lets you make a small portion of your drawing larger so that it is easier to work on. When you are done working on that section, you can zoom out so the drawing is normal size again. Look up *zoom out.*

> *"Danielle, how did you get those little white dots in your flowers? Every time I try to draw a pattern in my flowers, I can't get the mouse to stay inside the line of the petals," complained Janice.*
>
> *"That's easy to fix. Just use the* **zoom in** *feature to make your petal bigger. Then you can make any pattern you want," answered Danielle.*

zoom out When you *zoom out* of a picture on your computer screen, you can see more of the picture on your screen. Many drawing programs have a feature that lets you zoom in on a small area of your drawing so that it is easier to work on it. When you are done working on that section, you can zoom out so the drawing is normal size again. Look up *zoom in.*

"What are all those dots on your screen?" Greg asked Nancy.

"I'm working on a drawing."

"It doesn't look like a drawing to me," said Greg.

"That's because the picture is enlarged. Here, let me **zoom out**, *" said Nancy as she zoomed out of the picture.*

"Whoa! That's really neat. Your drawings look like a bunch of colored dots when you get really close," said Greg.

"That's right," laughed Nancy. "And then it looks like a picture again when I zoom out."

Answer Section

These are the answers to the games and puzzles throughout the book. Each puzzle can be found on the page number following the terms below. For example, the puzzle for *acronym* is found on page 19.

---

acronym, page 19. 1. D, 2. G, 3. I, 4. F, 5. H, 6. A, 7. J, 8. B, 9. E, 10. C.

---

arrow keys, page 27.

	A	B	C	D	E	F	G	H	
	→	→	↓	↑	←	←	→	↓	
Z	→	↓	→	→	↑	→	↑	↓	I
Y	↓	↓	→	→	→	→	↑	→	J
X	→	→	↑	←	←	↑	←	←	K
W	→	↓	→	→	→	↓	↓	←	L
V	←	↓	↓	↑	←	↓	↓	↑	M
U	↑	→	→	↓	↓	←	↓	←	N
	↑	←	←	←	↓	↑	←	↓	
		T	S	R	Q	P	O		

Enter Here	Exit Here
C	D
H	J
K	J
L	Q
N	Q
P	Q
W	V
X	J
Z	J

---

ascender, page 29. The ascenders in the alphabet are *b, d, f, h, k, l,* and *t.*

---

ascending order, page 29. Cynthia's list of all fifty states in ascending order, and each state's capital, is shown below.

State	Capital
Alabama	Montgomery
Alaska	Juneau
Arizona	Phoenix
Arkansas	Little Rock
California	Sacramento
Colorado	Denver
Connecticut	Hartford
Delaware	Dover
Florida	Tallahassee
Georgia	Atlanta
Hawaii	Honolulu
Idaho	Boise
Illinois	Springfield
Indiana	Indianapolis
Iowa	Des Moines
Kansas	Topeka
Kentucky	Frankfort
Louisiana	Baton Rouge
Maine	Augusta
Maryland	Annapolis
Massachusetts	Boston
Michigan	Lansing
Minnesota	St. Paul
Mississippi	Jackson
Missouri	Jefferson City
Montana	Helena
Nebraska	Lincoln
Nevada	Carson City
New York	Albany
New Jersey	Trenton
New Hampshire	Concord
New Mexico	Santa Fe
North Carolina	Raleigh
North Dakota	Bismark
Ohio	Columbus
Oklahoma	Oklahoma City
Oregon	Salem
Pennsylvania	Harrisburg
Rhode Island	Providence
South Carolina	Columbia
South Dakota	Pierre
Tennessee	Nashville
Texas	Austin
Utah	Salt Lake City
Vermont	Montpelier
Virginia	Richmond
Washington	Olympia
West Virginia	Charleston
Wisconsin	Madison
Wyoming	Cheyenne

baud rate, page 37. The chart shows how many letters (or characters) can be sent every second for each baud rate shown.

Baud Rate	Letters per second
28,800	3,600
14,400	1,800
9600	1,200
2400	300
1200	150

binary numbers, pages 38–39. The answers below show you how to count in binary.

1. 1	1 = 1
2. 111	4 + 2 + 1 = 7
3. 101	4 + 0 + 1 = 6
4. 100	4 + 0 + 0 = 4
5. 1100	8 + 4 + 0 + 0 = 12
6. 1001	8 + 0 + 0 + 1 = 9
7. 1010	8 + 0 + 2 + 0 = 10
8. 1111	8 + 4 + 2 + 1 = 15
9. 10000	16 + 0 + 0 + 0 + 0 = 16
10. 10100	16 + 0 + 4 + 0 + 0 = 20
11. 10101	16 + 0 + 4 + 0 + 1 = 21
12. 11111	16 + 8 + 4 + 2 + 1 = 31

cable, page 45. Did you find your way to the plug?

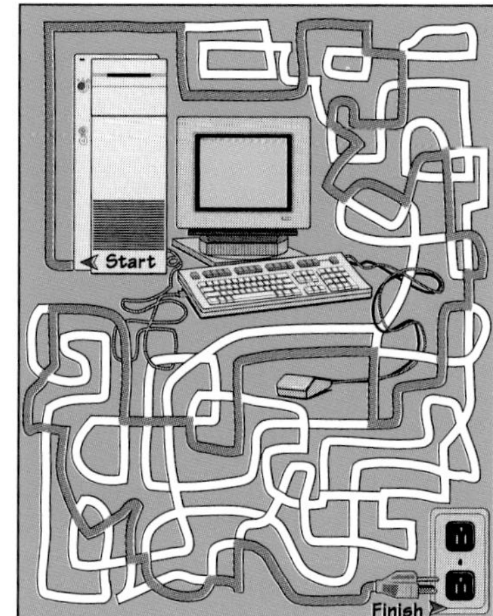

case sensitive, page 47. Ben's mistake is that he did not make his search and replace *case sensitive.* Ben replaced **mark** with **fred.** What Ben should have done was replace **Mark** with **Fred.**

CD-ROM, page 49. Did you figure out how many high-density, 3½-inch diskettes it takes to hold the same amount of information as one CD?

On a Mac: 542 diskettes
On a PC: 465 diskettes

characters per inch, page 51. As the font gets larger, there are less characters per inch.

1. 10 cpi 2. 8 cpi 3. 6 cpi 4. 5 cpi

chronological order, page 52. Here is a list of each invention, event, and inventor. Do you know of any other important events that took place in these years?

1450 – Printing press was invented by Johannes Gutenberg.
1492 – Columbus arrives in North America.
1776 – Declaration of Independence was signed.
1787 – Steamboat was invented by John Fitch.
1793 – Cotton gin was invented by Eli Whitney.
1796 – Smallpox vaccine was created by Edward Jenner.
1816 – Bicycle was invented by Karl D. Sauerbronn.
1835 – Revolver was invented by Samuel Colt.
1837 – Telegraph was invented by Samuel F. B. Morse.
1845 – Sewing machine was invented by Elias Howe.
1860 – Gas engine was invented by Etienne Lenoir.

1876 – Telephone was invented by Alexander Graham Bell.
1877 – Phonograph was invented by Thomas Alva Edison.
1879 – Cash register was invented by James Ritty.
1879 – Light bulb was patented by Thomas Alva Edison.
1893 – Movie projector was invented by Thomas Alva Edison.
1893 – Zipper was invented by W. L. Judson.
1903 – Airplane was invented by Orville and Wilbur Wright (the Wright brothers).
1911 – Air conditioning was invented by W. H. Carrier.
1925 – Television was invented by John Logie Baird.
1948 – Polaroid camera was invented by Edwin Land.
1950 – Color television was invented by Peter Carl Goldmark.
1954 – Polio vaccine was invented by Jonas Salk.
1956 – Videotape was invented by Charles Ginsberg.
1961 – First astronaut was launched into space.
1969 – First time an astronaut set foot on the moon.

clone, page 55. Did you find the clones? The clones are circled in the picture below.

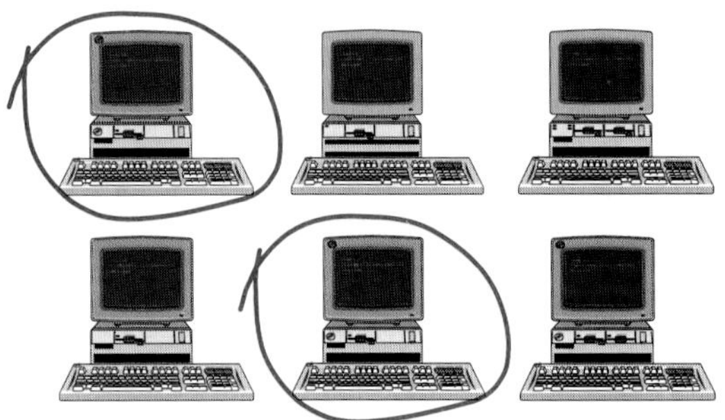

compatible, page 58. Did you find the things that do not belong?

1.

All others are just one hand.

2.

All others are electronic equipment.

3.

All others are not eating.

4.

All others are moving.

5.

All others are outdoor sports.

computer literate, page 62. Did you find all twenty computer terms?

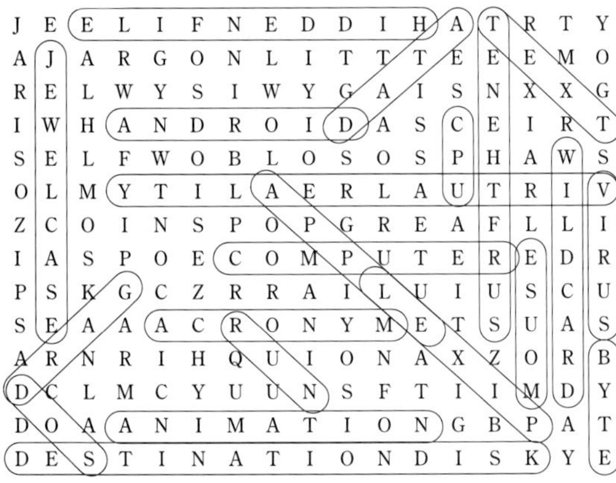

computer store, page 63. Did you locate the 14 items in the computer store that do not belong?

1. grapes
2. football
3. plant
4. toaster
5. binoculars
6. watermelon
7. baseball
8. owl
9. rocket
10. boat
11. suitcase
12. apple
13. basketball
14. octopus

data, page 72.

1. Colors.
2. Even numbers.
3. Towns in Pennsylvania.
4. Types of music.
5. Types of precipitation.
6. Computer games.
7. Names of U.S. presidents that are also the names of U.S. towns.

decrypt, page 78. Were you able to decrypt this excerpt from *Through the Looking Glass*?

"Who did you pass on the road?" the King went on, holding out his hand to the Messenger for some hay.

"Nobody," said the Messenger.

"Quite right," said the King, "this young lady saw him too. So of course Nobody walks slower than you."

—Lewis Carroll, *Through the Looking Glass*

descending order, page 82. Here is a descending list of Madeline's classmates.

Madeline Zubrowski
David Tang
Robert Stern
Brenna Sinclair
Jarik Quinn
Myra Josephs
Charlie Jewel
Kiki Hahn
Leah Cohen
Kenneth Brown

destination disk, page 83.

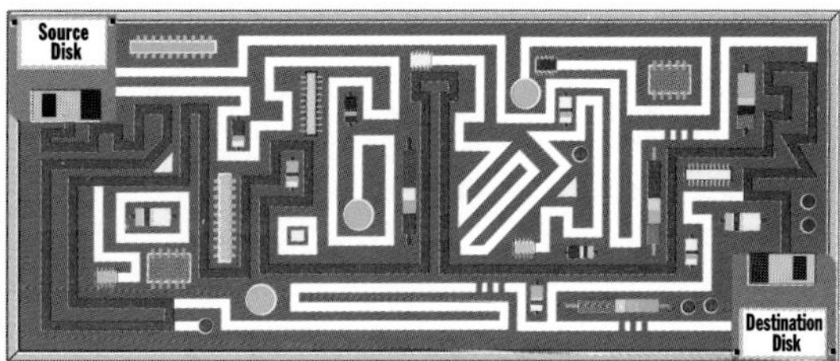

encrypt, page 103. Here is Sarita's encrypted poem.

Nbsz ibe b mjuumf mbnc,
Ijt cfe xbt cz uif ifbufs.
Cvu fwfsz ujnf if upttfe boe uvsofe,
If cvsou ijt xppmz tfbufs.

font style, page 117.

1. **Serif**
2. Serif
3. San serif
4. **San serif**
5. Serif
6. *Serif*
7. *San serif*
8. **SERIF**
9. **San serif**
10. **Serif**

function key, page 121.

Question: How can you keep an elephant from charging?
Answer: Take away his credit cards.

hardware, page 128.

1. Hardware.
2. Software.
3. Software.
4. Hardware.
5. Software.
6. Software.
7. Software.
8. Hardware.
9. Hardware.
10. Software.

hidden file, page 129.

input device, page 135. The computer items listed below are input devices.

1. Joystick.
2. Keyboard.
3. Mouse.
4. Scanner.

microprocessor, page 154. The words that we could find are shown below.

age / ages / ant / ape / apes
eat / eats / eon
gain / gait / gal / gals / gap / gape / gapes / gaps / gin / great
hoe / hoes / hop / hope / hopes / hops / hunk / hunks
keg / kegs
lag / lags / lager / lagers / lain / lap / laps / loan / lop / lope / lopes / lops
nag / nags / nap / naps / nape / napes / nit / nope / nosh / noun / nuke / nukes
oat
page / pager/ pagers / pages / pain / paint / pal / pals / pan / pant / pat / pea / peal / peals / peg / pegs / posh / pun / punk / punks / punker
reap / reaps / regain / repaint
shoe / shoes / shop / shops / shun / slag / slant / slap / slope / slopes / soap / soaps / son / sop / sops / soup /soups / span / spat / spun / spunk
tag / tags / tan / tap / taps / tape / tapes / taper / tapers / tie / tier / tiers / ties / tiger / tigers / tin

numerical order, page 165. The mistakes are *9, 19, 25,* and *27.*

9 Not prime because it can be divided by 3. 9 ÷ 3 = 3.
25 Not prime because it can be divided by 5. 25 ÷ 5 = 5.
27 Not prime because it can be divided by 3 and 9. 27 ÷ 9 = 3 and 27 ÷ 3 = 9.
19 Out of order. The number *19* should come after—not before—the number *17.*

Other prime numbers include 29, 31, 37, 41, 43, 47, 53, 59, 61, 67, 71, 73, 79, 83, 89, 97.

pointing device, page 178.

(a) Mouse.
(b) Trackball.
(c) Joystick.
(d) Flight controller yoke.

sneaker net, page 206.

	Receivers				
	Billy	Charlie	Jamal	Lauren	Mary
Senders Al	✍	X	X	X	X
Joseph	X	X	✍	X	X
Maria	X	X	X	✍	X
Simon	X	✍	X	X	X
Tommy	X	X	X	X	✍

sort, page 209.

Lizzy's Alphabetical Sort		
Name	**Grade**	**Birthday**
George Beam	5	1/3
Lizzy Cohen	6	10/16
Bernice Fisher	4	9/7
Kira Kalan	5	8/21
Zarek Kaminski	6	4/19
Rose Mary O'Brien	4	12/5
Harry Rizzo	5	7/7

Zarek's Chronological Sort		
Birthday	**Name**	**Grade**
1/3	George Beam	5
4/19	Zarek Kaminski	6
7/7	Harry Rizzo	5
8/21	Kira Kalan	5
9/7	Bernice Fisher	4
10/16	Lizzy Cohen	6
12/5	Rose Mary O'Brien	4

Kira's Numerical Sort		
Grade	**Name**	**Birthday**
6	Lizzy Cohen	10/16
6	Zarek Kaminski	4/19
5	Harry Rizzo	7/7
5	Kira Kalan	8/21
5	George Beam	1/3
4	Bernice Fisher	9/7
4	Rose Mary O'Brien	12/5